Conspicuous Feminism
on Television

Conspicuous Feminism on Television

Gender, Power, and #MeToo

Anna Marie Bautista

LEXINGTON BOOKS
Lanham • Boulder • New York • London

Published by Lexington Books
An imprint of The Rowman & Littlefield Publishing Group, Inc.

4501 Forbes Boulevard, Suite 200, Lanham, Maryland 20706
www.rowman.com

86-90 Paul Street, London EC2A 4NE, United Kingdom

Copyright © 2023 by The Rowman & Littlefield Publishing Group, Inc.

All rights reserved. No part of this book may be reproduced in any form or by any electronic or mechanical means, including information storage and retrieval systems, without written permission from the publisher, except by a reviewer who may quote passages in a review.

British Library Cataloguing in Publication Information Available

Library of Congress Cataloging-in-Publication Data Available

ISBN 9781666923001 (cloth) | ISBN 9781666923018 (epub)

Contents

List of Figures	vii
Acknowledgments	ix
Introduction	1
Chapter One: Negotiating Feminism on Television	17
Chapter Two: Exposing Abuse and Misogyny: *Big Little Lies*	41
Chapter Three: "Something Other Than A Mother or Housewife": Challenging Notions of Gendered Space in *The Marvelous Mrs. Maisel*	59
Chapter Four: Incorporating Intersectionality and Inclusivity: *Insecure*	85
Chapter Five: Resistance and Retaliation: *The Handmaid's Tale*	115
Chapter Six: Conclusion: Advocating and Commodifying Female Empowerment in Conspicuous Feminism	133
Bibliography	139
Index	157
About the Author	169

List of Figures

Figure I.1. Amy Schumer and the "Handmaids in the City" discussing sex and skincare on *Saturday Night Live*. *Saturday Night Live*, "Amy Schumer," Season 43, Episode 20.   2

Figure 2.1. Celeste (Nicole Kidman) discovers a bruise during a Skype conversation with Perry (Alexander Skarsgård). *Big Little Lies*, "Serious Mothering," Season 1, Episode 2.   46

Figure 2.2. Jane (Shailene Woodley) and Celeste (Nicole Kidman) share a moment after Perry's funeral. *Big Little Lies*, "You Get What You Need," Season 1, Episode 7.   50

Figure 3.1. Mrs. Maisel (Rachel Brosnahan) onstage at the Gaslight. *The Marvelous Mrs. Maisel*, "Thank You and Good Night," Season 1, Episode 8.   74

Figure 3.2. Susie (Alex Borstein) discloses her financial concerns and personal ambitions to Midge (Rachel Brosnahan). *The Marvelous Mrs. Maisel*, "It's the Sixties, Man!" Season 3, Episode 2.   78

Figure 4.1. Issa (Issa Rae) raps to her "mirror bitch." *Insecure*, "Messy as F**k," Season 1, Episode 2.   93

Figure 4.2. Issa (Issa Rae) listens to feedback from her co-workers at We Got Y'All. *Insecure*, "Insecure as F**k," Season 1, Episode 1.   97

Figure 5.1. June's (Elisabeth Moss) testimony against the
 Waterfords and Gilead begins in a long shot. *The Handmaid's
 Tale*, "Testimony," Season 4, Episode 8. 122

Figure 5.2. And ends in a close-up. *The Handmaid's Tale*,
 "Testimony," Season 4, Episode 8. 123

Acknowledgments

This book began as a PhD project on women and television some time ago and evolved significantly before my dissertation was finally completed with the support of a Research Postgraduate Studentship at the University of Hong Kong. After all the ups and downs in my PhD journey, it was extremely fulfilling to have the dissertation completed; to have it further developed and published as a book is a gift that I never imagined possible. I have to give thanks first and foremost to God for His grace and provision, which enabled me to keep going throughout the various stages of this project and continues to sustain me in all ways.

There are many people who helped me immensely in making this book come to fruition. Thanks first of all to my terrific acquisitions editor, Jessie Tepper, for her interest in the project—her input and support has been invaluable. Thanks also to Deja Ryland, Janine Faust, and the excellent team at Lexington Books for their assistance and efficiency. I am grateful also to the anonymous reviewer for their generous and constructive advice.

Thank you to Gina Marchetti, Monica Steinberg, and Amy Villarejo—a kind (and truly one of a kind) examining committee whose expert feedback guided me in approaching and revising my work in new and inspired ways.

Thank you to Alison Bartlett and Kendall Johnson for providing essential comments during different stages of this project.

Deepest gratitude to Tim Gruenewald, whose patience, encouragement, and critique were central to the realization of this project and the completion of my PhD. I could not hope for a better advisor.

My academic path would not be what it is without Staci Ford, whose support in all things has enriched me since the days of being her student to the great honor of now being able to call her my colleague and friend.

Many thanks to the many colleagues and students at the University of Hong Kong and at HKU SPACE that I have been privileged to work with—all of you continue to be a source of encouragement, joy, and motivation for me.

I am extraordinarily blessed to have so many friends and family members whose love and support I treasure. There is not enough space to thank all of you individually, but I am so very grateful to each of you.

My final thanks go to those whom no words can describe the depth of my love and gratitude for: Rebecca, Leandro, Andrew, Jasmine, Zeke, Jax, Poppy, Rose, and Alexa Bautista. This book would not have been possible without you.

This book is dedicated to my Lola, Elena Cortes, and to the memory of my Lola Rosalia Bautista and my Lolos, Candido Bautista and Avelino Cortes Sr.

I also dedicate this book to my parents, Rebecca and Leandro Bautista—thank you for your steadfast support and belief in me. I will always love watching TV with you.

Introduction

#METOO AND CONSPICUOUS FEMINISM: MANIFESTING ACTIVISM AND COMMERCIALISM

"Let's face it ladies, in 2018, *The Handmaid's Tale* is basically our *Sex and the City*," comedian Amy Schumer sardonically proclaims in a voiceover to the trailer for a faux television series, *Handmaids in the City* (*Saturday Night Live*, Season 43, Episode 20). The satirical fusion of HBO's *Sex and the City* (1998–2002) and Hulu's *The Handmaid's Tale* (2017–present) appeared as a skit on an episode of the variety sketch series *Saturday Night Live* (NBC, 1975–present), known for its parodies of contemporary politics and popular culture. The blending of the two series signifies the cultural significance of their representations of female empowerment in their respective eras, nearly twenty years apart. The result is a jarring parody that emphasizes the contrasts between the iconic HBO series' identification with feminist themes through commodification and sexual autonomy and the feminism expressed through depictions of abuse and sexual violence on Hulu's critically acclaimed adaptation of Margaret Atwood's 1985 dystopian novel.

Dressed in the handmaids' discernible red robes and white bonnets, Schumer and *SNL* cast members Aidy Bryant, Kate McKinnon, and Cecily Strong confer about their sex lives and skincare routines much like Carrie Bradshaw and her *Sex and the City* counterparts would during their weekly brunch dates at deluxe restaurants in Manhattan. However, this conversation takes place under the watch of the armed guards that frequently accompany the handmaids in Gilead, the fundamentalist dictatorship that has severely deprived women of their rights in *The Handmaid's Tale*. In the series, handmaids are fertile women assigned to the homes of Gilead's elite families in order to procreate for them. They are ritually raped by their masters at a monthly "Ceremony" in which their wives also participate, typically holding the handmaid down during the sanctified assault. Thus, the "threesomes" blithely discussed by Schumer and the *SNL* cast refer to the mandated

"Ceremony" and the skincare tips the handmaids offer to each other concern ways to conceal the bruises sustained during the beatings and assaults that the handmaids are subjected to.

This unsettling application of *Sex and the City*'s signature whimsical tone to dialogue about *The Handmaid's Tale*'s cruelties is indicative of how the #MeToo movement against abuse and gender inequality has impacted feminist discourse on television. #MeToo initially gained traction in 2017 from the allegations of sexual misconduct made against producer and executive Harvey Weinstein, but has since expanded to encompass all facets of gender-based inequality and injustice, in the media and culture industries and beyond. *SNL*'s incorporation of the two series signals their common themes of gender and power, while highlighting their distinctions by contrasting them. The discordant humor generated by the merging of *Sex and the City*'s perkiness with *The Handmaid's Tale*'s brutality caustically exploits the disparities between the feminist ideas undergirding both series and is an instance of how #MeToo has motivated representations of feminism on television series. The paradoxical tone of the sketch is also suggestive of how #MeToo's incentives are being leveraged in a manner resembling the commodification of female independence that has often been attributed to *Sex and the City*. This contrast highlights the key aspects of what I call "conspicuous feminism," which displays feminist issues in a distinct, militant, and accessible form that foregrounds misogyny and female oppression more emphatically than in previous eras.

Many of these representations have emerged on television, as exhibited by the volume of television series featuring female protagonists and reflecting

Figure I.1. Amy Schumer and the "Handmaids in the City" discussing sex and skincare on *Saturday Night Live*. *Saturday Night Live*, "Amy Schumer," Season 43, Episode 20. *Screenshot captured by author.*

themes palpably influenced by feminism. In addition to *The Handmaid's Tale*, these include HBO's *Big Little Lies* (2017–2019) and *Mare of Easttown* (2021), BBC's *Fleabag* (2016–2019) and *I May Destroy You* (2020), Hulu's *Little Fires Everywhere* (2020) and *Mrs. America* (2020), BBC America's *Killing Eve* (2018–2022), Apple TV's *The Morning Show* (2019–present), and Netflix's *The Queen's Gambit* (2020). These series and others depict complex female protagonists who encounter injustice, discrimination, harassment, and abuse that correspond to feminism's agenda of interrogating and dismantling sexism and sexist oppression. These issues have been at the forefront of the cultural discussion about gender, equality, and feminism that has emanated from #MeToo's major concerns with sexual harassment and gender inequality.

The impact of #MeToo on the larger cultural discourse has prompted an unprecedented and critical examination of misogyny on television that displays both the advocacy and popularizing facets of the movement. While misogyny is not an unfamiliar topic on television, #MeToo has instigated a greater number of depictions that interrogate issues of gender and power in more complex ways than in previous eras. *Conspicuous Feminism on Television: Gender, Power, and #MeToo* examines how the movement has impacted the portrayal of feminist themes relating to misogyny and abuse, the silencing and deceptions that are preserved in order to uphold gendered power relations, the challenging of established gender roles and identities, and the integration of intersectional perspectives in representations of women. By exploring these issues, I argue that the increased visibility and attention to gendered inequality prompted by #MeToo has been purposely incorporated into popular television narratives in order to reflect feminist concerns, as well as to capitalize on its prominence within the wider public discourse. I propose that these representations reflect a "conspicuous feminism" that is simultaneously perceptible, activist, and commodifying in its deliberation.

#METOO AND CONSPICUOUS FEMINISM

The #MeToo movement was originated in 2006 by activist Tarana Burke but gained prominence after the Weinstein allegations in 2017. The hashtag #MeToo attained viral status on various social media platforms in October 2017, following a post on Twitter by actor Alyssa Milano, exhorting women who have been sexually assaulted or harassed to post using the hashtag "MeToo" in order to heighten awareness of the extent of the issue. Milano's post was made in response to the exposure of the allegations leveled against Weinstein published in an article by Ronan Farrow in *The New Yorker* (Farrow

2017) days earlier and functioned as an attempt to disclose the magnitude of women that have similarly experienced harassment and assault. Twelve million Facebook posts using the hashtag were shared within twenty-four hours and nearly a million posts were shared on Twitter within forty-eight hours, including those made by high-profile Hollywood actresses Ashley Judd, Jennifer Lawrence, and Gwyneth Paltrow, among others.

The visibility of feminism has thus further expanded and evolved to concentrate on sexism and misogyny with the prominence of the #MeToo movement, which escalated in 2017 in response to the abundance of prominent cases concerning allegations of rape, assault, and harassment at various levels of society, the most prolific of which include men in positions of power such as Weinstein, actors Bill Cosby and Kevin Spacey. and then president of the United States Donald Trump. Following his inauguration in January 2017, the Women's Marches that took place globally (but largely in the United States and United Kingdom) with the aim of protesting Trump's election campaign rhetoric, which contained misogynistic overtones and the accusations of sexual misconduct that have been made against him, is a clear signifier of the collective vexation in the contemporary feminist movement (Harp 2019; Robson 2020). The #MeToo campaign and the "Silence Breakers" behind it were named *TIME* magazine's Person of the Year in 2017, indicating the weight and influence of feminism and women's issues surrounding the movement, as well as demonstrating the shift toward confronting misogyny as a focal point in media negotiations of feminism.

Prior to the ubiquity of #MeToo after the Weinstein allegations in 2017, feminist activism had become more easily accessible and was implemented through the multiplicity of channels available on online platforms. Forerunners to the movement developed on the feminist blogs and social media outlets enabled women to voice and disseminate their experiences and perspectives to a vast audience. The Everyday Sexism Twitter account, launched in 2012 by writer Laura Bates, describes individual women's everyday experiences of misogyny and is just one example that illustrates "the relationship between the personal and the political within an age of advancements of rapid communication and social media" (Chamberlain 2017, 15). Other examples include the #YesAllWomen hashtag, which broke out on Twitter in 2014, initially in response to the Isla Vista killings, which were motivated by misogyny but provided a platform for women to share their stories of sexism, violence, and harassment. When Alyssa Milano instigated women to post with the hashtag #MeToo on social media to express their experiences with sexual assault and harassment in October 2017, misogyny at various levels within society was subsequently exposed and discussed on social and mass media platforms.

The intensification of #MeToo has occurred alongside the increasing visibility of feminist influences in the media and popular culture, including the abundance of female narratives and representations on television. As Jessalyn Keller and Maureen E. Ryan observe in their analysis of the "emergent feminisms" attendant in media culture in 2018:

> Contemporary media culture is arguably producing more complicated, nuanced representations of feminine (and sometimes feminist) identities than perhaps were possible in earlier moments, partly as a result of some prominent female directors, screenwriters, and showrunners. Some of these nuanced feminine identities are articulated on popular quality dramas like *Girls*, *Transparent*, and *Orange is the New Black*, which deal with identity formation despite financial precarity (*Girls*), transgender politics and aging (*Transparent*), and an unjust prison system (*Orange is the New Black*). These texts have broadened the representational landscape of women's media and made new kinds of identities—ones that traverse the boundaries of race, class, and sexuality—increasingly visible and viable. (15)

These and other depictions of feminine identities on television and in the media have been facilitated by the recent feminist attention to issues of gendered inequality and female oppression, as well as the disparate circumstances in which women experience oppression, namely with regard to the intersectional facets of race, class, and sexuality.

The representations of conspicuous feminism central to this book are primarily concerned with reflecting these aspects of female oppression. The term suggests a distinctness and purposefulness in representing women's experiences of misogyny and inequality that has seemingly been influenced by the ubiquitous discourse around #MeToo. According to the Oxford Advanced Learner's Dictionary, the term *conspicuous* refers to elements that are "clearly visible" and "likely to attract attention." The representations of feminist issues in the television series examined in this book are similarly discernible and striking in their depiction and championing of female empowerment.

The term *conspicuous* also recalls economist and sociologist Thorstein Veblen's concept of "conspicuous consumption," which was originally applied to the consumption practices of the nouveau riche classes in 1899. Veblen's book *The Theory of the Leisure Class: An Economic Study in the Evolution of Institutions* (1899) examined the behavioral characteristics of the nouveau riche (new rich) classes that derived from the Second Industrial Revolution at the end of the nineteenth century. Key to his study are observations on their consumption practices, including that of conspicuous consumption, which became a principal indicator of wealth and social status. Veblen's theory asserts that conspicuous consumption transpires from the economic consumption of goods and services in order to exhibit wealth and status, in opposition to the consumption of basic necessities. Regarding conspicuous consumption and social status, Veblen states, "The basis on which good repute in any highly organized industrial community ultimately rests is pecuniary strength; and the means of showing pecuniary strength, and so of gaining or retaining a good name, are leisure and a conspicuous consumption of goods" ([1899] 1998, 64). Though Veblen's rendering of conspicuous consumption refers to status in relation to financial wealth, conspicuous feminism shares some of its characteristics in its visibility and explicitness. This visibility has largely been perceived on social media, following the expansion of #MeToo as a social media status update and its emergence from the corporate space of social media platforms, rather than from the social sphere itself.

In this regard, #MeToo has commonly been noted as a significant instance of "hashtag activism" (#hashtivism), which refers to "the act of showing support for a cause through a like, share, and etcetera, on any social media platform, such as Facebook or Twitter" (Mbabazhi and Mbabzahi 2018). Particularly after the significance of #MeToo, displaying a feminist position has garnered media and cultural influence, evoking Veblen's correlation of the visibility of wealth with social status. Much as Veblen emphasized the visible elements of conspicuous consumption, so is conspicuous feminism contingent on its perceptibility on social media and in popular culture. The term thus also encapsulates the variations between activism and commodification that conspicuous feminism conflates and manifests. As such, I assert that conspicuous feminism has been expressly incorporated into television representations and narratives in order to synchronize with the cultural concerns regarding women's issues stimulated by #MeToo.

Conspicuous feminism embodies features of Sarah Banet-Weiser's concept of "popular feminism" that she uses to construe various strands of popular culture, including on television. In spite of its ubiquity, Banet-Weiser articulates that, "The visibility of popular feminism, where examples appear on television, in film, on social media, and on bodies, is important, but it often stops there, as if seeing or purchasing feminism is the same thing as changing patriarchal structures" (2018, 15). There are problems in its representation as its substantial presence does not necessarily correspond to the structural transformation of gendered power relations. Banet-Weiser thus suggests that "popular feminism" is characterized by visibility rather than a substantial engagement with feminist politics and activism. Prolific illustrations of popular feminism include singer Beyoncé's performance amidst the backdrop of a luminous "Feminist" sign at the 2014 MTV Video Music Awards and the ubiquity of celebrities donning designer T-shirts featuring slogans such as "We Should All Be Feminists" and "The Future Is Female." The concept of female empowerment is central to portrayals of popular feminism but is typically employed in a simplified manner that does not interrogate the political and structural aspects of gender inequality, reiterating Banet-Weiser's assertion that "popular feminism circulates in an economy of visibility" (2018, 18), in lieu of implementing specific goals and action.

This visibility has thus been broadly delimited to manifestations of feminism that have economic and commercial appeal. In her discussion of the burgeoning phenomenon of celebrity feminism since the mid 2010s, Nicola Rivers proposes that the visibility of feminism has been heightened by its cooptation into the commercial arena:

> ... it is certainly true that the renewed popularity of feminism(s) has both influenced and been influenced by the commercialization of the movement. In short, currently feminism sells, or at least those strands of feminism uncomplicatedly promoting the neoliberal principles of agency, choice, and empowerment do. (2017, 57)

This corresponds to Banet-Weiser's claim that, "those feminisms that are most easily commodified and branded are those that become most visible. This means, most of the time, that the popular feminism that is most visible is that which is white, middle-class, cis-gendered, and heterosexual" (2018, 21). Rivers cites UN Women Global Goodwill ambassador Emma Watson for the HeForShe initiative advocating gender equality, alongside similarly "white, cis-gendered, and heterosexual" celebrities Jennifer Lawrence and Taylor Swift as key exemplars of celebrity feminism, reinforcing how the visibility of feminism has been dominated by those who possess the means to publicize it. Thereby, the feminist movement itself becomes depoliticized in favor of its market potential. Popular and celebrity feminism has also provided ample opportunities for consumerism and "femvertising," defined by lifestyle and digital media company She Knows Media in 2004 as "advertising that employs pro-female talent, messages, and imagery to empower women and girls" (SheMedia 2004), as well as enabling feminist reflection and incorporation. However, a distinct advocacy for female empowerment distinguishes conspicuous feminism from constructions of popular feminism so that they retain the latter's visibility and commercial viability of feminist themes but also incorporate an activist component that is engendered by the influence of #MeToo.

Conspicuous feminism also diverges from the "neoliberal principles" identified by Rivers in relation to the media visibility of feminism and female empowerment. Neoliberal feminism commonly defines feminism and empowerment in terms of individual success rather than solidarity and collaboration. Catherine Rottenberg describes the neoliberal feminist subject:

> Individuated in the extreme, this subject is feminist in the sense that she is distinctly aware of particular inequalities between men and women. This same

subject is, however, simultaneously neoliberal, not only because she disavows the social, cultural, and economic forces producing this inequality but also because she accepts full responsibility for her own well-being and self-care, which is increasingly predicated on crafting a felicitous work-family balance based on a cost-benefit calculus. The neoliberal feminist subject is thus mobilized to convert continued gender inequality from a structural problem into an individual affair. (2018, 55)

While retaining the elements of visibility that characterize instances of popular and neoliberal feminism, depictions of conspicuous feminism integrate a more nuanced perspective to feminist concerns by incorporating greater complexity and diversity, as well as more pronounced opposition to systemic misogyny, which has been instigated by the salience of the #MeToo movement.

The combativeness that has articulated constructions of conspicuous feminism following the impact of #MeToo is also apparent in feminist campaigns concentrated on issues of bodily autonomy. "Bans Off My Body," a Planned Parenthood campaign initially launched in 2019 in response to bans and restrictions on abortions enacted across several US states, became resurgent in May 2022 following the uproar over the discovery of a leaked US Supreme Court document suggesting that the court would overturn the landmark *Roe vs. Wade* case, which legalized abortion in 1972. In June 2022, *Roe vs. Wade* was officially overturned, giving individual states the right to ban abortions. At the time of writing, half of the states in the United States are expected to introduce new bans or restrictions on the reproductive rights of women. The fall of *Roe vs. Wade* has further fomented feminist concerns for the state of women's rights as evidenced by the numerous protests and rallies that have taken place across the United States since the Supreme Court ruling. The antagonism fostered by #MeToo has ostensibly been heightened, portending the possibility of increased and more complex conceptions of conspicuous feminism.

The militant and commodifying facets central to examples of conspicuous feminism are embodied in the cultural phenomenon of *The Handmaid's Tale*. In addition to the Hulu series' pronounced representation of resistance to female oppression and abuse, the image of the handmaid has become a recognizable symbol of female protest and defiance, which has been utilized for commercial purposes, as in the aforementioned *SNL* skit. The idiosyncratic synthesis between activism and commodification that characterizes conspicuous feminism is strikingly captured by the presence of people dressed as handmaids at various protests for women's rights, particularly in relation to abortion and reproductive rights. Handmaids appeared most recently following the overturning of *Roe vs. Wade* in June 2022. In these cases, the image of the handmaid has been evoked to signify resistance to patriarchal institutions that oppress women, but there have been instances in which handmaids have been visually employed purely for marketing purposes, such as in Hulu's campaign for the 2017 Emmy Awards. It involved stationing handmaids in various locations across Los Angeles, including landmarks such as the Beverly Wilshire Hotel and the Los Angeles County Museum of Art. Commenting on Hulu's brazen strategy in its "For Your Consideration" Emmy campaign that year, Stephanie Eckhardt notes that "There's a fine line between smart, socially-conscious marketing and exploitative tactics that capitalize on the very real fears women face in America's political climate today" (2017). This appropriation of the image of the handmaid symbolizes the inclination to address matters of abuse and inequality that have become pronounced in the #MeToo era, while also illustrating how gendered oppression has been commoditized in the media and popular culture, eliciting the tensions that conspicuous feminism straddles in its concomitant championing and exploitation of feminist issues.

VISIBLE NARRATIVES

The pervasiveness of the specter of #MeToo suggests an assimilation of the movement into manifestations of conspicuous feminism, such as the considerable number of television series incorporating narratives of violence and assault toward women. Karen Boyle contends that the distinct visibility of #MeToo has enabled the representation of these narratives to become more customary, as well as to become an effective means of expressing feminist concerns:

> [#MeToo] is also a mainstream news story, involving many competing voices attempting to determine, assert and limit the meanings and significance of the outpouring of evidence of gendered violence and harassment associated with the hashtag. These stories may—as Banet-Weiser's analysis of popular feminism demonstrates—do feminist work, but focusing simply on the most visible stories as representative of contemporary feminism is profoundly distorting. (2019, 4)

Boyle attests that the ubiquity of #MeToo establishes the presence of gendered inequality and abuse but the narratives that are given prominence circumscribe its capacity to reflect feminist motivations.

#MeToo's consonance with constructions of conspicuous feminism also ensues from the movement's initially predominant associations with the media and entertainment industries. There has been significant coverage of celebrities' stories of abuse and sexual misconduct within the entertainment industry, namely in relation to the Weinstein allegations and subsequent criminal trial, with noted actresses including Rose McGowan, Annabella Sciorra, and Mira Sorvino among the most outspoken in their detailing of their respective experiences. As such, the #MeToo movement has largely been more closely aligned with these celebrity testimonies than with activist and sexual harassment survivor Tarana Burke, who originated the phrase in 2006 in order to gain recognition for women of color who have experienced sexual abuse and to foster solidarity for and among them. Though Burke was not cited in Milano's initial Twitter post, she has since been acknowledged for her conception of the phrase and has been a leading figure in the advancement of the movement. However, though she was featured in the *TIME* magazine article, she was not included on the magazine's cover and her initial appeals for an intersectional awareness of sexual abuse and harassment have not been critically scrutinized in media constructions of the movement overall.

Though feminist issues have become more prominent in the media and popular culture, there have been concerns as to how far they apply to the circumstances of all women, particularly those who do not embody the particular classed and racialized identities that media constructions typically favor. In this regard, the concept of intersectional feminism has become crucial for critiques of media constructions of femininity, resulting in scrutiny of the limitations in prominent renderings of feminism, which include "the primacy of whiteness in postfeminist popular culture" (Keller and Ryan 2018, 6). Feminism itself has been increasingly interrogated in intersectional terms in order to account for distinctions in race, class, and sexualities, particularly as they relate to dynamics of power in contemporary culture.

Coined by race theorist and activist Kimberlé Crenshaw in 1989, "intersectionality is the concept and metaphor used to describe how people who occupy multiple marginalized social positions experience oppression that is qualitatively (not simply quantitatively) different from those with fewer social disadvantages" (Hunt 2017, 121). Intersectional feminism, then, is concerned not only with inequality and marginalization correlating to gender but also with how other factors that can constitute inequality and marginalization, such as race, converge with it to produce multiple and intersecting levels of disparity, disadvantage, and oppression. As Crenshaw explicates in relation to the instance of black women, "[they] experience discrimination in ways that are both similar to and different from those experienced by white women and Black men" (1989, 149). The discrimination faced by women of color cannot simply be categorized in terms of race or gender but must be considered with respect to the overlapping and intersecting nature of the prejudice and inequity stemming from the power dynamics intrinsic to both race and gender relations.

Since Crenshaw's designation of the term, the influence of intersectionality has been evident in figurations of feminism, with diversity commonly being incorporated in portrayals of female strength and empowerment. Notable examples include Beyoncé, whose image and music plainly invoke a consciousness of feminist and racial politics (e.g., "Run the World (Girls)" 2013, "Formation" 2016, "Freedom" 2016, and other songs) and advertising campaigns for women's beauty and cosmetic brands such as Dove's "Real Beauty" (2004) and L'Oréal's "All Worth It" campaigns, which featured women of varying body types and ethnicities. Although these and other examples indicate a discernment for and commitment to presenting diversity in popular culture, a number of scholars have suggested that they merely utilize race and ethnicity to function as a commodified element in popular and consumer culture (Banet-Weiser 2007; Butler 2014; Kanai 2020; Nakamura 2008). Banet-Weiser contends that both race and gender are often employed as a specific "flava" in popular culture texts in order to appeal to diversified audiences, claiming that "Like race, gender identity is constructed in the present 'postfeminist' cultural economy as a 'flava,' a flexible, celebratory identity category that is presented in all its various manifestations as a kind of product one can buy or try on" (2007, 202). Thus, the visibility of difference and diversity in popular culture signifies an awareness of intersectional identities, but not necessarily a deliberate engagement with the systemic variations that underlie them.

This presence and operation of diversity in media and popular culture recalls Anna Carastathis's concerns over the complications involved in endeavoring to integrate intersectionality into feminist discourse:

> . . . its easy appropriation means that often the aims of intersectionality are inverted, its theoretical content is oversimplified, and its political force is therefore effaced. This occurs in both critical and celebratory accounts, in which the metaphor is variously reduced to an additive junction of essentialist categories, upheld or dismissed as a naïve form of identity politics, fetishized as the guarantor of political or theoretical inclusion, or aggrandized as a unified theory of "multiple oppressions." (2016, 8)

Carastathis's perspective reflects the apprehension that while intersectionality accords a greater recognition of diverse identity categories and experiences, it also raises the possibility that they can be easily reduced to distinctive modes or trends that can be simply identified and at times, commodified. Barbara Tomlinson augments this in her avowal that "merely recognizing and condemning gendered, racialized, classed, and sexualized power does not protect us from unwittingly deploying terms and tools that are saturated with power and structured in dominance" (2019, 2). Thus, while the visibility of diverse identity groups in the media has increased, it has not consequently altered the systems of dominance and disparity that structure them, just as the visibility of feminism does not necessarily prompt a more comprehensive understanding of systems of gendered inequality.

Although #MeToo has enacted a platform for women to share their experiences, there has been concern as to which experiences are more extensively heard and thus granted greater visibility. In this sense, the movement has effected a conspicuous feminism in that it is those narratives that have more potential for media interest that are foregrounded. This recalls Michel Foucault's contention that "Visibility is a trap" (1979, 200), referring to his description of Jeremy Bentham's (1843) "Panopticon," in which prisoners of an institution are unable to determine when they are being watched, despite their constant visibility. This corresponds to the media's leverage in its transmission of #MeToo, in that individuals who are afforded visibility are conferred a certain level of power as a result, but this visibility and power is ultimately controlled by dominant forces. Rosalind Gill and Shani Orgad ponder how far #MeToo's prominence has implications in terms of the movement itself as opposed to its media attraction:

> It concerns the question of whether the movement's popularity and visibility are indeed due to its call for justice, or because of the salacious content of the stories it has brought to light. To put it somewhat crudely, is it sexism or sex that "sells"? How should we understand the role of a mainstream media that suddenly seems to believe [some] women, after decades of trivializing and undermining us? Does this represent a genuine shift? Is a backlash coming? (2018, 1320)

Concern over the disproportionate attention given to the stories of women in positions of relative power and privilege thus constitutes a component of the "backlash" that Gill and Orgad envisage, as the experiences of minority, non-heterosexual, and economically disadvantaged women are marginalized. The media's inclination to reflect issues of sexual assault and harassment could be a consequence of #MeToo's conspicuousness, rather than an impetus to galvanize the movement itself.

Thus, themes of assault and harassment have been foregrounded in representations of conspicuous feminism in the media, including on television. The enlarged focus on these issues can be attributed to the pervasiveness of #MeToo and is comparable to the general media constructions of the movement; television negotiations of sexual violence and misdemeanors have generally been confined to female narratives with visibility and intrigue. However, in spite of its insufficiency in portraying narratives that do not necessarily employ an encompassing and intersectional focus, #MeToo has broadened television representations of feminist issues and incorporated an activist sentiment that was not previously so distinct. Reflections of conspicuous feminism implement this activist perspective in its exceptional inspection of systemic gender inequality, paralleling the advocacy for awareness and change that the movement has elicited.

Conspicuous Feminism on Television: Gender, Power, and #MeToo examines how #MeToo has influenced the representation of conspicuous feminism on television in its heightening of the cultural momentum toward addressing gendered inequality. Chapter one, "Negotiating Feminism on Television," provides a broad overview of prominent television series that have featured feminist themes, ranging from *The Mary Tyler Moore Show* (CBS, 1970–1977) to *Sex and the City* (HBO, 1998–2004) to *Orange Is the New Black* (Netflix, 2013–2019), focusing on the social, cultural, and industrial developments that have preceded television constructions of conspicuous feminism. The last half of the chapter considers the evolution of "quality television" amidst the developments in television reception and distribution into the "peak TV" era that have also facilitated the expansion of depictions of conspicuous feminism on television. The increase in female showrunners and producers has coincided with the vast changes that have transpired in television distribution and reception, most notably the presence of streaming platforms offering original television content that have enabled the multiplicity and diversity of female representations on television to flourish. As a result, constructions of conspicuous feminism on television have become more complex and nuanced in their reflections of female independence and empowerment as more series ponder the configurations of feminism that imbue cultural notions and representations of feminine identity.

In the following chapters, close analysis of four contemporary quality television series will demonstrate how the prominence of #MeToo has provoked the palpable, assertive, and commodified constructions of female empowerment that are characteristic of conspicuous feminism. Chapter two, "Exposing Abuse and Misogyny: *Big Little Lies*," considers the themes of gender and power featured in HBO's *Big Little Lies*. Based on Liane Moriarty's 2014 novel, the series offers a compelling portrayal of the realities that are often behind the exteriors that frame dominant expectations in relation to contemporary female identities, reflecting #MeToo's determination to expose misogynistic structures within society. One of the fundamental issues that the series tackles pertains to abuse and the unequal gender relations that can exist beneath immaculate exterior appearances and that often remain implicit. Indeed, its notable depiction of domestic abuse and sexual assault associates it with feminism, particularly in the #MeToo era, which has propelled more women to speak out about violence and misogyny. The incorporation of themes of female solidarity and empowerment also reiterate the movement's motivation for collective awareness and consideration of women's experiences with misogyny. The undertaking of these themes constitutes it as a key illustration of conspicuous feminism as feminist issues are simultaneously being accentuated and commodified in response to the influence of #MeToo.

Chapter three, "'Something Other Than a Mother or a Housewife': Challenging Notions of Gendered Space in *the Marvelous Mrs. Maisel*," examines how Amazon Prime's *The Marvelous Mrs. Maisel (2017–present) incorporates elements of conspicuous feminism in its depiction of a daring female protagonist intent on devising her own path during the 1950s–1960s, when gender demarcations were sharply circumscribed. In its representation of a woman seeking achievement and recognition outside of the domestic sphere and attempting to access the male-dominated profession of stand up comedy, the series illustrates how closely ideals of femininity were tied to traditionally gendered constructions of home and domesticity, and provides an opportunity to reflect on their relevance in the contemporary era. The series' treatment of gender and power dynamics has resounded in the #MeToo era and has demonstrated how elements of sexism and misogyny that were common in the 1950s have persisted, particularly in relation to the gendered roles and spaces that have delimited women's presence in the public sphere.*

Chapter four, "Incorporating Intersectionality and Inclusivity: *Insecure*" considers how the comparative infrequency of black female protagonists on television mirrors the concerns over #MeToo's perceived deficiency in addressing intersectional issues. Although the movement was originated by a black woman in 2006 in response to the abuse of underprivileged and minority women, the incidents highlighted by the media have predominantly focused on the experiences of high-profile white women and have largely not considered aspects of race and class. The black female protagonists on HBO's *Insecure* (2016–2021) produce an opportunity for the stories of black women to be foregrounded as a notable example of conspicuous feminism and for their experiences of discrimination to be depicted in an effort to reposition feminist and media practices that have dominantly centered on whiteness. The series' depiction of black women and the intersectional concerns that significantly comprise their everyday experiences reflects black feminist themes of intersectionality in their expression of conspicuous feminism.

Chapter five, "Resistance and Retaliation—*The Handmaid's Tale*," discusses how the unequivocal depiction of the cruelties inflicted on women in Hulu's *The Handmaid's Tale* (2016–present) engenders acute representations of conspicuous feminism, particularly in relation to resistance against the oppression of women. *The Handmaid's Tale* evokes the issues of sexual violence and gendered power structures that are being interrogated in the era of #MeToo, and Hulu's critically acclaimed adaptation of Margaret Atwood's

1985 dystopian novel has been notable in the resurgence of women's narratives and perspectives on television. The image of the handmaids has served as a symbolic reminder of patriarchal oppression, as well as resistance to it. The phenomenon of the series has thus correspondingly developed amidst a renewed cognizance of women's experience of sexism and gendered power relations, namely demonstrated by the surge in activist movements, such as #MeToo and #TimesUp.

Chapter six, "Conclusion: Advocating and Commodifying Female Empowerment in Conspicuous Feminism," reflects on how the cultural attention toward misogyny and gender inequality generated by the #MeToo movement has contributed to the portrayals of conspicuous feminism in television series that foreground misogyny and female oppression more emphatically than series in previous eras. The series examined in this book all incorporate the characteristics of conspicuous feminism in their depictions of female empowerment and have been influenced by the social and cultural impact of #MeToo. The movement's exposure of abuse and misogyny within various levels of society has engendered representations of a conspicuous feminism that unequivocally portrays aspects of gender inequality in a combative manner, alerting viewers to instances of sexism and female oppression. The themes of female empowerment in these series also integrate elements of commodification as conspicuous feminism capitalizes on the ubiquity of the #MeToo movement.

Chapter One

Negotiating Feminism on Television

In November 2019, Apple launched their streaming service platform Apple TV+ with a slate of seven original programs, including *The Morning Show*, a drama that prominently featured narratives pertinent to #MeToo. The series centers on the repercussions faced by a popular morning news program when its male co-host Mitch Kessler (Steve Carrell) is fired due to allegations of sexual misconduct. Although the series was originally based on Brian Stelters's 2013 book *Top Of The Morning: Inside the Cutthroat World of Morning TV* and developed before the #MeToo movement's growth, the plotline echoes the real-life misconduct allegations of 2017 that culminated in the firing of prominent veteran news anchors Matt Lauer and Charlie Rose of NBC's *Today* and CBS's *This Morning*, respectively (Strause 2019). As showrunner Kerri Ehrens expressed to the *Atlantic*, "If you're doing a story about morning news right now, how do you not do #MeToo?" (Li 2019). The series' exploration of the gendered power dynamics that regulate the news network's operations, and of the challenges faced by women working in the industry in particular, reverberates with the concerns that #MeToo has disclosed, exemplifying how conspicuous feminism is being mediated on television as a consequence of the movement's impact.

Feminism has impacted US television representations since its "second wave," corresponding to the re-evaluation of women's roles in US culture in the 1960s and 1970s, following the expanding social awareness of new and varied roles for women outside of the domestic space. Feminism's second wave is widely construed as advancing the first wave's attempts in the late nineteenth and early twentiethth centuries to grant women access to the public sphere they had largely been restricted from due to their equivalence with the "cult of domesticity" that broadly designated women's roles during this period. The second wave is also characterized by activism that extended the first wave's aspirations toward gender equality with regards to suffrage.

In contrast, after the various achievements made for women in the public arena during the second wave, the third wave of feminism that developed in the 1990s has commonly been associated with female empowerment in terms of women's individual choices, although this wave has also been identified with a more pointed consideration of intersectional differences (Dicker 2016; Hewitt 2010; LeGates 1996). Lauren Rabinovitz states in her assessment of the uneven and contradictory reflections of feminism on television until the 1990s that, "Feminism's capacity to disrupt and upset cultural categories has always been so ambiguously presented on television that it lends itself to a range of political interpretations" (1999, 145). Notable examples of television's "ambiguous" presentation of feminism include *Ally McBeal* (FOX 1997–2002) and *Sex and the City* (HBO 1998–2004), which celebrated female independence through the protagonists' individual choices relating to personal (vs. political) issues such as relationships, marriage, career aspirations, and motherhood.

These representations and others are indicative of Lynn Spangler's assertion that "television into the twenty-first century is primarily a postfeminist world where equal rights are assumed and problems are between individuals, not systemic" (2003, 241). Shows such as *Ally McBeal* and *Sex and the City* reflect feminism, but its influence is less discernible and not explicitly expressed. Indeed, the inclusion of the fictional television character Ally McBeal (Calista Flockhart) on the front cover of the June 29, 1998, issue of *TIME* magazine alongside prominent feminists Susan B. Anthony, Betty Friedan, and Gloria Steinem accompanied by the headline "Is Feminism Dead?" signified the ambivalence that had come to infuse constructions of feminism by the late 1990s. The accompanying article suggested that feminism was being construed on *Ally McBeal* in terms of women's individual choices relating to issues such as marriage, motherhood, and careers in contrast to the politicized feminist objectives commonly associated with Anthony, Friedan, and Steinem such as voting, employment, and reproductive rights.

In contrast, Nicola Rivers postulated in 2017 that "Feminism may be back, occupying a more prominent or celebrated position in popular culture" (2017, 152), and the increase in female narratives on television is one illustration. These portrayals are evocative of the new feminist visibilities that have seemingly heralded feminism's fourth wave, which is broadly constituted by confrontation and outspokenness regarding misogyny and the victimization of women (e.g., in the #MeToo and #TimesUp hashtags and in "call out culture"), diverging from the postfeminist constructions that had largely distinguished representations of female empowerment in terms of choice and individuality (Genz and Brabon 2009; Gill 2007b; McRobbie 2004). In addition to Rivers, Prudence Chamberlain (2017) and Kira Cochrane (2013) have also described the fourth wave's focus on workplace harassment, intersectionality, body positivity, and the use of digital technology and social media. The renewed feminist visibility has largely centered on the pronounced exposure of the presence of misogyny in culture and has mainly been attributed to how feminist activism has become more easily accessible and implemented through the multiplicity of channels available on online platforms. The representations of conspicuous feminism on television can thus be regarded as a part of the activist sensibilities central to fourth-wave expressions, though the commodifying facets compelled by the commercial imperatives of television also diverge from them somewhat.

The unprecedented growth in the range and diversity of female representations on television has increased the possibilities for feminist interpretations and perspectives. In the 2020–2021 season, 45% of major characters on television series were women across broadcast/cable networks and streaming platforms (Lauzen 2021). As more women have become involved in the creation of these series as writers, producers, and performers, the possibilities for feminist interpretations and for the heterogeneity of female narratives to be further explored have also increases. In 2020–2021, women working as creators, producers, directors, writers, editors, and directors of photography accounted for 31% of behind-the-scenes personnel on television series on broadcast/cable networks and 33% across streaming platforms. The percentage of women creators on streaming programs was significantly higher than those on broadcast networks (30% vs. 22%). Notably higher percentages of women were also hired as directors on streaming programs (31% vs. 19% on broadcast networks) (Lauzen 2021). These trends suggest increased opportunities for women to be employed in leadership roles on streaming platforms. Noted female showrunners include Micaela Cole (*Chewing Gum* and *I May Destroy You*), Lena Dunham (*Girls*), Mindy Kaling (*The Mindy Project*), Jenji Kohan (*Orange Is the New Black*), Issa Rae (*Insecure*), Shonda Rhimes (*Grey's Anatomy, Scandal, How to Get Away with Murder*, and *Bridgerton*), Amy Sherman-Palladino (*Gilmore Girls* and *The Marvelous Mrs. Maisel*), and Phoebe Waller Bridge (*Fleabag*), with the majority of their series created for streaming channels.

This increase in female showrunners and producers has coincided with the vast changes that have transpired in television distribution and reception. Television streaming was introduced in the mid-2000s, which Amanda Lotz distinguishes as "internet-distributed television that enables protocols related to its nonlinearity and user specificity [and that] introduces strategies for distribution unavailable to previous mechanisms of television distribution" (2017). Notable examples of streaming platforms offering original television content include Amazon Prime, Disney Plus, HBO Max, Hulu, and Netflix, which have enabled the multiplicity and diversity of female representations on television. Hulu and Netflix launched streaming services in 2007, followed by Amazon Prime in 2013, Disney Plus in 2019, and HBO Max in 2020. Viewer subscriptions to these platforms have increased exponentially, and by March 2020, Netflix reported 183 million subscribers, while Disney Plus and Hulu reported 50 million and 30 million subscribers, respectively (Conklin 2020).

These trends signify the enduring relevance of "Peak TV in America," as proclaimed by FX network CEO John Landgraf in 2015 (James 2015). Taylor Nygaard and Jorie Lagerwey define the term *peak TV* as "a celebration of original scripted television content being distributed across broadcast, cable, and increasingly streaming video platforms, which is said to be revolutionizing the textual characteristics, industrial practices, audience behaviors, and cultural understandings of contemporary television" (2020, 47). The importance of streaming platforms in the peak TV era further increased as a result of the global repercussions wrought by the Covid-19 pandemic. Media production and distribution practices were significantly altered as the pandemic forced global shutdowns across various industries and instigated a shift toward television streaming platforms as major channels for distributing and exhibiting products (Fortmueller 2021). Viewership for television streaming correspondingly increased as Netflix and other platforms experienced an upsurge in subscribers as a result of social distancing and lockdown restrictions implemented worldwide to curb the spread of the pandemic (Fortmueller 2021; Vlassis 2021).

These developments have escalated the demand for original programming on streaming channels, yielding increased opportunities for female narratives and reflections of feminist themes, as well as creating more space and freedom for women in television production itself. These progressions have largely coincided with the proliferation of #MeToo, indicating that television representations of conspicuous feminism have been amplified by the various developments ensuing from these transformations alongside the enlarged media and cultural visibility of feminism itself. Before examining how feminist concerns have become more definitively portrayed on television as a consequence of #MeToo's impact, the following section broadly considers how television depictions of feminism have seemingly evolved alongside the social and cultural developments that motivate them.

INFLUENCE OF SECOND-WAVE FEMINISM IN THE 1960S AND 1970S

Several scholars maintain that themes and tropes of feminism have been reflected in television series since the 1970s, corresponding to the presence of second-wave feminism in the 1960s and 1970s (Brunsdon 2000; D'Acci 1994; Dow 1994; Johnson 2007; Spigel 2001). The women's rights movement that developed during this period raised and encouraged women's incentive to explore their options apart from the traditional role of wife/mother and the recognition of these options eventually moved into various aspects of popular culture, including television intent on targeting the market potential of independent working women. Prominent examples of television heroines inspired by feminist discourses included Ann Marie (Marlo Thomas) in *That Girl* (ABC, 1961–1967), Mary Richards (Mary Tyler Moore) in *The Mary Tyler Moore Show* (CBS, 1970–1977), and Laverne DeFazio (Penny Marshall) and Shirley Feeney (Cindy Williams) in *Laverne and Shirley* (ABC, 1976–1983), who were mainly characterized by their unmarried status and career ambitions, setting them in direct contrast to the happy housewives that had previously delineated women's roles on television. *The Mary Tyler Moore Show* is particularly endorsed as being among the first series to suggest that a career outside of the home could be a source of satisfaction for women in itself, instead of merely being a substitute for marriage and a family (Bathrick 2003; Dow 1996). Protagonist Mary Richards was depicted as focused and driven by her career as associate producer on a television news program without the need of a man to depend on financially or emotionally. Bonnie Dow argues that

> Mary Tyler Moore created important parameters for future television discourse representing feminism, parameters that include a focus on working women (and a concomitant avoidance of a critique of the traditional patriarchal family), the depiction of women's lives without male romantic partners, the enactment of a "feminist lifestyle" by young, attractive, white, heterosexual, female characters, and a reliance on the tenets of second-wave liberal or equity feminism. (1996, 26)

Though there were clear limitations to feminist narratives during this period, female protagonists such as Mary Richards were a direct contrast to the "happy housewife" construction that had become prevalent on television during the years following World War II.

This period ushered in the "network era" dominated by three principal networks, NBC, CBS, and ABC, which became synonymous with US television culture (Boddy 2004; Haralovich 1999; Lipsitz 2003; Lotz 2007; Spigel 2001). Lotz (2007) categorized the modifications within the American television broadcasting context in terms of three broad stages, commonly identified as the "network era" (1952–mid-1980s), the "multichannel transition" (mid-1980s–mid-2000s) and the "post-network era" (mid-2000s–present). The network era's credence on these three broadcast networks was defined by content and programming targeted toward a mass audience, formulaic structures within genres and representations, and limited options in terms of viewing and scheduling. Thus, the scope of female portrayals was significantly narrower during the early days of television and the primary stages of the network era due to the limitations on narrative variety and specificity. Television was a symbolic element of the period of postwar prosperity and contributed much to the ideal of suburban comfort and prosperity in delineating the American Dream (Samuel 2001; Spigel 2001).

Spangler documents that "As the popularity of television grew, so did American families and the idyllic myth of the housewife" (2003, 25). It is unsurprising, then, that television roles for women during this period were largely restricted to the domestic setting, clearly positioning them as wives and mothers. This would also correspond with the rise of advertising and consumerism in the years of postwar prosperity, with the happy housewife a keen target for advertisers marketing household products deemed essential to the maintenance of a blissful home and family. Notable contributors to the idyllic myth of the housewife were Harriet Nelson in *The Adventures of Ozzie and Harriet* (ABC, 1952–1966), Margaret Anderson (Jane Wyatt) in *Father Knows Best* (CBS/NBC, 1955–1960), June Cleaver (Barbara Billingsley) in *Leave It to Beaver* (CBS/ABC, 1957–1963), Donna Stone (Donna Reed) in *The Donna Reed Show* (ABC, 1959–1966), and Laura Petrie (Mary Tyler Moore) in *The Dick Van Dyke Show* (CBS, 1961–1966). Despite marginal differences in each of these iconic housewife portrayals, all reflected the distinct cultural expectations thrust on women in the immediate postwar era to "specialize in meeting expressive needs and routine tasks within the family" (Benson 2014, 16), and are rarely, if ever, depicted outside the space of the home. This image of the happy housewife was also clearly demarcated in terms of race and class, as evidenced in their exclusively white, middle class constructions.

One of the most iconic and beloved television housewives and mothers of the period, Lucy Ricardo (Lucille Ball) in *I Love Lucy* (CBS, 1951–1957), is commonly singled out for her feminist potential in her repeated and comic attempts to escape the position of housewife and the domestic space allotted to her. Each episode of the immensely popular series would focus on Lucy's hapless efforts to thwart the wishes and demands of her bandleader husband Ricky (Ball's real-life husband Desi Arnaz) and to enter into the public space outside the home. She makes several attempts to become a part of Ricky's nightclub act throughout the series, as well as attempting various other forms of employment, most memorably and humorously with friend and sidekick Ethel Mertz (Vivian Vance) in a candy factory ("Job Switching," Season 2, Episode 4). Lucy is clearly not content to be defined by domesticity, but by the close of each episode, she agreeably acquiesces to Ricky's will and is securely restored to her housewife role. However, several critics have commented that Lucy is a critical housewife figure in her resistance to the domestic role. Lori Landay describes her as "a model of female ambition that is relentless in its craving for freedom, participation and equality" (1998, 193). This presence of "female ambition" in a 1950s television housewife is noteworthy and important, although it is contained within Ball's brilliant slapstick comedy and the lesson in each episode that, "ultimately, [the wife/mother role] is what makes her most happy and she cannot successfully have both a career and a family life" (Spangler 2003, 34).

Ball's performance in *I Love Lucy* hints at the components of "trans gender queer" that Quinlan Miller argues were present in sitcom television programming of the 1950s and 1960s. Miller contends that the concept operated within the apparently fixed gendered constructions that characterized television representations during that period, including on iconic series such as *The Dick Van Dyke Show*, that challenged dominant representational modes of sexuality and race. *I Love Lucy* is indicative of the "parody of gender norms" (2019, 5) that Miller attributes to the "trans gender queer camp," constructions that were contained in sitcom performances that ostensibly appeared to conform to dominant norms of gender and sexuality. Lucy's defiance toward the happy housewife image reflects Miller's allegation that "camp" and "drag" aspects permeated the normalized conceptions of gender featured in 1950s and 1960s sitcoms that deftly critiqued the gendered norms being accentuated. According to Miller, the emphasis placed on signifiers of normalized traits of gender and sexuality served to challenge and satirize the models being presented, implying that the potential for subverting gendered norms was functioning even before second-wave feminism influenced gendered representations on television more directly.

The second-wave feminist movement of the 1960s and 1970s responded to Betty Friedan's positing of a "problem with no name" (1963, 29) in her book *The Feminine Mystique* (1963) regarding women's traditional circumscription to the home and domesticity by lobbying to increase and enhance women's access to the public space. Challenging these constructions, Friedan claimed that women were afflicted with an identity plight concerning their (re)inscription to the private space in the decades following World War II:

> Can the problem that has no name be somehow related to the domestic routine of the housewife? When a woman tries to put the problem into words, she often merely describes the daily life she leads. What is there in this recital of comfortable domestic detail that could possibly cause such a feeling of desperation? Is she trapped simply by the enormous demands of her role as modern housewife: wife, mistress, mother, nurse, consumer, cook, chauffeur, expert on interior decoration, childcare, appliance repair, furniture refinishing, nutrition, and

education? We can no longer ignore that voice within women that says: "I want something more than my husband and my children and my home." (1963, 29)

The second-wave feminist movement specifically challenged the validity of domesticity as the sole identity for women in favor of Friedan's notion of "a real identity" formed through the pursuit of "higher education, achieving a rewarding career and performing a meaningful role in the public sphere" (Gillis and Hollows 2009, 7). During the 1960s and 1970s, series such as *That Girl* and *The Mary Tyler Moore Show* would reflect the possibilities outside of domesticity in their negotiations of women in the public space.

A number of women's groups were founded during this period, most notably the National Organization of Women (NOW) in 1966 and the Women's Equity Action League (WEAL) in 1968. These and other organizations focused on consciousness raising among women of all ages concerning issues including work, child care, women's health and sexuality, and violence against women. Notable achievements included the Equal Pay Act in 1963, Title VII of the Civil Rights Act in 1964 (which prohibited gender discrimination in employment), and Title IX of the Higher Act in 1972 (which prohibited gender discrimination within the educational arena). Other acts aided women in regards to sexuality and reproduction, most notably in the success of the Supreme Court case *Roe vs. Wade,* which legalized abortion in 1972 (Gilmore 2008; Hewitt 2010). (As noted in the Introduction, *Roe vs. Wade* was overturned by the Supreme Court in June 2022.)

Women's issues and the presence of feminism was summarily acknowledged on television during this period though the wife/mother characters that largely continued to conform to traditional notions of gender and domesticity. Carol Brady (Florence Henderson) in *The Brady Bunch* (ABC, 1969–1974), Edith Bunker (Jean Stapleton) in *All in the Family* (CBS, 1971–1979), and Marion Cunningham (Marion Ross) in *Happy Days* (ABC, 1974–1984) were all versions of the smiling and unassuming wife/mother, satisfied with her role in the domestic space. One of the most memorable housewives of this era was also not merely a housewife at all—Samantha Stephens (Elizabeth Montgomery) in *Bewitched* (ABC, 1964–1972) literally charmed audiences with her portrayal of a witch/suburban wife and mother, happily ensconced within the domestic environment. It is equivocal that Samantha willingly chooses a life of domesticity to care for her hapless husband Darrin (Dick York, replaced by Dick Sargent after 1969) and their children, despite her numerous and considerable options due to her infinite powers of witchcraft, suggesting that even with the multitude of options open to them (even magic!), women are most content and suited to the realm of domesticity. *All in the Family* was also noteworthy in its inclusion of social issues that had not previously been featured in primetime television sitcoms, such as breast cancer ("Edith's Christmas Story," Season 4, Episode 15) and rape ("Edith's 50th Birthday," Season 8, Episode 4). Though the issues are dealt with lightly and humorously—in the first instance, matriarch Edith ultimately discovers that she does not have cancer, and in the second she is able to fend off her attacker with a cake pan—the episodes do indicate the influence of feminism and the raised consciousness of women's issues.

The 1960s and 1970s generally witnessed a marked decrease in television representations of housewives and stay-at-home mothers, due to the influence of second-wave feminism and the expanding social awareness of new and varied roles for women outside of the domestic space. One exception was Maude Findley (Beatrice Arthur) on *Maude* (CBS, 1972–1978), noted for being the first primetime television series to portray a character opting to have an abortion in 1972 ("Maude's Dilemma," Season 1, Episode 9/10), just months before the *Roe vs. Wade* Supreme Court ruling (Beale 1992). Housewife Maude was also characterized by her outspokenness regarding feminist and civil rights issues. In general, feminism was more likely to be reflected in characters and narratives that were not defined by domesticity and the family. Widowed and divorced single mothers such as Julia Baker (Diahann Caroll) on *Julia* (NBC, 1968–1971), Alice Spivak Hyatt (Linda Lavin) on *Alice* (CBS, 1976–1986) and Ann Romano (Bonnie Franklin) on *One Day at a Time* (CBS, 1975–1984) embodied feminist dispositions in their negotiations of both the private and public space. *Julia* was also notable for being the first television sitcom to feature a black female protagonist (Bodroghovsky 2003; Opinde 2019).

The Mary Tyler Moore Show arguably established the single working woman series as the "preferred fictional site for a 'feminist' subject position'" (Rabinovitz 1999, 3). It reflected the influence of second-wave feminism's achievements as the character of Mary Richards was able to explore possibilities outside of domesticity and the home. However, the success and popularity of the show has often been attributed to the ways in which it was able to blend a feminist perspective with traditional patriarchal ideals (Dow 1996; Gitlin 1982; Taylor 1989). Although the series is primarily set in the workplace outside of the home, Mary Richards still embodies constructions of femininity associated with domesticity in her encompassing of the caretaker role among her dominantly male colleagues. As Dow notes in her analysis of the influence of feminism in the series,

> Within her family of co-workers, Mary functions in the recognizable roles of mother, wife, and daughter—roles familiar from decades of reinforcement in popular culture generally and sitcom specifically. Mary alternately nurtures, mediates, facilitates and submits. . . . . In *Mary Tyler Moore*, "woman's place" is transformed from a matter of location to one of function. (1996, 40)

In spite of featuring a female protagonist that is not defined by the space of the home and domesticity, traditional characteristics associated with it are still reproduced and simply transferred to the workplace, suggesting that women could find gratification outside of the home without disrupting gendered ideals affiliated with it. This conception of feminism would continue to influence television representations of women outside of the home as feminine traits commonly identified with domesticity were reconfigured in alternative settings.

"BACKLASH" AND THE 1980S

The television industry underwent substantial developments during the 1980s, establishing Lotz's (2006) demarcation of the multichannel transition and the end of the network era. The multichannel transition is widely identified with the growth of cable television programming that began to rival the dominance of the broadcast networks, as well as significant technological advancements that impacted television consumption and viewing practices, such as remote control devices and video cassette recorders (Walker and Bellamy 1993). Two of the three networks were sold to major corporations (ABC to Capital Communications Inc. and NBC to General Electric; CBS would be acquired by The Westinghouse Electrical Corporation in the mid-1990s). Amidst these administrative conversions, new broadcast networks emerged as viable competitors to the previously dominant networks, notably FOX in 1986. The Lifetime cable network became the first network to explicitly target female viewers upon its launch in 1984. This increase in choice created an unprecedented climate of greater viewer control, leading to the shift toward "narrowcasting" as the increased variety in programming encouraged audience fragmentation and polarization. These changes would have a considerable impact on television representations, offering much more heterogeneity and possibilities in programming, content, narratives, and characterization, including those concerning women, feminist thought, and social change.

The inclination toward representing independent and successful women continued with viewers captivated by the antics of the ensemble in *Designing Women* (CBS, 1986–1983), Murphy Brown (Candice Bergen) in *Murphy Brown* (CBS, 1988–1998), as well as the female lawyers and career women on *LA Law* (NBC, 1986–1994) and *Thirtysomething* (ABC, 1987–1991), amongst others. *LA Law* and *Thirtysomething* were representative of the accession of the hour-long ensemble dramatic series in the 1980s, a genre that continues to dominate primetime television programming. *Cagney and Lacey* (CBS, 1981–1988), focusing on the experiences and relationship between two female police officers (Sharon Gless and Tyne Daly) is consistently hailed as a landmark series for female representation and is believed to have shaped cultural definitions of womanhood on television in its relentless representation of women's issues including sexual harassment, rape, abortion, and breast cancer (D'Acci 1994). These series and others could be seen as representative of television's pursuance in the 1980s of the female market, resulting in images of women occupying the public space outside of the home becoming more commonplace and familiar.

However, certain ideologies concerning women's place continued to linger despite the frequency of these representations in that the career success of these female characters is often tempered by the relative lack in their personal lives—Murphy Brown, in particular, is "depicted as a woman who had paid a price for her success in terms of the barrenness of her personal life and her lack of traditionally feminine attributes" (Dow 1996, 386). This interrogating of "feminism's success" is indicative of the "backlash" discourse identified by Susan Faludi. Her book detailed a range of media texts in the 1980s and 1990s that seemingly rendered the "sad plight of millions of unhappy and unsatisfied women" as a result of the feminist movement:

> Professional women are suffering "burnout" and succumbing to an "infertility epidemic." Single women are grieving from a "man shortage" . . . Childless women are "depressed and confused" and their ranks are swelling . . . Unwed women are "hysterical" and crumbling under a profound crisis of confidence" . . . High powered career women are stricken with unprecedented outbreaks of "stress-induced disorders. . . ." (1992, 1–2)

According to the backlash discourse, women have suffered on account of the social changes effected by feminist ideals, resulting in the myriad female crises constituted above and the fluctuating representations of women and feminist considerations on television.

In spite of these backlash depictions of working women, representations of the wife/mother primarily defined by her domestic and household duties were even more scarce during the 1980s. Mothers on television were often working mothers—notable examples include Elyse Keaton (Meredith Baxter Birney) in *Family Ties* (NBC, 1982–1989), Clair Huxtable (Phylicia Rashad) in *The Cosby Show* (NBC, 1984–1992), and Maggie Seaver (Joanna Kerns) in *Growing Pains* (ABC, 1985–1992). All are successful career women (Elyse Keaton is an architect, Clair Huxtable is a lawyer, and Maggie Seaver is a journalist), yet television narratives presented them mostly in the domestic setting in their roles as wives and mothers. This echoes Susan Douglas's assertion that "although women may be shown to work outside the home, they continue to perform the duties of the homemaker so that their status is ambiguous" (2010, 108). This ambiguity allowed for more realistic representations of working women and acknowledged the impact of feminism, yet simultaneously upheld traditional ideals concerning gender and femininity. Cultural backlash anxieties relating to working women and their impact on conventional constructions of motherhood and domesticity could also be allayed through such modes of representation. In Dow's (1996) examination of how backlash narratives impacted depictions of feminism in television series during the 1980s, she notes that media coverage of working women typically focused on concerns relating to difficulties in fulfilling their domestic responsibilities, marriage problems, finding adequate day care services, and infertility issues (1996, 94).

In contrast, perhaps the most contentious wife/mother television figure of the era was Roseanne Connor (Roseanne Barr) in *Roseanne* (ABC, 1988–1997). Always scrutinized in sharp contrast to the other successful, attractive, and dignified television mothers of the time, Roseanne is observed for her crude and brash demeanor, as well as her physical appearance, which did not conform to the svelte and cultivated images of conventional television heroines. In her ironic and self-proclaimed interpretation of the term "domestic goddess," Roseanne was a prime example of Kathleen Rowe's (1995) concept of the "unruly woman" who is intent on demolishing the tropes of femininity that produce conceptions of the "ideal" wife and mother. The Connor family's working-class background, unkempt household, and caustic family interactions, as well as Roseanne's biting sarcasm, confirm Spangler's remark, in citing television critic David Bianculli, that the series is not "concerned with proper behavior, language and role models" (2003, 169). In its rejection of traditional ideals of femininity, "Roseanne (was) a reminder that feminist arguments continue to be relevant, important and necessary" (White 2017, 248), and the series received critical praise for its representation of the gritty realities of working-class life and was fundamental to illustrating the actual difficulties of conforming to the paradigm of the happy housewife myth, especially in particular social and class contexts.

POSTFEMINISM IN THE 1990S AND 2000S

The term *postfeminism* became widely used after the 1980s as women's presence in the public space continued to increase, and feminism became plagued by concerns over its relevance for contemporary women. As Shelley Budgeon asserts, "as feminism has become institutionalized, its presence as an oppositional social movement has waned" (2011, 35), and she argues that women are now directed "towards subjectivities defined by choice, empowerment, and individuality" (2011, 51). Perceptions of choice and individuality were central to denotations of postfeminism and constructions of femininity, in contrast to the more collective constitution of second-wave feminism. In this way, postfeminism is also distinguished from postmodern feminism, which is largely characterized by its attention toward differences between women and by the predication that gender and femininity are constructed through systems of language (Assiter 1996; Butler 1990; Hekman 1992). The elements of postmodern feminism are broadly specified by a rejection of essentialist and universalist norms that have defined women and femininity through traditional patriarchal constructs and an emphasis on empowerment through choice.

Yvonne Tasker and Diane Negra claim that "Postfeminism is . . . inherently contradictory, characterized by a double discourse that works to construct feminism as a phenomenon of the past, traces of which can be found (and sometimes even valued) in the present" (2007, 8), suggesting that postfeminism can be defined by the "traces" of feminism that have been retained in its figurations. Stephanie Genz and Benjamin Brabon similarly claim that postfeminism can be "read as a healthy rewriting of feminism, a sign that the women's movement is continuously in process, transforming and changing itself" (2009, 11–12). Ann Brooks has also positively characterized postfeminism as "feminism's 'coming of age,' its maturity into a confident body of theory and politics, representing pluralism and difference" (1997, 1). Negra also accentuates postfeminism's simultaneous continuation of and shift away from second-wave feminism by postulating that

> This widely-applied and highly contradictory term performs as if it is commonsensical and presents itself as pleasingly moderated in contrast to a "shrill" feminism. Crucially, postfeminism often functions as a means of registering and superficially resolving the persistence of "choice" dilemmas for American women. (2009, 2)

In the 1990s and 2000s, these "choice dilemmas" were often embodied in the typically contradictory and diverse media and cultural representations of women's identities and the numerous roles afforded to them. The protagonists on series such as *Ally McBeal* and *Sex and the City* manifested the predicaments of choice associated with postfeminism.

Themes of choice and individuality were inherent in the multiplicity of female representations that flourished on television in the 1990s. The "multichannel transition" seamlessly segued into the "post-network" era, which Lotz distinguishes as "the erosion of (network) control over how and when viewers watch particular programs" (2006, 15). By the mid-1990s, network dominance had consistently been dissolved by multiple industry mergers, as well as continuous competition from new broadcast networks (namely UPN and the WB in 1995) and the rapid expansion of cable television. The 1990s witnessed the ascendancy of HBO, which has been heralded as a principal innovator in its programming and representations, including those of women. Two more cable channels explicitly targeting female viewers were launched (Women's Entertainment in 1997 and Oxygen in 2000) and along with the previously established channel Lifetime, increased in prominence with their popular rosters of daytime talk shows, reality series, and syndicated programming.

The 1990s saw an increase in dramatic series focused on female narratives and experiences (Lotz 2006, 6). Indeed, the era is known for its "representation of competent professional women in ensemble dramas such as *ER* (NBC, 1994–2009), *The X-Files* (FOX, 1993–2002) and *The Practice* (ABC, 1997–2004)" (Dow 1996, 389), indicating television's continuing adherence to portraying women outside of the domestic space. One prolific example was Ally McBeal (Calista Flockhart) in *Ally McBeal*. The polemical Ally divided feminists between those who praised her rendering of a capable and successful lawyer thriving in the workplace and those who deplored her obsessiveness with her romantic life (or lack thereof). Indeed, the series would reiterate the female prototypes of the 1960s and 1970s in that a woman's navigation of the public space would ultimately center on the "feminine" realms of love, relationships, and personal issues typically related to the private sphere of sociality and emotions.

Ally was a forerunner of the women of *Sex and the City*, the series that is commonly lauded as the preeminent postfeminist television text. The four female protagonists inhabit the public space (The City) in a manner never previously witnessed on network television, not only in their professional attainments (all are established career women at the start of the series), but more notably in their romantic and sexual exploits. Indeed, the explicit sexual encounters and frank conversations about sex the characters routinely engage in would not have found an avenue on broadcast television, which was just one of the ways HBO distinguished itself from its broadcast network competition. Carrie Bradshaw (Sarah Jessica Parker) and her counterparts were not restricted to the private sphere of family and domesticity—in their typical and habitual occupation of the public sphere, they enthralled and provoked viewers with their audacity toward the gendered nature of the public/private divide and the characteristics commonly associated with each. In the pilot episode, Carrie asserts that having "sex like a man" equated to "own(ing) the city" (*Sex and the City,* Season 1, Episode 1), suggesting that the traits affiliated with women and the private sphere have shifted in accordance with the shifting qualities of the public and the private.

The popularity of *Sex and the City* confirmed Rebecca Munford and Melanie Waters's contention that "postfeminism has become the lens through which contemporary discussions of the relationship between popular culture and feminism are most often refracted" (2014, 13). In addition to Ally and the women of *Sex and the City*, television representations of women that are not defined by traditional constructions of femininity and domesticity include Olivia Benson (Mariska Hargitay) on *Law and Order: SVU* (NBC 1999–present), Lorelai Gilmore (Lauren Graham) on *Gilmore Girls* (The WB, 2000–2006 and the CW, 2006–2007), Meredith Grey (Ellen Pompeo) and her medical colleagues on *Grey's Anatomy* (ABC, 2005–present), Carrie Mathison (Claire Danes) on *Homeland* (Showtime, 2011–2020), Hannah Horvath (Lena Dunham) and her fellow *Girls* (HBO, 2012–2017), Mindy Lahiri (Mindy Kaling) on *The Mindy Project* (Fox, 2012–2017), Olivia Pope (Kerry Washington) on *Scandal* (ABC, 2012–2018), Selina Meyer (Julia Louis-Dreyfus) on *Veep* (HBO, 2012–2019), Annalise Keating (Viola Davis) on *How to Get Away with Murder* (ABC, 2014–2020), and Issa Dee (Issa Rae) on *Insecure* (HBO, 2016–2021). The multiplicity of female representations in popular culture confirms that constructions of femininity are no longer confined to the space of the home and that reflections of feminism have become more complex and varied as a result of expanded narrative possibilities.

However, these postfeminist depictions have summarily "been viewed by many as a 'selling out' of feminist principles and their co-option as a marketing device" (Genz and Brabon 2009, 5) that serves a distinctively commercial rather than feminist purpose. Budgeon similarly observes that the growth in women's opportunities and autonomy has not eliminated "traditional expectations regarding what constitutes 'proper' femininity" (2011, 61) and that postfeminism has reinforced rather than restructured these expectations concerning women's place. Postfeminism has also been strongly aligned with "a variety of popular practices and forms of cultural consumption [so that] femininity and its associations with passivity, dependency, domesticity, and investment in physical attractiveness have been seen to contribute to the production of a feminine identity that makes women blind to their participation in their own oppression" (Hollows 2000, 20). This can be surmised in Budgeon's affirmation that "ideally, women must be assertive, autonomous, and self-determining, but they must also retain aspects of traditional femininity, including heterosexual desirability and emotional sensitivity to others" (2011, 54), further emphasizing that even though women have the autonomy to make their own choices, conventionally ascribed gender traits still retain the potential to restrict their options.

A spatial confusion that characterizes women's roles can thus be evinced in popular television's reverting of female characters back to the domestic space. In the midst of the constantly evolving and multiple roles that emerged for women in the postfeminist era, there has been a renewed focus on domesticity, albeit in a manner that distinctly contradicts and denies the nostalgia that is commonly associated with earlier constructions of the happy housewife. Indeed, the popular media have been saturated with images of the housewife—notable examples range from the ubiquitous *Desperate Housewives* of the hit ABC television drama (ABC, 2004–2012) to the glamourous and provocative escapades of *the Real Housewives* on the titillating Bravo reality series (2006–present). Although domesticity is seemingly enjoying a revival of sorts within popular culture, its presentation definitively varies from its earlier idealization in the postwar era. According to *Desperate Housewives* creator Marc Cherry, the postfeminist era has resulted in confusion and ambivalence in interpretations of the housewife role:

> The women's movement said, "Let's get the gals out working." Next the women realized you can't have it all. Most of the time you have to make a choice. What I'm doing is having women make the choice to live in the suburbs, but that things aren't going well at all. (McCabe and Akass 2006, 9)

The postfeminist rhetoric of choice has largely informed the cultural visibility of the housewife, which has increased as a consequence of the success of *Desperate Housewives* and other shows that portray the various tribulations experienced by women within the domestic space. The prominence of businesswoman and television personality Martha Stewart's domestic empire (*Martha Stewart Living* 1993–2004 [syndicated] and *The Martha Stewart Show* NBC, 2005–2012) also elevated domesticity to a form of expertise, augmenting the status of the private sphere of the home within culture. However, this renewed focus on domesticity is notably different from the 1950s "cult of motherhood" (Dow 1996, 90), in that women are not generally presented as naturally disposed to the domestic sphere, challenging the assumptions that uphold conceptions of gendered space.

Other important depictions of women that embody these renewed constructions of domesticity include Carmela Soprano (Edie Falco) on *The Sopranos* (HBO, 1999–2007), Ruth Fisher (Frances Conroy) on *Six Feet Under* (HBO 2001–2004), Nancy Botwin (Mary Louise Parker) on *Weeds* (Showtime 2005–2012), Betty Draper (January Jones) on *Mad Men* (AMC, 2007–2015), and Skyler White (Anna Gunn) on *Breaking Bad* (AMC, 2009–2013). While these characterizations suggest that domesticity and motherhood might still be idealized in many ways, the efforts required to achieve these ideals are also exposed. In these representations, the domestic space has seemingly transformed from a site typically associated with safety, sentimentality, and nostalgia (Massey 1994, 13) to a rather more unstable and precarious terrain. For instance, Nancy Botwin on *Weeds* largely conducts her business as a marijuana dealer in the private space of the home, and Betty Draper's misery in domesticity is amply documented on *Mad Men*. These regenerated renderings of the domestic space distinctly interrogate the "naturalized distinctions between public/private and masculinity/femininity that work to maintain sexual difference by subordinating women in the home" (Nathanson 2013, 12) and further complicate the traditional associations between female identities and domesticity.

Thus, in spite of the various options available to women outside of the home, there is still ambivalence regarding Friedan's 1963 contention that the key to women's emancipation was in access to the public space. Instead, Munford and Waters suggest that ideals of femininity are being shaped by a "postfeminist mystique," which "reactivates modes of feminine identity that were 'proper to a former age,' but which seem 'out of harmony' with a present that has ... reaped all the benefits of second wave feminism" (2014, 10). This reinforces the postfeminist characteristic of "choice" and Elspeth Probyn's contention that "binding women and choice together gives a construction of women as thinking about choice but unable to choose" (1995, 262). These confusing and at times anachronistic configurations of women's roles have continued to inform representations of feminine identity and constructions of feminism on television and in popular culture. However, #MeToo has modified the constructions of feminism that proliferated on television and in the media since the mid-2010s. The themes of female strength and empowerment that have been consistently featured in female narratives on television since the second wave have been enhanced by the resistance to misogyny that the movement engendered, producing reflections of a conspicuous feminism that are more complex and explicit in their conviction.

STREAMING CONSPICUOUS FEMINISM AND #METOO ON QUALITY TELEVISION

In the title of her opinion piece published in May 2019, Yomi Adegoke claimed that "We're in a golden age of feminist TV" (*The Guardian* 2019), referring to the numerous television series featuring female protagonists and reflecting themes palpably influenced by feminism, including *Big Little Lies*, *Broad City* (Comedy Central, 2014–2019), *Fleabag*, *Glow* (Netflix, 2017–2019) and *Killing Eve*. This "golden age" was enabled by the transformations in television distribution and reception that occurred during the 2010s. The post-network era distinguished by Lotz (2006) as commencing in the mid-2000s has been identified with the growth of premium cable television programming and television streaming platforms. In 2021, 559 scripted television series were aired, reflecting a 13% growth in comparison to the previous year, which was largely due to the pervasiveness of streaming services

(Romanchick 2022). The dominance of streaming and cable platforms at prestigious television awards shows also affirms their association with models of "quality television." In 2021, HBO garnered 130 nominations at the Primetime Emmy Awards, followed closely by Netflix with 129 (Fung 2021). The original programming provided on these distribution channels associated with the concept of "quality television" has yielded increased opportunities for female narratives and reflections of feminist themes, as well as created more space and freedom for women in television production.

Jonathan Bignell defines quality television programming as the "kinds of programme that are perceived as more expensively produced and, especially, more culturally worthwhile than other programmes" (2004, 176). As such, quality television has also been defined by its narrative, technical, and aesthetic capacities that frequently garner critical acclaim and by a niche target audience that prefers viewing that is "'progressive' and socially challenging, versus identifying programmes which perpetuate formerly dominant social conventions and support the status quo" (Bignell 2004, 181). Series such as *Big Little Lies*, *The Marvelous Mrs. Maisel*, *Insecure*, and *The Handmaid's Tale* thus offer deeper possibilities for the interrogation of feminist issues and for richer representations of women's narratives.

Bignell's definition of quality develops from Jane Feuer's (1985) identification of quality television as a concept intentionally adopted by US network television in the 1970s, referencing the success of MTM productions and its *The Mary Tyler Moore Show* as a primary example of a production studio that attempted to confer status and cachet specifically to the television sitcom genre. Building on Feuer's work, Kristen Lentz argues that quality was accorded to *Mary Tyler Moore* due to its conscious engagement with feminist issues:

> The discourse of "quality" television found the burgeoning discourses of feminism to be useful tools in the project of improving television's public image. If 1970s feminism, broadly speaking, sought to champion the "rights" of women, drawing attention to the inequities of gender role socialization and attempting either to revalue or to eschew femininity, 1970s television was similarly enmeshed in an attempt to resist its inferior status in relation to other media (especially cinema) and to revalue or reverse its associations with femininity. The strategies of "quality" television were therefore strangely allied with some forms of feminism. "Quality" had as one of its goals nothing less than the "emancipation" of television. (2000, 49)

The integration of second-wave feminist discourses comprised the denotation of quality in *Mary Tyler Moore*, which was particularly notable for a sitcom, a genre not typically regarded for social relevance or complexity, and allotted a sense of modernity and relevance to the television medium itself. In this way, Lentz's explication of the concept of quality maintains its affiliation with television constructions of conspicuous feminism that have been activated by the prominence of #MeToo.

The definition of quality television has since been debated by various scholars, with most referring to Feuer's signification of the term as a starting point (McCabe and Akass 2007a). Robert J. Thompson draws on Feuer in his description of the growth of quality television in the early 1980s, which he defined as not "regular" (1996, 13) TV but "better, more sophisticated, and more artistic than the usual network fare" (12). Indeed, quality television, particularly after the post-network era of the 1990s, has largely been identified with non-network programming and, in contrast to Lentz's intimations on quality and the incorporation of feminist themes, was initially associated with more progressive and complex constructions of masculinity with depictions that embodied more emotional depth and moral ambiguity than was previously afforded to male protagonists. Notable examples include Tony Soprano (James Gandolfini) on *The Sopranos* (HBO, 1999–2007), Enoch "Nucky" Thompson (Steve Buscemi) on *Boardwalk Empire* (HBO, 2010–2014), Don Draper (Jon Hamm) on *Mad Men* (AMC, 2007–2015), and Walter White (Bryan Cranston) on *Breaking Bad* (AMC, 2008–2013). These performances and their affiliated series were all critically lauded and deemed representative of the cinematic features often accredited to quality television:

> Quality programmes' creative imagination, authenticity or relevance might instead suggest links with cinema, visual art or theatre, and thus quality comes to mean "not-like-television." The distinctive use of style is a reason why generic programmes can become labelled as "quality" television drama. Stereo sound, CGI and post-production effects technology have offered further opportunities for making visually distinctive narratives. (Bignell 2004, 187)

Quality television also became synonymous with the specific brand being endorsed by the respective network or streaming platform, as illustrated by the figuration of *The Sopranos* as emblematic of HBO's brand identity as "It's Not TV." David Thorburn describes the series as "a brilliant hybrid culmination of film and television, and an originating text as well, among the first complex expressions of the digital future now impending" (2008, 69), emphasizing quality television's distinctiveness in terms of style, visuals, narrative, and characterization.

Amidst quality television's earlier correlations with innovative constructions of masculinity, HBO's *Sex and the City* has frequently been recognized as one of quality television's first examples to impact female culture and generate discussions on women's roles and constructions of femininity in popular culture in its bold depictions of "sexualities, reproductive 'choice,' and feminine embodiment" (Nash and Grant 2015, 976). However, Astrid Henry notes that the series' "vision of female empowerment is severely limited by the fact that all four of its protagonists are white, heterosexual, thin, conventionally attractive and, importantly, economically well off" (2004, 70). The racial, sexual. and economic privilege that Carrie Bradshaw and her counterparts possess produces a figuration of feminism that neglects consideration of certain identities.

Fifteen years after the premiere of *Sex And The City*, *Girls* debuted on HBO in 2012. Also featuring four protagonists living in New York City, the series has garnered multiple comparisons to its predecessor but has also enlarged its feminist scope. Created, directed, and starring self-proclaimed feminist Lena Dunham, the series has been praised for portraying a protagonist that does not conform to expected models of physical appearance, and is dysfunctional and struggling, as well as being empowered and hopeful. As Jessica Ford attests in her article on Dunham's series:

> None of the characters are having the kind of "empowering" sexual encounters depicted in *Sex and the City*, but rather they are continually confronted by how they have internalized the misogyny of their culture. . . . the series uses irony and reflexivity to reinforce that the authors are aware of the various ways that characters and the series are indebted to and enabled by second wave feminism and earlier feminist television series. (2016, 1033)

In contrast to the focus on empowerment, choice, and individuality that *Sex and the City's* construction of feminism is typically associated with, *Girls* has contemplated feminist issues ranging from body image concerns, sexual relationships, female reproductive issues, and constructions of masculinity to harassment and assault, illustrating a wider and more complex vision of feminism than that offered by its predecessor.

The themes of empowerment and independence are present but enacted without the gloss and confidence that largely defined *Sex and the City*, reiterating Meredith Nash and Ruby Grant's observation that "the women of *Girls* are similarly white and entitled but unambitious, mostly unemployed and financially unstable" (2015, 979). Uncertainty and shame are frequent markers of main protagonist Hannah Horvath's (Dunham) experiences as denoted by repeated and often humiliating disappointments in her career goals, relationships, and sexual encounters. The series' relentless concentration on the failures of Hannah and her friends has been identified as a distinctive iteration of feminism (Householder 2015; Nash and Grant 2015; Silverman and Hagelin 2018) that "rewrites our cultural narratives about women's productivity and self-improvement" (Silverman and Hagelin 2018, 881). In this way, *Girls* has been commended for expanding and complicating postfeminism's affiliations with ostensible demarcations of choice, independence, and empowerment.

The demand for specified content precipitated by the ascension of television streaming options has also increased the opportunities for female showrunners and other women in the industry, producing more female-centered narratives and integrating feminist themes. Business and distribution models generated by the growth of digital television technologies and developments in television viewing practices have become significantly more diverse and specified (Lotz 2017), and as a result, several series featuring female narratives have since attempted to portray more inclusive and comprehensive reflections of feminist issues. This enlarging of feminist themes on quality television has also been attributed to the growth in opportunities for women in television production, as evidenced by the expanding numbers of female showrunners. Joy Press describes the considerable amount of control and responsibility granted to the showrunner of a series:

> Today showrunner is an elastic term that can encompass varying degrees of creative and managerial control over a TV series. That might mean developing the original concept, overseeing a cast and crew, shepherding a writers' room, consulting with directors, editing episodes, maintaining a budget, and negotiating with studios and networks. The showrunner is the visionary in chief, operations manager, and financial officer all rolled into one. (2018, 23)

The presence of more women in the role has engendered more prospects for female perspectives to be incorporated into narratives displaying feminist concerns and has corresponded to the heightened visibility of feminism in the media and culture. As Press observes, "This mainstreaming of feminism dovetailed perfectly with the new wave of woman-powered television, shows that offered varied representations of female life and often engaged with serious issues such as abortion, equal pay, and violence against women" (31).

Jenji Kohan's *Orange Is the New Black* (Netflix, 2013–2019) is regularly referenced as indicative of the variety of female narratives and representations offered on streaming platforms. Indeed, Netflix is the prime example of the prevalence of television streaming characterized by Lotz (2017) as "portals" that disseminate television programming through the internet. The Netflix brand in particular has been associated with an ability to cater to diverse audiences and "multiple taste groups" (Lotz 2017), and narratives engaging with feminist concerns are a key aspect of this diversity. *Orange Is the New Black* was Netflix's first female-centered original series and an initial example of conspicuous feminism, featuring intriguing portrayals of the female inmates at the fictional Litchfield Penitentiary. In addition to main protagonist Piper

Chapman (Taylor Schilling), an upper-class young woman sentenced to fifteen months for attempting to smuggle drugs out of the country on behalf of her girlfriend Alex (played by Laura Prepon and also an inmate sentenced at Litchfield), other inmates include the transgender Sofia Burset (Laverne Cox), prison "mother" Red Reznikov (Kate Mulgrew), the volatile Suzanne "Crazy Eyes" Warren (Uzo Aduba), and the hyperfeminine romantic idealist Lorna Morello (Yael Stone), among others. The series' "explicit[ness] about sex, violence, corruption and racial and ethnic divisions within the prison system" (Walters 2017, 201) has received critical recognition and employed a more intersectional perspective to its negotiation of conspicuous feminism, as well as expanded the multiplicity and diversity of women's stories being told on popular television.

In spite of the eminence of *Orange Is the New Black* and other series renowned for featuring representations of diversity such as *Insecure* and *I May Destroy You*, there is still apprehension regarding how diversity has generally been depicted and accommodated within the multiple outlets featuring heterogeneous narratives that have become available via the growth in streaming channels. Scholars have noted the particular means by which diversity has been incorporated into television narratives, such as Shonda Rhimes's use of "blindcasting" (Warner 2015) for the roles in her hit series, which can merely symbolize a "plastic representation" (Warner 2017) that largely delivers a superficial portrayal of difference and racial issues and does not fundamentally provoke dominant power structures. Although streaming platforms have offered more opportunities for diverse perspectives and content, these representations have also been consciously commodified and accommodated in order to appeal to global audiences (Lobato 2019; Nygaard and Lagerwey 2020; Petruska and Woods 2019). For example, *And Just Like That . . .*, HBO's 2021 revival of *Sex and the City*, attempted to redress the privilege that was largely unacknowledged on the original show by pointedly including narratives and characters featuring issues of cultural, racial, and sexual diversity. However, these endeavors were largely derided by critics, who perceived the inclusion of these themes as a calculated bid to incorporate intersectional motifs for their topicality and currency (Corry 2022; Patten 2021).

In his study on branding and intersectionality on streaming television, Aymar Jean Christian posits that "Intersectional stories still remain outliers on corporate platforms, which seek surplus value from attracting underserved audiences" (2018, 460), suggesting that streaming platforms still largely adhere to moderate depictions of race and diversity due to persisting discourses in television that privilege certain constructions of gender and race. Although the opportunities for a multiplicity of narratives and perspectives have flourished in the peak TV era, the methods and mindsets used to integrate them have not consequently done so.

The prominence of #MeToo has coincided with the proliferation of conspicuous feminism on television, producing more sensitive and complex portrayals of sexual violence. The lack of censorship restrictions on sexual content on cable and streaming platforms has led to more explicit representations in the quality television series that are distributed on them (McCabe and Akass 2007b). Graphic depictions of violence toward women have been included in quality series such as *The Sopranos* and *Game of Thrones* (HBO, 2011–2019), but the influence of #MeToo has since rendered more perceptive representations that reflect the complexity of the specific situations being depicted, particularly as they pertain to elements of trauma and shame that have in the past not typically been considered in depth. As Zarah Moeggenberg and Sarah Solomon contend in their article on the influence of #MeToo on Hulu's adaptation of *The Handmaid's Tale*, an "axis from which women are questioning the normalization and silencing of sexual violence against women has been through television" (2018, 6). In addition to *The Handmaid's Tale*, a number of renowned series have recently featured themes of sexual violence, including *Big Little Lies*, *Jessica Jones* (Netflix, 2015–2019), *Orange Is the New Black*, *Sharp Objects* (HBO, 2018), *13 Reasons Why* (Netflix, 2017–present), *Westworld* (HBO, 2016–present), *Unbelievable* (Netflix, 2019), and *I May Destroy You* (HBO, 2020). *The Affair* (Showtime, 2014–2019), *Grey's Anatomy,* and *The Good Fight* (CBS, 2017–present) all explored the violation of boundaries signaled by #MeToo that designate instances of workplace harassment and allegations of sexual misconduct, particularly where the abuse of power is concerned.

As Laura Collier Hillstrom describes from the perspective of the movement's proponents, #MeToo has raised awareness of the various forms and circumstances in which misogyny is present in that it

> has brought much-needed public attention to the pervasiveness of sexual harassment and assault. They view it as a long-overdue reckoning that shed[s] light on forms of degradation and abuse that women had always silently endured in order to keep their jobs, or secretly warned each other about through "whisper networks," or reluctantly altered their lives to avoid. They marvel at the fact that two words empowered women around the world to join together and speak out against sexism, misogyny and discrimination. (2019, 6)

The salient cultural focus on women's experiences of misogyny has expanded to representations on quality television series whose incorporation of depth and specified focus enables a more comprehensive approach to portraying female-centered narratives. These narratives have been particularly salient and compelling due to television's noted ability to generate affect toward viewers within its texts, including those pertaining to issues of misogyny and abuse. As Misha Kavka remarks, "television fulfils its function as a technology of intimacy; by bringing things spatially, temporally and emotionally close," (2008, 7) and this sense of "intimacy" enables viewers to perceive the concerns of #MeToo beyond its use as a hashtag on social media. The affective responses that can be engendered by television representations of #MeToo's themes render television series a powerful and dynamic mode for transmitting and comprehending conspicuous feminism.

These developments in television production, distribution, and reception have thus instigated the representations of conspicuous feminism that became more noted alongside the prominence of the #MeToo movement. The shift toward more nuanced depictions of feminist themes, such as women's roles and constructions of femininity, intersectionality, and sexual abuse, were already occurring as a result of the demand for diversified content on streaming platforms and the increasing presence of female showrunners. The influence of #MeToo then heightened the awareness of and interest in these issues, expanding representations of conspicuous feminism on television.

Acknowledgment: A portion of this chapter is derived from Bautista, Anna Marie. 2014. "'Quiet Desperation': The 'Retreat' and Recuperation of the Housewife and Stay-at-Home Mother on Popular Television." In Stay-at-Home Mothers: Dialogues and Debates, *edited by Elizabeth Reid-Boyd and Gayle Letherby, 223–241. Bradford, Ontario: Demeter Press.*

Chapter Two

Exposing Abuse and Misogyny
Big Little Lies

At the close of the first season of HBO's *Big Little Lies*, the series' protagonists Bonnie Carlson, (Zoë Kravitz), Jane Chapman (Shailene Woodley), Renata Klein (Laura Dern), Madeline McKenzie (Reese Witherspoon), and Celeste Wright (Nicole Kidman) attribute the death of Celeste's husband Perry (Alexander Skarsgård) to an accidental fall, covering up that it was Bonnie herself that had deliberately pushed him down the flight of stairs. That the women had discovered that he was a rapist and abuser just moments prior to the incident is a key facet to the "lies" that characterize the women's narratives and experiences throughout the series. This lie becomes pivotal to the entire series, particularly in the second season, where the women's friendships virtually hinge on sustaining their complicity in it, underlining *Big Little Lies'* motivation to expose the private deceptions that enable unequal and even dangerous gendered power dynamics to be upheld within the home and elsewhere.

Based on Liane Moriarty's 2014 novel, *Big Little Lies* contemplates the indelible relationship between domesticity and feminine identity, particularly with regard to the deceptions that are sustained in order to present ideals of domestic fulfilment. The series' intricate representation of feminist issues including domestic abuse and assault has garnered critical acclaim in its acute portrayal of elements behind the exteriors previously not often glimpsed in television representations of motherhood, marriage, and relationships. The series' examination of the silencing and "lies" that are maintained in order to uphold ideals of femininity and gendered power dynamics reiterate #MeToo's objectives in exposing and denouncing elements of misogyny that were previously unquestioned.

The first season garnered critical acclaim upon its release in 2017, earning eight Emmy awards and four Golden Globe awards, including Outstanding Limited Series and Best Miniseries or Television Film, respectively. Laura

Dern, Nicole Kidman, and Alexander Skarsgård were also recognized with awards for their performances in the series. Originally conceived as a limited series, its success prompted the release of a second season in 2019, which heavily promoted Academy Award winner Meryl Streep joining the already illustrious ensemble cast. Written and created by David E. Kelley and directed by Jean-Marc Vallée (season one) and Andrea Arnold (season 2), the series has been lauded not only for its award-winning credentials but also for its complex portrayal of abuse and female empowerment, rendering it a notable example of the increasing visibility and significance of feminist issues in television narratives.

Set in an affluent community in Monterey, California, the protagonists of *Big Little Lies* are repeatedly shown in sumptuous homes, wearing designer clothing and frequenting upscale restaurants and cafes, accentuating the motif of unmasking the truths beneath surface appearances that the series is concerned with. Apart from these exterior displays of elegance and luxury, the women each harbor pretenses below the archetypal characteristics of motherhood and femininity that they respectively embody. Madeline McKenzie is the perfectionist who insists on being involved in most matters in the community; Renata Klein is the high-powered and driven working mother; Celeste Wright is pictured as the embodiment of blissful family life with a beautiful home, twin sons, and an envied marriage to a handsome and successful businessman; and Bonnie Carlson is the exotic and bohemian second wife to Madeline's ex-husband Nathan (James Tupper). New arrival to Monterey Jane Chapman is presented as distinctly set apart from the other women due to her status as a single mother and her moderate financial resources, as signified by her comparatively less glamorous and impeccable appearance. The series soon makes it clear, however, that the impressive veneers are masking the various domestic plights that each woman endures.

There have been other prominent television portrayals of the complications behind the traditional gendered expectations concerning women and domesticity. Another dramatic mystery series previously noted for its feminist considerations in depicting the private adversities of its characters is ABC's *Desperate Housewives* (2004–2012). Also featuring five protagonists dealing with conflicts pertaining to social expectations of domesticity, marriage, and motherhood, the series was likewise celebrated for its portrayal of the actuality behind the cliché of the happy housewife. Just as *Big Little Lies* opens with a crime scene investigation at the site of Perry Wright's fatal accident, *Desperate Housewives* similarly begins with the death of a key character, the posthumous narrator Mary Alice Young (Brenda Strong), and centers on uncovering the circumstances of her demise. The parallels between the series also extend to their settings. Comparable to the exclusivity of Monterey, *Desperate Housewives* exposed the secrets of its protagonists within the homes in the pristine and equally privileged neighborhood of Wisteria Lane. Elizabeth Kaufer Busch asserts that *"Desperate Housewives* suggests a greater complexity in women's search for fulfillment, as children, homes, and husbands alone are insufficient sources of happiness for women. Wives cannot expect fidelity, protection, or loyalty from their husbands" (2009, 96). While *Desperate Housewives* illustrated the difficulties and desperation within domesticity and the private space for women, *Big Little Lies* expands on these themes by emphasizing the efforts and consequences of concealing these plights from the public.

As with *Desperate Housewives*, the negotiation of feminist themes on *Big Little Lies* largely rests on the individual concerns of the key characters, and does not consider broader issues of collectivity or diversity. Only one of the protagonists is a woman of color, suggesting that the series does not substantially diverge from the white and economically privileged contexts typically manifested in constructions of popular feminism. Representations of female empowerment in the media and popular culture are recurrently constructed in terms of wealth and whiteness, including on television series such as *Sex and the City* (Wilkes 2015). Thus, the series' focus on empowerment in terms of personal issues overlooks the possibilities for intersectional critiques of race and class structures in the process.

The constructions of female empowerment that the series presents approximate Banet-Weiser's assertion that empowerment within "popular feminism" is highly individualized and personal:

> Within popular feminism, empowerment is the central logic; with little to no specification as to what we want to empower women to do, popular feminism often restructures the politics of feminism to focus on the individual empowered woman. Here, the historical feminist politics of "the personal is the political" are often understood in the reverse, as "the political is the personal." (2018, 24)

While the series seems to depict women's issues in a complex and provocative manner, its reluctance to look beyond the scope of "the individual empowered woman" may undermine its overall feminist potential, as there is little inquiry into the experiences of women who do not occupy the particular racial and class positions that *Big Little Lies* pictures.

Rosalind Gill has equated *Big Little Lies* and representations of femininity in other contemporary series with her notion of "feminist gloss" on television, which she defines as

> the emptying out of feminism as something superficial and the high production values . . . It is really good to see women's friendships being foregrounded and forms of relating that are not—or not only—about meanness, rivalry or

competitiveness. At the same time, I think the shows invite us into a highly limited world of privilege and glossy empowerment that doesn't suggest any need to change the structures of racialised, patriarchal capitalism. (quoted in Jones 2019)

Indeed, in spite of the series' concentration on feminist themes and female narratives, the protagonists do inhabit a veritably entitled milieu and embody the polished empowerment and privilege that Gill describes, establishing an integration of feminist issues that has marketable and mainstream appeal. Thus, although the series' resolute engagement with themes of misogyny and abuse expands and complicates the premises of "feminist gloss" and "popular feminism," its' featuring of these topical issues also retains the commercial imperatives that have propelled the visibility of conspicuous feminism in the media.

EXPOSING ABUSE AND TRAUMA

The central theme of abuse and assault surrounds the key deception in *Big Little Lies* and is depicted in Celeste Wright's narrative as she attempts to reconcile her dangerous domestic situation with the ideals of marriage and motherhood that she desires to emulate. That she keeps the abuse hidden, as does Jane Chapman in a parallel narrative centering on her rape at the hands of Perry Wright, also illustrates the series' pertinence to #MeToo, which has encouraged numerous women to come forward and express their experiences of assault and abuse. The series' treatment of Celeste and Jane's affliction and the eventual revelation of their respective experiences indicates a commitment to raising awareness of sexual abuse and violence that #MeToo is also keen on exposing and scrutinizing.

The popular and critical recognition of the series transpired amidst a revived public sensibility toward women's experiences of sexism and gendered power relations that has been engendered by the influence of #MeToo. The first season of *Big Little Lies* was released in February 2017, months prior to the allegations made against Harvey Weinstein that would trigger the spotlight on #MeToo. The series' themes of abuse and misogyny resonated strongly with the public attention garnered by the movement during its critical awards success the following year. Nicole Kidman directly alluded to the movement in her acceptance speech for Best Actress in a Limited Series at the 2018 Golden Globe Awards:

> This character that I played represents something that is the center of our conversation right now: abuse. I do believe, and I hope, we can elicit change through the stories we tell and the way we tell them. (McDermott 2018)

When the second season aired in June 2019, the series was solidly associated with #MeToo. The series' depiction of the trauma sustained by survivors of abuse, as well as the possibilities for abusive tendencies to be transmitted across generations, also deepens its representation of misogyny and gender inequality.

The bullying inflicted on six-year-old Amabella Klein (Ivy George), daughter of Renata and Gordon Klein, is disclosed in the pilot episode, foreshadowing the theme of abuse that is fundamental throughout the series. The episode reveals that Amabella has been the victim of a choking attempt on the first day at school, but she refuses to reveal the true identity of the fellow first grader that has attacked her and falsely identifies Jane Chapman's son Ziggy (Iain Armitage) as the aggressor. Subsequent episodes affirm that the abuse continues throughout the school term as bite marks are found on her shoulder, yet fear prevents her from disclosing who her abuser is, reiterating the silence that is often correlated with victims of assault. Overturning this silence is a key motivation of #MeToo, reflecting conspicuous feminism's instigation to "speak out" loudly against misogyny and abuse. This resonates with feminist practices of speaking out in response to sexual violence and the transformative potential of women sharing their personal narratives to generate more awareness of and action against abuse and misogyny (Serisier 2018). Stressing the importance of speaking out to feminist interventions against sexual violence, Boyle attests that "the feminist project of speaking out is not an end in itself, rather it is a step towards challenging, and ultimately ending, men's violence against women. But for speech to have an impact, it has to be heard" (2019, 24). *Big Little Lies'* intention to unearth the silence that often covers instances of abuse reiterates the aims of the feminist project to eventually end violence by first naming it. The final episode of the first season concedes that it is Max Wright, one of Celeste and Perry's twin sons, who has been hurting Amabella, a revelation that takes on particular significance as the series illustrates that Celeste has been routinely abused by Perry throughout their marriage.

At the outset, Celeste and Perry are presented as the perfect couple with a blissful marriage envied by other parents in the community. Described as "elegant" and "volcanic" by seemingly jealous mothers, Celeste was an attorney who gave up her career upon marrying Perry and is now a full-time mother to twins Josh and Max. Though he is outwardly amiable, Perry's violent tendencies are hinted at in the first episode with his abrupt mood swings, even in tender moments with his wife and children. His dark side is confirmed in the following episode with the swift slap delivered to Celeste's face in the midst of packing for one of his business trips, as he accuses her of not informing him of his sons' school schedule. The shock of the slap is immediately followed by Celeste striking Perry across the face; he then retaliates by throwing her roughly against a closet. Following a brief struggle by Celeste, the couple proceed to engage in rough sex, and it is ambiguous whether or not it is consensual. This instance is a precursor to a number of scenes that depict Perry's violence toward Celeste, each of them distressing and impactful as he strikes and at times chokes her in graphic detail. That sexual intercourse is often mingled with these occurrences illustrates the ambivalence that underlies the violence in their marriage. An intimate Skype conversation while Perry is away on business inadvertently and abruptly reveals a large bruise on Celeste's shoulder ("Serious Mothering," Season 1, Episode 2), dramatically shifting the tone of the scene, as frequently occurs in their interactions. The bite marks found on Amabella's shoulder two episodes later parallel Celeste's bruises, starkly symbolizing the physical scars of abuse, as well as its continuation over generations.

These scenes occasionally evoke Sarah Projansky's description of the ambiguities often contained within the depictions of sexualized violence in popular culture that blur the outlines of consent. In her discussion of the representations of rape in film and television, Projansky deliberates on the "examples of sexualized violence that draw on many of the same narrative and representational conventions as do more literal rape films. Thus, the pervasiveness of rape in film naturalizes the existence of all these other forms

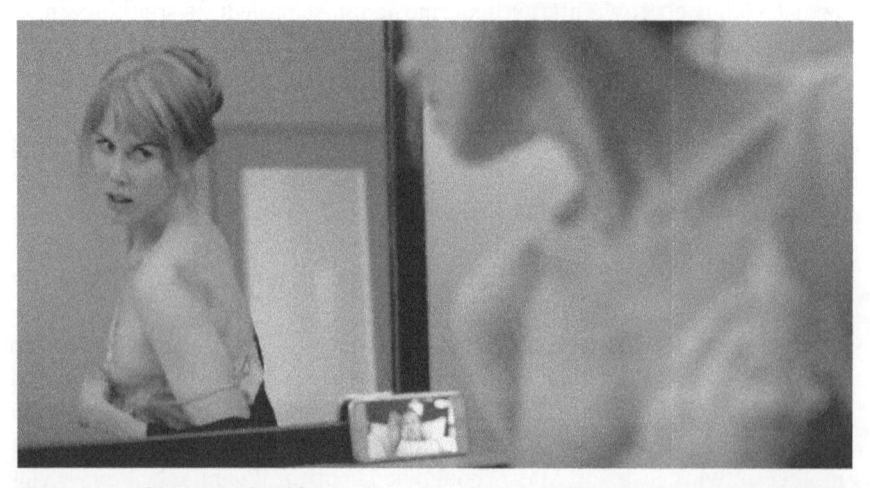

Figure 2.1. Celeste (Nicole Kidman) discovers a bruise during a Skype conversation with Perry (Alexander Skarsgård). *Big Little Lies*, "Serious Mothering," Season 1, Episode 2. *Screenshot captured by author.*

of sexual violence" (2001, 64). The portrayal of sexual violence in Celeste and Perry's relationship invokes these indeterminate boundaries, but *Big Little Lies* plainly conveys the dynamics that prescribe Celeste's vulnerable position. The unsettling dynamics of their relationship are rendered by interactions depicted as both loving and abusive, often simultaneously. However, through the documenting of Celeste's unrest throughout the series, the sinister angle to their interactions is evident, eliciting Lisa M. Cuklanz's observation that the more complex portrayals of sexual violence "sometimes leave the question of consent open to viewer understanding, leaving ambiguities in the dialogue and visual representations that can be filled in by specific viewpoints and experiences" (2000, 61–62). The series' detailing of Celeste's trauma and shame enable an access and comprehension to the female protagonist's viewpoint that has largely been absent in popular culture's obscure depictions of sexualized violence.

The societal pressures to uphold the immaculate impressions related to marriage and motherhood prevent Celeste from communicating her predicament, even to herself. Paula Nicolson argues that "There are many psychological reasons that make women stay with violent men, such as shame, fear and the social pressure not to declare the abuse" (2010, 4), reflecting Celeste's reluctance to speak out about her situation. She often characterizes the relationship as "complicated" and appears to believe that these incidents of violence are a facet of the love and passion in her relationship and that she herself is complicit in. As she attempts to explain the complexities of her marriage to her mother-in-law Mary Louise (Meryl Streep), she insists of her role in these encounters, "I'm not saying I was blameless. I'm just telling you we were violent with each other, and sometimes—sometimes, it would lead to sex. . . . We loved each other. We were . . . we had a sickness" ("Tell-Tale Hearts," Season 2, Episode 2). Celeste's refusal to view herself as a victim, even as her therapist specifically stresses that she is being hurt and is in danger, evokes both the concealment and the ambiguity that often surrounds domestic abuse. *Big Little Lies'* sensitive portrayal of the shame and ambivalence experienced by Celeste indicates the series' motivation to provide a more nuanced treatment of women's issues that are often unexpressed due to social compulsions to maintain illusions of domestic bliss that keep them silenced (Buchbinder and Eiskovitz 2003; Hoff 2009; Nicolson 2010).

The complex portrayal of Celeste and Perry's situation attests to the uncommonly delicate approach employed by *Big Little Lies* in its representation of domestic violence. By illustrating Celeste's perceived complicity in the abuse and the accompanying pain and humiliation, the series attempts to represent the spectrum of sexual violence, the scope of which the #MeToo movement has been intent on fostering recognition of. Liz Kelly identified the "continuum" of sexual violence, which she defines as "a continuous series of elements or events that pass into one another and cannot be readily distinguished" (1988, 76), indicating that instances of sexual violence cannot be contemplated as individual occurrences but that they must be construed in terms of how they operate together in the context of patriarchal power imbalances in order to more fully comprehend their repercussions in individual women's experiences. As such, #MeToo has striven to acknowledge the numerous and diverse incidents experienced by different women and to forge some connection between them, a disposition that is increasingly being reflected in media representations of abuse and harassment, including on television.

Kelly's notion of the "continuum" can be applied to *Big Little Lies'* depiction of Celeste's ambivalent attitude toward the violence in her marriage. As Boyle states in her explication of Kelly's concept:

> it allows us to establish a common character between different experiences and to understand the continuous nature of women's experiences of sexual violation in patriarchal culture, which can make it difficult for women to articulate where individual acts against them begin and end. . . . the continuum allows us to see how individual acts of sexual aggression are embedded within existing relationships and power structures. In this context, apparently consensual sex with a partner who has previously been abusive may be difficult for a woman to disentangle from a prior experience of being raped by this man. The rape creates the context for these later interactions; it shapes the woman's ability to give consent because she knows where refusal may lead. (2019, 53–54)

Big Little Lies illustrates this continuity in how women can experience instances of sexual violence in patriarchal culture through Celeste's narrative in that she is unable to articulate where and how the violence in her marriage begins and ends. The power structures inherent in her relationship with Perry prevent her from expressing, or even completely realizing, her own oppression as she endeavors to maintain the façade of being the ideal wife and mother. In rendering the complicated degrees of Celeste's situation, the series offers an astute delineation of the continuum of facets that function together in experiences of sexual violence in patriarchal culture.

The abuse escalates as Celeste gradually gains more independence and confidence, largely through revisiting her career as a lawyer as she assists Madeline in legal matters concerning the performance of the controversial musical *Avenue Q* by the community theatre. The experience gives her more self-possession and the idea of resuming her professional career is exhilarating, as she admits to Madeline that she does not feel fulfilled in her identity as wife and mother ("Push Comes To Shove," Season 1, Episode 4). This realization of possibilities outside of her domestic position enables her to begin to stand up to her husband and resist his assertions of control, and to finally make contingency plans for leaving him after repeated urgings from her therapist.

Her newfound boldness incites more rage and violence from Perry as he is unable to maintain authority over her actions, recalling Kate Manne's observations on misogyny toward women with power and autonomy. Manne posits that "Misogyny stems from the desire to take women down, to put them in their place again. So the higher they climb, the farther they may be made to fall because of it" (2018, 77). Celeste is literally "made to fall," as evidenced in the opening moments of the final episode of season one, in which she is pictured crumpled on the bathroom floor after a beating from Perry, who had been quietly upset the previous evening upon his wife nonchalantly leaving the house for a dinner appointment. The more she acts upon her growing self-possession, the more the abuse intensifies as Perry suspects he is losing his control over her, as intimated by the therapist at their sessions. As Melissa Jeltsen specifies in her discussion of the portrayal of domestic abuse in the series, "At its core, domestic violence is about maintaining power and control over another person. It is clear that Perry's need to dominate Celeste is at the root of their problems" (2017). When he discovers that she has made concrete plans to leave him and has rented an apartment for herself and her sons, he realizes that he no longer has the power to dominate her, resulting in their final argument on the way to the school Trivia Night event, which concludes with his death.

Thus, the first season ends with Perry lying at the bottom of a set of stairs outside the school and the women conspiring to cover up that it was Bonnie who pushed Perry down after a protracted struggle in which Perry attempted to attack Celeste. The incident occurs amidst the mutual recognition that he is also Jane Chapman's rapist, whose identity she has been searching for throughout the first season. The theme of assault is replicated in Jane's narrative as it focuses on her ongoing trauma from the incident and her determination to care for her son Ziggy, the product of the rape. Jane's characterization differs drastically from those of the other protagonists, namely due to her different economic circumstances, delineated via her comparatively modest home and wardrobe. Unlike the other protagonists, Jane is the sole provider for herself and her son, and her employment in bookkeeping and later in the local aquarium in the second season is a financial necessity, in contrast to the work situations of the other women.

Although Jane does not recognize that Perry is her rapist until the final moments of the first season, the revelation that both she and Celeste are victims of his abuse signifies that abuse and violence occur regardless of contrasting social, economic, and familial situations. As Jo Johnson contends in her commentary on the representation of contemporary womanhood in the series:

> *Big Little Lies'* viewers are exposed to a group of women for whom sexual violence transcends class, age, and socio-economic status in devastatingly destructive ways. And we're reminded that this sort of violence can monopolize women's thoughts—burrowing down and manifesting as our darkest of secrets. (2017)

Through the portrayal of Jane's struggles to move on from the assault, *Big Little Lies* corresponds to the tenets of the #MeToo movement in its attempt to provide an outlet for victims to work through and express their trauma (Strauss Swanson and Szymanksi 2020). Jane's trauma is depicted largely through flashbacks and nightmares of the incident and her fantasies of shooting her attacker with the gun that she keeps by her bedside. In spite of their disparate economic and familial positions, Celeste and Jane share the same repression of abuse and violence that is essential to both their narratives, echoing the scope of women's experiences with assault that #MeToo aspires to encompass and the corresponding experiences of shame and secrecy that *Big Little Lies* attempts to illuminate.

Celeste and Jane deal with the aftermath of their ordeals in very contrasting ways, as is delineated in the second season, which portrays both women continuing to grapple with the consequences of Perry's abuse even after his death. Apart from maintaining the conspiracy to hide the circumstances of his

Figure 2.2. Jane (Shailene Woodley) and Celeste (Nicole Kidman) share a moment after Perry's funeral. *Big Little Lies,* **"You Get What You Need," Season 1, Episode 7. Screenshot captured by author.**

fall, both women must still contend with the repercussions of his violence, and the distinctions in how they do so are indicative of the differences in their respective economic and social positions. Anxious to preserve the appearance of the flawless family life she has cultivated, Celeste persists in hiding Perry's abuse and its impacts, particularly from her sons, while Jane is relatively more candid in her admissions of her trauma. The series depicts Jane as being more adept at moving on as she openly discusses the circumstances of his paternity with son Ziggy and attempts to be honest about her past in a burgeoning relationship with her co-worker Corey (Douglas Smith) at the Monterey Bay Aquarium.

Meanwhile, Celeste is depicted in the early episodes of the season fondly reminiscing about her husband, both alone and with her sons, insisting to them that "Your daddy was a wonderful person. A beautiful person. He could be weak . . . like we all can. He could make mistakes, but your . . . your daddy was a beautiful . . . wonderful man" ("Tell-Tale Hearts," Season 2, Episode 2) when she addresses their questions about his violent tendencies. While outwardly concealing the realities of the abuse, she is clearly inwardly suffering, as evidenced by her nightmares and risky behaviors she attempts to keep hidden, such as a growing dependence on alcohol and sleeping medications, as well as engaging in indiscriminate sexual encounters. The differences in how both women process their afflictions attest to how the series suggests that social and economic privilege can mask numerous deceptions and may even add to the pressure to keep them hidden. Jane's position as a relative outsider to the wealth and status of the Monterey community also enables her to confront the trauma of her abuse more honestly due to her lesser regard toward maintaining surface appearances.

The instability Celeste exhibits with regard to her marriage and subsequent liaisons is heavily scrutinized, particularly by her mother-in-law Mary Louise and in the court trial for the custody battle that she executes for full custody of her grandsons. Mary Louise's refusal to acknowledge her son's abusive behavior further illustrates *Big Little Lies'* observations on the social taboos around speaking of domestic violence. Throughout the second season, she acts as an antagonist to the "Monterey Five" as she seeks to uncover the truth behind the events surrounding her son's death. Even as it is recognized that Celeste was a victim of domestic abuse, Mary Louise uses the trial to exploit the notion that she does not comply with traditional ideals of good motherhood, such as those described by Rebecca Feasey as "romanticised, idealised and indeed conservative images of selfless and satisfied 'good' mothers who conform to the ideology of intensive mothering" (2012, 3). A typical line of questioning sustained by Celeste throughout the trial alludes to her capacity to be a secure parent to her sons:

Judge: Tell me why you stayed.

Celeste: Um, because I loved him, and I thought—And but I—I just always thought he would get better.

Judge: But he didn't.

Celeste: No, he didn't. And when I was happy, I stayed because I was happy and when I was depressed, I stayed because I was depressed. I mean, either way, I was afraid if I left him of what he might do. I was afraid how he would react. I was afraid of being alone. I was—So I stayed. I stayed to survive. I stayed for my boys. ("The Bad Mother" Season 2, Episode 6)

Celeste's testimony is reinforced by the presentation of a home video to the court covertly taken by her sons that depicts Perry hitting and dragging her. It is also revealed that Perry was abused by his mother as a child, diminishing Mary Louise's claims to being a more suitable guardian to the boys, which leads to Celeste receiving full custody. Mary Louise immediately responds to Celeste's declaration of Perry's account of the abuse by vehemently denying it, "That's a lie! That's a lie. . . . You're a liar" ("I Want To Know," Season 2, Episode 7), returning to the theme of deception that resounds throughout the series. The revelation of Mary Louise's abuse of Perry also reinforces the series' complex representation of abuse in its communication that abusive tendencies can be reproduced across generations. In its inspection of Celeste's competence as a mother, the trial further underscores the aspects of repression, shame, and fear she endured in relation to the domestic abuse, and which she kept hidden in order to adhere to conventional ideals concerning femininity, marriage, and motherhood.

Mary Louise's staunch conviction of Perry's and her own blamelessness extends to her skepticism toward Jane Chapman's allegations that Perry had raped her, resulting in the birth of Ziggy. As Mary Louise attempts to forge some connection with her newly discovered grandson, she challenges Jane as to her recollections of the assault, again raising the matter of public skepticism that often afflicts victims of abuse and that *Big Little Lies* is keen to address:

Mary Louise: Celeste has shared with me that she and Perry had a—a complicated sex life—one that included violence.

Jane: She shared that with you?

Mary Louise: Yes. And I'm—It makes me wonder if, perhaps, he misinterpreted or misread a signal from you.

Jane: Your son raped me and as he was doing so, I was screaming for him to get off. I don't think that you "misread" that. ("The End Of The World," Season 2, Episode 3)

Mary Louise's suggestion that Jane initiated the encounter with Perry elicits the matter of "victim blaming," which frequently discredits allegations of abuse and assault (Ullman 2010). Her interrogation of Jane's role in the attack is thus indicative of the series' intention to confront the tendency to cast blame and doubt on victims and to more accurately portray the experiences of assault survivors, thereby challenging the systemic biases against them.

#MeToo's key motivations for voicing the hidden presence of sexual abuse and violence are displayed in the narratives of both Jane and Celeste. The juxtaposition of Celeste and Jane's experiences of assault reiterate #MeToo's inclination to convey that abuse can take place in a variety of contexts and that the nature of and responses to the abuse do not conform to any pattern. Paralleling Boyle's profession that the testimonies shared via #MeToo, "can mean making visible as violence experiences which have not previously been understood in this way" (2019, 25), *Big Little Lies* elucidates that sexual violence can be present and hidden in a variety of socioeconomic contexts.

ELIDING RACE IN ABUSE NARRATIVES

The theme of abuse is further developed in the second season in relation to Bonnie Carlson's narrative and explains the context for her pushing Perry down the stairs to his death at the close of season one. She is on the periphery of the main narratives for much of season one, where she is depicted as an outsider in the community—Nathan Carlson's second wife is younger than Madeline and her more relaxed and uninhibited personality contrasts her with the other protagonists. Her depiction in the first season mostly serves as a juxtaposition to Madeline's abrasiveness, until she delivers the fatal push.

The second season explores Bonnie's situation in more depth and provides the context for her actions. The season finds her pensive and somber in contrast to her breezy disposition in the first season. She is also withdrawn with the other members of the "Monterey Five," which she attributes in her profession to Madeline to her discomfiture over the "lie" they are harboring. When Bonnie's mother Elizabeth (Crystal Fox) arrives in Monterey at the request of Nathan, who is perturbed by his wife's sudden sullen and melancholy temperament, it is revealed that Bonnie was abused by her mother as a child. The abuse is disclosed through flashbacks to her childhood that alternate between tender moments of mother and daughter walking on the beach to images of Elizabeth violently shaking and hitting the child Bonnie.

When Elizabeth suffers a seizure that leaves her hospitalized in a coma, several scenes depict Bonnie fantasizing about smothering her with a pillow as she grapples with her memories of the abuse. Eventually Elizabeth dies of the brain tumor she was diagnosed with after Bonnie privately confesses to her that she killed Perry as a result of the abuse she suffered from her mother ("The Bad Mother," Season 2, Episode 6). The repercussions of abuse are again foregrounded through Bonnie's admissions and accentuate how such experiences are often buried or brushed away in service of "lies" such as those that the series portrays.

Although Bonnie's story is given much more detail in the second season, the series does not probe into aspects of her racial identity, particularly in relation to the other protagonists' whiteness. In fact, her preservation of the "lie" and acknowledgment of her own abuse largely takes place apart from the narratives of abuse concerning Celeste and Jane. *Big Little Lies* does not interrogate the impact of maternal abuse specifically or examine how race might influence Bonnie's contending with it, reflecting Sujata Moorti's contention that "there is no space to discuss the intersection of race and gender within the language and representational system of television" (2002, 2009). The fatal push Bonnie commits serves as symbolic of the five women overthrowing various forms of abuse and misogyny, but her own experience of abuse at the hands of a woman and the significance of her racial identity are overlooked.

Throughout the entire series, only one reference is made to Bonnie being a woman of color, when Elizabeth questions her daughter's place in the community, "You are out here surrounded by people who don't even get you. They don't look like you. I haven't seen one other black person since I've been out here" ("Tell-Tale Hearts," Season 2, Episode 2). This refusal to engage with issues of race and class raises some of the problematic elements of conspicuous feminism as designated in *Big Little Lies*. As Bonnie herself wryly notes in response to Madeline's daughter Chloe's (Katherine Watson) concern about violence committed by gang members, "There are no gangs in Monterey" ("She Knows," Season 2, Episode 4), highlighting the privilege and affluence that is depicted throughout the series. The unwillingness to delve deeper into how race functions in Bonnie's representation of female identity is a missed opportunity for the series to investigate the intersectional dynamics that influence her experience of marriage and motherhood, particularly in relation to the delusions that frame constructions of femininity.

The symbiotic denouements of female solidarity across race and class do not extensively address the intersectional differences between the women that belie their particular experiences of misogyny and abuse. Thus, though feminist concerns and women's issues are deliberated on in a complex and sensitive manner, it is a feminism that is only applied to a specific category of women that maintains paramount visibility in media representations. In this way, *Big Little Lies* reflects a perplexing feminist position as it does not critique issues of race and class in relation to patriarchy and misogyny, preferring instead to comply with constructions relating to "the most visible popular feminism . . . within the arena of consent: it consents to heteronormativity, to the universality of whiteness, to dominant economic formations, to a trajectory of capitalist 'success'" (Banet-Weiser 2018, 23). This accords with the criticisms of the media conflation of #MeToo with narratives of visibility and privilege (Griffin 2019).

The final episode of the second season ("I Want To Know," Season 2, Episode 7) thickly underlines the theme of deception that circumscribes the whole series. The ending of the episode depicts the five women walking together into the Monterey police department after receiving an off-screen text message from Bonnie, suggesting that the conspiracy that has been maintained throughout the series is finally going to be uncovered. As Celeste says to Madeline, "The lie is the friendship," insinuating that they have all contrived to uphold the pretenses regarding the death of Perry, as well as the deceits related to the various figurations and ideals of femininity that the series interrogates.

The series intimates that the murder of Perry is an inevitable response to the abuse suffered by the women, and their pact to hide it signifies the female bonds forged through common experiences of misogyny and abuse that #MeToo aims to propagate. The central "lie" concerning the circumstances of Perry's death can be denotative of the women's collective response to their individual situations of gendered inequality and their tacit agreement to keep the incident a secret suggests a shared solidarity in their experiences.

The endings to both seasons indicate a close affiliation between the women, as they are depicted companionably reposing at the beach with their children and unitedly entering the police department in the closing scenes of the first and second seasons, respectively. Though the women are pictured in the absence of male intervention in both season finales, this is undercut by the employment of long camera shots, which transmit the visual implication that they are being watched. In this way, the series delivers an obscure conclusion, suggesting that female empowerment has not been fully liberated from patriarchal observation, as the ongoing efforts of #MeToo testify. This also recalls the conflict over creative control of the series' second season, which appeals to the misogynistic structures that continue to underlie the media and television industries. Andrea Arnold's role as director of the second season was undercut by showrunner David Kelley's decision to reinvolve first-season director Jean-Marc Vallée in the creative process, without Arnold's prior knowledge, in order to maintain the visual aesthetic established in the first season (O'Falt 2019). This queries the extent of the series' reflection of feminist themes as conceived through male perspectives and authority, resulting in the ambiguous contemplation of conspicuous feminism at the close of the second season.

Conspicuous feminism as presented in *Big Little Lies* can also be ascribed to the celebrity power associated with the series. The protagonists are all portrayed by well-known Hollywood actors and the casting of the critically venerated Meryl Streep in the role of Mary Louise in the second season further enhanced its prestige as quality television. Again, the media conspicuousness of the series elicits Banet-Weiser's assertion of popular feminism as "that (which) seizes the spotlight in an economy of visibility and renders other feminisms less visible" (2018, 21). The visual emphasis on the scenic Monterey landscape and the elegant homes adds to a sense of indulgence in viewing the series, and also reinforces Gill's notions of "feminist gloss" that it is identified with (Jones 2019).

Visual presentation plays a key function in *Big Little Lies'* promotional campaigns, which utilize perceptions of feminine glamour combined with the notions of female empowerment that define representations of conspicuous feminism. Advertising for the series has centered on glossy images of the A-list cast and its picturesque Monterey location, downplaying its concentration on misogyny and sexual abuse. Instead, the female empowerment being marketed focuses on the themes of female solidarity and achievement as evidenced by HBO's partnership with The Wing, an international network of community and work spaces specifically designed for women, to launch the second season of *Big Little Lies*. The partnership coordinated events such as live panel discussions with the series' stars and collaborations with women-owned brands to create custom retail collections, a portion of the proceeds of which would be donated to the National Network to End Domestic Violence, expanding the series' advocacy to persevere against female oppression and to promote women's initiatives (Yang 2019). The synergy between female accomplishment, consumerism, and fundraising conceived by the partnership also accentuates the inspiring, commodified, and activist facets to *Big Little Lies'* contemplation of conspicuous feminism.

Big Little Lies' representation of female empowerment is ultimately varied and ambiguous, even as it tackles the vital issues that have been heightened through the #MeToo movement. Its protracted focus on feminist issues foregrounding white, affluent, and heterosexual protagonists prevents a thorough analysis of less visible feminist considerations regarding race, class, and sexuality. At the same time, the series enables its protagonists to find actualization as they work through the "lies" that define their specific narrative trajectories, allowing important themes of motherhood and marriage as well as abuse and assault to be considered deftly and evocatively. The "lies" that the series uncovers relate to the deceptions upheld by women in order to maintain traditional ideals of femininity that support misogynistic structures, namely with regard to the silencing that typically circumscribes experiences of assault and domestic violence. The series' representation of the shame and trauma that result from abuse reproduces #MeToo's incentive to raise awareness of these repercussions and to seek vindication for injustice, as well as to reveal the realities of abuse hidden beneath the politically correct facade of business, politics, and the entertainment industry. As such, *Big Little Lies* offers a compelling example of the impact of #MeToo's generation of conspicuous feminism on television, as it approaches these female narratives in a manner that is simultaneously inspiring, commodifying, and disturbing in its depiction of female identities and experiences.

Acknowledgment: This chapter is derived in part from an article published in Feminist Media Studies, *published online on January 5, 2022, copyright Taylor & Francis. Available online: https://www.tandfonline.com/doi/abs/10.1080/14680777.2021.1996417.*

Chapter Three

"Something Other Than A Mother or Housewife"

Challenging Notions of Gendered Space in *The Marvelous Mrs. Maisel*

In its portrayal of protagonist Miriam "Midge" Maisel (Rachel Brosnahan), a housewife attempting to forge a career in stand-up comedy in New York City in the late 1950s, *The Marvelous Mrs. Maisel* (Prime Video, 2017–present) negotiates the commonly prescribed roles for women. After her husband leaves her for his secretary, Midge has to navigate her options outside of the home and domesticity, which she had comfortably inhabited in the conventional role of wife and mother. Her manager Susie Myerson's (Alex Borstein) querying of her desire to be "something other than a mother or housewife" in the pilot episode after her first impromptu comedy set clearly ruminates on the expectations and perceptions regarding domesticity and women's roles. Indeed, the charm and effervescence that characterizes the series often belies the feminist potential of Mrs. Maisel in her pursuit of success and fulfillment apart from her domestic identity. The series' premise of a housewife breaking out of the domestic space to pursue her goals as a female stand-up comedian generates opportunities for ebullience and humor, but also occasions the possibility for critique and interrogation of conventional gender roles.

The series incorporates elements of conspicuous feminism in its depiction of a daring protagonist intent on devising her own path at a time when gender demarcations were sharply circumscribed. In its representation of a woman seeking achievement and recognition outside of the domestic sphere and to access a male-dominated profession, *The Marvelous Mrs. Maisel* illustrates how closely ideals of femininity were tied to traditionally gendered constructions of home and domesticity, and the series provides an opportunity to reflect on their relevance in the contemporary era. Although creator Amy Sherman-Palladino did not originally envision the series as a counterpart to the tenets of #MeToo, its depiction of the obstacles Midge faces in her efforts to attain recognition in a male-dominated field, as well as the traditional expectations concerning women's roles that she attempts to subvert, have granted it a resonance with the movement. The series' treatment of gender and power dynamics has resounded in the #MeToo era and has demonstrated how elements of sexism and misogyny that were common in the 1950s have continued to persist, particularly in relation to the gendered roles and spaces that have delimited women's presence in the public sphere. The vibrant and amiable tone that characterizes *The Marvelous Mrs. Maisel* often obscures the gendered power dynamics that it queries, rendering it a notable example of a television series contending with contemporary feminist themes being (dis)placed in its 1950s period setting.

Premiering on Amazon Prime Video in March 2017, the series immediately achieved critical acclaim, garnering several critics awards, including the Peabody Award in 2017 and awards at the Emmys and Golden Globes, for Best Comedy Series and Best Actress for Brosnahan in 2018 and 2019, respectively. Sherman-Palladino is noted for producing series with prominent female characters, ranging from her time as a writer on *Roseanne* to her success as creator and executive producer of *Gilmore Girls* (WB, 2000–2007 and Netflix, 2016). Inspired by Sherman-Palladino's memories of her father's experience as a stand-up comedian in New York City, *The Marvelous Mrs. Maisel* follows Midge's journey as she pursues the unconventional career of a female stand-up comedian, while coping with the demise of her marriage and social expectations regarding her role as wife and mother. The first season centers on Midge's discovery of her ambitions and the initial actions she takes in pursuit of them, while dealing with the disintegration of her marriage to husband Joel (Michael Zegan) and finding an identity outside of that of wife and mother. Subsequent seasons find Midge becoming more confident in her craft as she enters the local comedy circuit, embarks on a new romantic relationship with eligible doctor Benjamin Ettenberg (Zachary Levi), and experiences further professional success as she goes on tour with popular singer Shy Baldwin (Leroy McClain) as his opening act. The series also focuses extensively on Midge's relationships with manager Susie and with her parents Abe (Tony Shalhoub) and Rose (Marin Hinkle), who are frequently perplexed and at times distressed by their daughter's stand-up aspirations and transgressing of gendered norms.

The field of comedy has traditionally been perceived as an arena where social conventions can be mocked and interrogated through humor and performance, such as in Mikhail Bakhtin's (1965) work on the "carnival" literary mode, which employs humor and chaos to challenge dominant styles and structures, and Henri Bergson's (1911) essay on the use of comedy and laughter to comment on social events. In this respect, several writers have also examined how female comedy can be viewed as a feminist mechanism, as female comedians often perform from a marginal position in a male-dominated field. By portraying Midge's pursuit of her dreams of success on the stand-up stage, *The Marvelous Mrs. Maisel* also challenges traditional gendered attitudes by addressing the "social myths that a woman's proper or natural role is to appreciate male humor rather than speak her own truth through comedy" (Mizejewski and Sturtevant 2017, 4). Apart from Sophie Lennon (Jane Lynch), who quickly becomes a rival rather than an ally on the comedy circuit, Midge's fellow comedians are all men, illustrating Linda Mizejewski and Victoria Sturtevant's contention that "the idea that women aren't funny persists because it symptomizes a much larger gender problem" (2017, 3) that presumes women cannot eclipse men in generating humor due to gendered expectations that have traditionally positioned women as the subject, rather than the object, of stand-up comedy. Placing Midge on the comedy stage effects the series portrayal of conspicuous feminism in its critique of constructions of female roles and identities via her performances, which typically center on the frustrations experienced in her identity as wife and mother and are vigorously expressed through her stage persona "Mrs. Maisel." Her literal performing of a feminist position aligns with the exhibitive characteristics of conspicuous feminism.

The Marvelous Mrs. Maisel thus exhibits conspicuous feminism in its concentration on the self-actualization, empowerment, and fortitude of women. The series features strong female relationships rather than established delineations of heterosexual romance. Indeed, the partnership of Midge and Susie functions as the primary relationship within the series and enables Midge to realize her goals, in contrast to their being constrained within her marriage to Joel. Midge's desire to deviate from prescribed norms and expectations of femininity is reflected in her disavowal of the traditional feminine realms of romance, marriage, and domesticity and is expanded in her attempts to attain gratification and achievement outside of them. The series explicitly portrays Midge's pursuit of fulfillment in her stand-up career as a recasting of the traditional feminine roles of wife and mother and clearly suggests that women do not need to be situated in the domestic realm in order to be content.

In spite of the distinct representation of female strength and capability, *The Marvelous Mrs. Maisel* has been criticized for its limiting of these depictions to characters of a particular social class. Midge Maisel's relative resources and privilege have drawn comparisons to similar assessments of the privileged feminist dispositions characterized on Sherman-Palladino's other celebrated female-centered series, *Gilmore Girls* (Friedlander 2016). Both series evoke the individualist discourses often associated with postfeminist constructions, which Stephanie Genz and Benjamin Brabon designate as a "brand of feminism [that] does not ensure that all women should receive ample opportunities and choices and, in so doing, it guarantees that a power and privilege imbalance persists to exist among them" (2009, 38). Indeed, Midge Maisel is able to aspire toward her goals without considerable concern for issues pertaining to finances or childcare, due to the social and class privileges she inhabits. Thus, the series' aim to destabilize preconceived ideals pertaining to women's roles is moderated by concerns over the lack of heterogeneous viewpoints and intersectional engagement. However, the series does begin to interrogate intersectional matters of race, class, and sexuality in its third season alongside its portrayal of feminism and female empowerment, thereby querying the various entitlements that "Mrs. Maisel" seemingly takes for granted.

CHALLENGING IDEALS OF FEMININITY AND DOMESTICITY

Female domesticity has generally had an uneasy relationship with feminism, particularly after second-wave feminism's challenging of the "doctrine of feminine domesticity" (Oakley 1990, 49), which claimed that domesticity and the home were incompatible with feminism. Indeed, the figure of the housewife, who is largely defined by her propensity to the home and domestic space, has typically had an antagonistic relationship with the tenets of second-wave feminism. Betty Friedan's *The Feminine Mystique* fostered a feminist agenda that challenged women's then conventional circumscription to the domestic arena. Friedan's book attributed the "problem that has no name" (1963, 29) to women's dissatisfaction over the prevailing ideals relating femininity to domesticity and the prescribed options of the traditional roles of wife and mother. Friedan describes the "feminine mystique" that women subscribed to in the post–World War II era:

> But the new image this mystique gives to American women is the old image: "Occupation: housewife." The new mystique makes the housewife-mothers, who never had a chance to be anything else, the model for all women; it presupposes that history has reached a final and glorious end in the here and now, as far as women are concerned. Beneath the sophisticated trappings, it simply makes certain concrete, finite, domestic aspects of feminine existence—as it was lived by women whose lives were confined, by necessity, to cooking, cleaning, washing, bearing children—into a religion, a pattern by which all women must now live or deny their femininity. (1963, 84–85)

Friedan's book charged that the "problem with no name" was a direct result of the "feminine mystique" created and cultivated by the media and advertising, which reinforced and glorified women's positions as wife, mother, and homemaker. However, she argued that in actuality, women were unfulfilled, uninspired, and unhappy with the domestic role, prompting the desire to seek "something more" outside the realm of domesticity. Midge Maisel's attempts at self-actualization apart from her roles as wife and mother echo Friedan's proposition of women demanding more. The series offers an insightful and complex commentary on how closely women's identities were associated with notions of domesticity, as well as illustrating feminist contentions of the liberating potential of rupturing these associations for women (de Beauvoir 1949; Greer 1970; Oakley 1974).

From the outset of the series, Midge would appear to be the embodiment of the 1950s "quintessential white middle class housewife who stayed home" (Meyerowitz 1994, 1). Portending her stand-up comedy career, the pilot episode introduces Midge in the midst of delivering a playful speech at her own wedding, where she clearly relishes commanding the attention of an audience. The speech professes that the attractive and spirited Midge graduated from Bryn Mawr College with a degree in Russian literature but that her college experiences were "simply the preamble to [her] ultimate destiny" of "meet[ing] a man, a perfect man" ("Pilot," Season 1, Episode 1). Cut to four years later in 1958 and Midge is pictured as a blithe housewife to husband Joel, with two children and living in an Upper Westside apartment above her parents, Abe and Rose Weissman. A nostalgic aesthetic of the 1950s is vibrantly established in distinctive detail, from the musical soundtrack to the full skirts and pastel colors in Midge's wardrobe. The renown of the series' signature style was evident when its designs and costumes were featured in an exhibit at the Paley Center for Media in New York City called "Making Maisel Marvelous" in August–September 2019. According to production designer Bill Groom, the vintage set decoration and costuming aimed to recall the ambience and genial mode of 1950s- and 1960s-era Doris Day films, reiterating Sherman-Palladino's trademark vivacious and buoyant style (Zuckerman 2017).

The surface breeziness that frequently characterizes Sherman-Palladino's work complements Midge's tacit conforming to expected gender norms, while concealing the more sobering themes that the series confronts. Her penchant for the color pink, as visible in her dresses and hats and her Pyrex dish, also evokes conventional notions of femininity. She is apparently content in her role as mother and housewife—she dutifully supports Joel's ambition to be a stand-up comic, as she takes notes on his performances and cooks brisket for the staff at the Gaslight, in order to negotiate better performance time slots for him. After a particularly disastrous set in front of their friends Archie and Imogene (Joel Johnstone and Bailey De Young), he unceremoniously announces to Midge that he has been having an affair with his secretary and leaves her in the improbable predicament of being without a husband, much to her parents' chagrin.

This abrupt dissolving of Midge's idyllic life leads to her drunkenly taking the subway in her nightgown back to the Gaslight and unwittingly performing her first stand-up act. The set becomes a scathing indictment of Joel and his affair with secretary Penny Pann (Holly Curran) in which she vents her anger at Joel's decision to leave in spite of the initiative she poured into their family: "I'll tell you this much. I was a great wife. I was fun. I planned theme nights. I dressed in costumes. I gave him kids—a boy and a girl" ("Pilot," Season 1, Episode 1). The spontaneous performance ends with Midge topless onstage, one instance of her transgressing notions of female propriety, leading to her arrest and brief jail stint and effectively establishing that the series will progress very differently from the idealized portrait of home and domesticity depicted in the pilot episode's opening moments. Locating the inception of Midge's career at the Gaslight is also significant due to its countercultural associations in the 1950s (Walsh 2017). The Gaslight is based on the Gaslight Café in Greenwich Village, an establishment that was famous for its origins as a "basket house" where unpaid performers would pass around a basket for donations after each set. Notable performers included musician Bob Dylan, beat poet Allen Ginsburg, and comedian Joan Rivers.

Her unpremeditated foray onto the stand-up comedy stage instigates Midge's realization that there are options outside of the domestic role that she has been prepared for, and this is particularly radical in the 1950s context of the series. As Susan Lynn notes, "The prevalent image of American women in the years immediately following World War II was that of the suburban housewife who centered her life on marriage and children" (1994, 104) and this was the ultimate predestination that Midge believed she had already achieved. In her unwavering support of Joel's ambitions in the field, it has never occurred to her that she herself could be onstage, and the breakdown of their marriage fuels the discovery of her own talent and potential, thereby reconceptualizing the image and possibilities outside of domesticity for the 1950s housewife.

Midge's ponderings on the "natural(ness)" of motherhood for women during another improvised comedy set early in the first season distinctly conjures conventional associations of femininity with childrearing, domesticity, and the home:

> What if I wasn't supposed to be a mother? What if I picked the wrong profession? If you're afraid of blood, you don't become a surgeon. If you don't like to fly, you don't join Pan Am. I—I can't change my mind and donate my kids to

the library, like I'm gonna do with this book. Oh, my God, I'm awful. I mean, women are supposed to be mothers. It's supposed to be natural. It comes with the tits, right? The equipment is pre-installed. I mean, are there exceptions? What if some of us are just supposed to travel a lot? Or run 24-hour diners out in rural areas wearing coveralls? What if some of us are supposed to just talk to adults our entire life? Oh, I never thought about any of this before tonight. ("Because You Left,"Season 1, Episode 3)

Her musings on possibilities outside of the domestic role anticipate her efforts to define herself outside the roles of mother and housewife and are illustrative of how *The Marvelous Mrs. Maisel* explores the gendered nature of home and domesticity. In this way, Midge further challenges the image of the 1950s housewife and her comic meditations on motherhood vividly demonstrate "the competing voices within the public discourse on women and the internal contradictions that undermined and destabilized the domestic stereotype even as it was constructed" (Meyerowitz 1994, 2).

Prior to discovering her talent for stand-up comedy, Midge's identity largely revolved around Joel and their two children, Ethan (Matteo and Nunzio Pascale) and Esther. Her father Abe's immediate response to Midge upon hearing of Joel's infidelity and departure is that she should "Find him and make him come back home" ("Pilot," Season 1, Episode 1), clearly illustrating how central the role of wife/mother is to female identity. Both Abe and Rose spend much of the first season attempting to reconcile Midge and Joel's relationship, for fear of their daughter being left without the security and protection of a man. Rose explains Joel's absence to neighbors as due to his traveling as a result of a job promotion and constantly encourages Midge to look her best whenever she will be seeing Joel:

Rose: And what are you gonna wear?

Midge: Why?

Rose: Wear your red dress

Midge: That's an evening dress.

Rose: It's dinner. That's evening.

Midge: Mama . . .

Rose: If you have to see Joel, then he has to see you, and if he has to see you, he should see what he's missing.

Midge: That is not what this dinner's for.

Rose: You're a single woman now. That's what every dinner's for. ("Ya Shivu v Bolshom Dome Na Kholme," Season 1, Episode 2)

For her parents, there is never any question that Midge must have a man in her life and the responsibility for retrieving and then keeping Joel in the marriage is clearly hers, an undertaking she is apparently content to have at the outset of the series. Apart from her role as homemaker and her dutiful encouragement of his stand-up career dreams in spite of his questionable lack of talent, Midge also takes undoubted pride in and effort to maintain her physical appearance, a crucial element to their marriage, as indicated by Rose's prescription to her daughter that "he should see what he's missing." In this context, Rose is adamant that Midge should capitalize on her physical appearance in order to recapture her husband, but ultimately Joel's failure to "see" beyond it and recognize her own talent and ambitions result in the collapse of their relationship, although the third season suggests that Joel has become less one-dimensional in this respect.

Conventional expectations regarding femininity and female appearance are exemplified in Midge's daily ritual body measurements and the painstaking efforts she takes during her marriage to ensure that Joel never sees her without her hair and makeup done, perfecting an elaborate nightly beauty routine that is entirely conducted while Joel is asleep. These routines are also practiced by Rose while Abe sleeps, indicating that these exercises have been passed down from mother to daughter ("The Disappointment of the Dionne Quintuplets," Season 1, Episode 4). Midge's persistent attention toward the size of her infant's daughter's forehead also attests to the importance assigned to femininity and female appearance.

The depiction of these beauty rituals underscores Genz's postfeminist conceptions regarding discipline and self-surveillance, which she professes are tantamount to notions of domesticity and to preferred constructions of femininity:

> Instead of regarding caring, nurturing or motherhood as central to femininity (all of course highly problematic and exclusionary), in today's media, possession of a "sexy body" is presented as women's key (if not sole) source of identity. The body is presented simultaneously as women's source of power and always unruly, requiring constant monitoring, surveillance, discipline and remodeling (and consumer spending) in order to conform to ever-narrower judgements of female attractiveness. (2009, 149)

The vigilance and control required to maintain ideal standards of female physical appearance in media representations have summarily "been viewed by many as a 'selling out' of feminist principles and their co-option as a marketing device" (Genz and Brabon 2009b, 5) that serves a distinctively commercial rather than feminist purpose. Rachel Brosnahan's charming appearance and Midge's stylish vintage wardrobe of fit-and-flare dresses and colorful accessories also contribute to the series' visual appeal, thereby conflating her empowerment and self-determination with her physical attractiveness. As such, the conspicuous feminism displayed on *The Marvelous Mrs. Maisel* implies that even if women have the autonomy to make their own choices, conventionally ascribed gender traits and standards of femininity are still being strategically employed.

These traits also pertain to gendered expectations concerning marriage and the series' depiction of Midge's romantic relationships. The decisions she makes between her career and relationships reflect the "choice" dilemmas discussed in the Introduction that are central to postfeminist narratives. Budgeon declares that "Increased levels of autonomy and demands for the right to self-realization co-exist with traditional expectations regarding what constitutes 'proper' femininity" (2011, 61). Midge discovers that in order to find success and fulfillment outside of the domestic space, she must still contend with these expectations regarding the constitution of "proper femininity," namely in the realms of romance and relationships, whereby both personal and professional fulfillment are seemingly incompatible. When Midge begins dating eligible doctor Benjamin Ettenberg (Zachary Levi) in the second season, Rose frets over the possible ramifications of her daughter's career ambitions on the relationship's progression:

> Yes, uh well, she's um, pursuing a career in comedy, which is bad enough in itself, but there's a very viable man in the picture now, and I am so worried that this career will be the downfall of this relationship. ("All Alone," Season 2, Episode 10).

Although Benjamin, the "very viable man" that Midge meets during a family vacation in the Catskills and becomes engaged to at the end of the second season, is supportive of her career and aspirations, in contrast to ex-husband Joel, both Rose and Abe are concerned that a career outside of the home will be detrimental to her future romantic prospects.

In the series, idealized femininity rests on constructions of domesticity and female beauty that preclude work outside of the domestic space. Both parents are aghast when she takes a job as a salesgirl at the makeup counter at B. Altman Department Store and are even more dismayed when they discover her comedy career in the second season. Abe unwittingly stumbles upon one of her particularly racy performances while they are vacationing in the Catskills, in which he and Rose are the subject of her risqué jokes ("Midnight at the Concord," Season 2, Episode 5). Midge's determination to persist in her stand-up career in spite of her father's chagrin illustrates her willingness to repudiate (and ridicule) her parents' conventional (patriarchal) expectations in order to pursue her career aspirations. Abe initially refuses to consider her career a possibility, referring to it as a "hobby" and an "absurd thing . . . pursuing a life as a foul-mouth comic" ("Let's Face The Music And Dance," Season 2, Episode 6). Rose is similarly astounded, but by the end of season two, both parents are curiously accepting of Midge's goals and Abe even exhibits pride when watching her perform during her slot on a charity telethon ("Vote For Kennedy, Vote For Kennedy," Season 2, Episode 9).

The first three seasons of the series continued to speculate on the possibilities of Midge and Joel reviving their relationship, but these were averted largely due to his ambivalence toward her career aspirations. Early in the first season, she refuses his proposal to take her back, much to his own and her parents' incredulity that she would readily relinquish the security of marriage in favor of forging a future on her own terms ("Because You Left," Season 1, Episode 3). Although Joel recognizes Midge's talent, he is not able to accommodate her career with their relationship. After unexpectedly spending the night together after Ethan's birthday party, there is the possibility of reconciliation between them, but it evaporates when he inadvertently hears a bootleg recording of one of Midge's sets at the Gaslight, in which she humorously shares intimate details about their marriage ("Thank You And Good Night," Season 1, Episode 8). When Midge declares her love for him early in the second season, he tells her that "for us to be together, you'd have to give it up. . . . I can't be in a marriage where my wife is going off and talking about me to a room full of strangers, talking about my faults, my mistakes, my failures. . . . Maybe another man could, but I just can't be a joke" ("Simone," Season 2, Episode 1).

The third season witnesses Midge and Joel getting divorced ("It's The Sixties, Man!" Season 3, Episode 2) and getting remarried after a drunken night while Midge is on tour in Las Vegas ("Hands!" Season 3, Episode 4). Though both acknowledge that this remarriage was unwittingly undertaken by both parties and must be terminated again, the event ensures that Midge is still "Mrs. Maisel," both on and offstage. Though there is genuine affection between them, her inhabiting the stage instead of the domestic space does not fit his gendered ideals for marriage. As much as it causes her pain, Midge accepts this and moves on in her steadfast refusal to give up her aims and to conform to his patriarchal expectations for marriage. This contradicts Michele Schreiber's contention that "popular culture perpetually reinforces the notion that romantic love is integral to a fulfilling life" (2014, 12) and suggests that Midge can pursue paths of fulfillment other than those within of the traditional feminine realms of domesticity, marriage, and motherhood.

Midge's desire to pursue professional in place of personal and romantic fulfillment is evidenced when she abruptly breaks off her engagement to Benjamin at the close of the second season, again forfeiting the chance for domestic and financial assurance. Instead of heeding her father's advice to "marry somebody and everything will be fine" ("Someday," Season 2, Episode 8), she barely hesitates to accept the offer to go on tour as the opening act for singer Shy Baldwin (Leroy McClain), prompting her understanding that this could end her relationship with Benjamin:

> He wants me to go on tour with him. He says I'll be gone six months. And I said yes. Just like that—didn't even think about it. Didn't think about anything or anyone. Just yes. And I understand now. Everything's different. I can't go back to Jell-O molds. There won't be three before thirty for me. I just made a choice. I am gonna be alone for the rest of my life. ("All Alone," Season 2, Episode 10)

Midge recognizes that in pursuing her professional ambitions, she must forge a feminine identity that does not incorporate the "Jello-O molds" and "three before thirty" mindset that governs the domestic experiences of her peers, such as her friend Imogene, with who she had previously relished participating in the experiences of motherhood and marriage alongside. Her decree that she will prioritize her career over her personal life is also reflected in the hints throughout the series at a possible romance with fellow comedian Lenny Bruce (Luke Kirby), whose pursuit she initially rebuffs but eventually reciprocates in the fourth season. This relationship never compromises her professional goals and perhaps Lenny's simultaneous competitiveness and encouragement even propels it, underlining her conviction that her dreams of a successful comedy career are not compatible with the ideals of femininity that had formerly confined her to the domestic sphere in a relationship.

"TITS UP": WOMEN AND STAND-UP COMEDY

Midge and Susie's signature aphorism "tits up" before each stand-up performance is an evident innuendo for her access to the traditionally male-dominated field of stand-up comedy, as well as inferring an affirmation of femininity as a source of empowerment. This challenges feminist critiques of traditional modes and signifiers of femininity that are perceived to connote oppression in conforming to patriarchal ideals of feminine presentation (Bartky 1990; Bordo 1997; Brownmiller 1984; Wolf 1990). Midge's performance of stand-up transgresses conventional norms in that she occupies a male arena and embraces established traits of femininity while doing so. Joanne Gilbert claims that "Like other marginalized performers, the female comic simultaneously affirms and subverts the status quo" (2004, 33) and Midge Maisel's performances similarly consider and critique social structures in their comical and provocative interrogation of sanctioned gender roles.

Midge's performances typically remonstrate and lament social expectations relating to femininity and women's roles, summoning Judy Little's argument that female humor can create "a radical reordering of social structures, a real rather than temporary and merely playful redefinition of sex identity" (1983, 2). The topics of Midge's performances typically center on various feminist critiques relating to femininity and female identity, such as the constraints imposed on the female body by the assorted undergarments women are required to wear:

> It's the bras, right? It's the bras. And the girdles and the corsets, all designed to cut off the circulation to your brain, so you walk around on the verge of passing out, and you look at your husband, and he tells you things, and you just believe them. ("Ya Shivu v Bolshom Dome Na Kholme," Season 1, Episode 2)

These constraints also extend to social pressures accorded to women regarding their marital status (or lack thereof) and their tendency toward self-denial due to common perceptions of femininity:

> So what if I get divorced? So what if I'm alone? Why do women care about how people look at them or see them? All women. Beautiful women, successful women. ("Put That On Your Plate!" Season 1, Episode 7)

> Why do women have to pretend to be something that they're not? Why do we have to pretend to be stupid when we're not stupid? Why do we have to pretend to be helpless when we're not helpless? Why do we have to pretend to be sorry when we have nothing to be sorry about? Why do we have to pretend we're not hungry when we're hungry? ("Put That On Your Plate!" Season 1, Episode 7)

Midge's onstage diatribes about gender stereotypes and assumptions utilize Rebecca Krefting's idea of "charged humor," which appropriates comedy to raise awareness about and challenge social inequalities. In her wry and indignant observations on gender inequalities, Midge "charges audience members with complicity toward social inequities" (Krefting 2014, 25) and her honesty and exasperation evoke Rowe's concept of the "unruly woman" comedic character. The "unruly woman" is defined by her willful transgression of conventional gendered expectations and forthrightness in self-expression. Her inclination toward outrageousness and imprudence can be applied to Midge as she "disrupts the norms of femininity and the social hierarchy of male over female through excess and outrageousness" (Rowe 1995, 30) in her stand-up performances and endeavors to define herself outside of the traditionally prescribed domestic role.

Mrs. Maisel is conceived in the tradition of Jewish female comics who are largely recognized for their proclivity to accentuate women's issues and experiences through humor. In her overview of Jewish female comedians, Joyce Antler details their influence:

> there has been a veritable tradition of Jewish women's humor. From Yiddish theater and film, to vaudeville and burlesque, to nightclubs, improv and stand-up clubs, radio, television, the Broadway stage, and Hollywood cinema, Jewish women have made us laugh in a myriad of performance venues. In each of these arenas, they challenged conventional modes of joking. When they speak up, stand-up, or even sit-down. . . . these women create humor by speaking through their female sensibilities. (2010, 124)

Antler includes prominent Jewish female comedians in her study, such as Fanny Brice, Gilda Radner, Wendy Wasserstein, and Sarah Silverman. Though Midge Maisel has no real-life counterpart, comparisons are often made to Joan Rivers, who became renowned as a female comic in the mid 1960s, some years after Midge launches her stand-up career (Fousiannes 2018). Rivers's persona and stage performance consists of self-deprecation, bawdiness, and caustic criticism of gender expectations that interrogates conventional masculine discourses (Mills 2011; Mock 2019; Waisanen 2011). Her routines foregrounded issues of female sexuality and challenged female stereotypes, which was still considered particularly audacious in the 1960s, similar to the reception to Midge's typically racy performances, which unsettle the traditionally male space of the stand-up comedy stage. Incorporating Rivers's mode and content of humor into the character of Midge in the 1950s devises a further feminist reimagining of the possibilities for women and comedy that were not available during that time period.

As Gerard Matte and Ian McFadyen state, "Stand-up comedy, however, routinely deals with themes that are controversial—sexuality, race, politics and religion" (2011, 163) and these themes are commonly tackled by male performers. Lenny Bruce, featured prominently as one of Midge's cohorts on the stand-up circuit in *The Marvelous Mrs. Maisel*, was notorious for his satirical critique of politics and religion, as well as the obscenity and profanity that characterized his performances. His utilization of sexual innuendo and crude language often precipitated his arrests for obscenity, as the series documents. When Midge incorporates similarly controversial and raunchy elements in her sets, the series illustrates the general disquiet surrounding women and humor, particularly in relation to sexuality. Jennifer Foy asserts:

> It is a cultural commonplace that, for women, joking converges with promiscuity. This axiom is useful as a lens through which to evaluate the social disorder created by female comics who not only use humor, but whose comedy comes in some way from sexual aggressiveness. This social disorder manifests most immediately in the female comic's relationship with her audience when she

makes sexual jokes. Given the sexual conventional social disapproval of promiscuous women, sexual joking threatens the female stand-up's relationship with her audience in a way that it does not for male stand-up comics. (2015, 703)

Midge's intrepidness in integrating sexual content in her stage act further illustrates the singularity of a female performer so boldly participating in such a male-dominated arena, which was particularly inconceivable in the 1950s period.

Midge's transgressions of feminine norms in her performances clearly do not comply with societal expectations. She receives frequent heckling from (mostly) male audience members, such as "Hey, go home and clean the kitchen!" "Women aren't funny!" and "You're a dumb bitch" ("Thank You and Good Night," Season 1, Episode 8), as well as a few stints in jail due to arrest for public impropriety. She is even pulled offstage at one performance for speaking about childbirth and pregnancy, taboo subjects due their being "female stuff, it's private" ("All Alone," Season 2, Episode 10). Regenia Gagnier elucidates the social encroachment enacted by female comics:

> Men fear women's humor for much the same reason that they fear women's sexual freedom—because they encourage women's sexual aggression and promiscuity and thus disrupt the social order; that therefore men desire to control women's humor just as they desire to control women's sexuality—to wit, in the public domain. (1988, 137)

Midge's performance threatens the social order in her brazen declaration and critique of the social conventions that regulate feminine ideals and the behavior of women. In this way, she is explicitly challenging the circumscription of women's actions, namely relating to sexuality, that uphold patriarchal paradigms.

Correspondingly, the opposition Midge encounters to her stand-up efforts recalls Mizejewski and Sturtevant's description of the "woman comedian as an angry, powerful, mythical creature crashing a boys' club . . . an apt metaphor for the ways women comics are still required to prove themselves" (2017, 30), reiterating the advice dispensed to Midge by her rival and veteran female comedian Sophie Lennon, who notes the obstacles faced by women in comedy and emphasizes the challenges Midge faces in a profession traditionally dominated by men:

> Darling, look at you. I mean, really. Men don't want to laugh at you. They want to fuck you. You can't go up there and be a woman. You've got to be a thing. You want to get ahead in comedy? Cover up that hole. ("Put That On Your Plate!" Season 1, Episode 7)

Sophie Lennon's trademark "thing" is a caricature of a working-class, overweight and overbearing housewife with the signature catchphrase "Put that on your plate!" enacting Pamela Robertson's perceptions relating to "gender parody," which "takes as its object not the image of the woman, but the idea" (1996, 12). Midge learns that Sophie's persona is indeed an act upon visiting her extravagant home and witnessing the luxury and svelteness of Sophie's reality—"It's a very successful charade, isn't it? It's all fat suit and makeup" ("Put That On Your Plate!" Season 1, Episode 7). Sophie's act is thus able to maintain gendered power dynamics as she becomes an object of ridicule even as she commands the stage.

Her routine draws parallels to real-life comedian Phyllis Diller, who achieved success in the late 1950s and early 1960s with a similarly self-deprecating housewife persona, replete with gaudy humor and baggy dresses to suggest a larger figure (Zinoman 2012). This is also reminiscent of the distinctions between Diller and Joan Rivers who, like Midge, attempted to transgress the male boundaries of comedy without conforming to traditional female archetypes, in comparison to Diller (and Sophie), who yield to disparaging stereotypes of the housewife to draw laughs. In contrast, Midge's onstage "character" Mrs. Maisel is drawn from herself and her own experiences, enabling her to satirize the gendered social norms of her everyday existence instead of playing a role to do so. When Midge protests that Lenny Bruce and Bob Hope are successful comedians without a "character," Sophie pointedly references their gender and intuits that Midge is at an even greater disadvantage due to her physical appearance.

Midge indeed challenges the "pretty/funny" binary that has often characterized female comedians. As Mizejewski explains, "woman comics, no matter what they look like, have been located in opposition to 'pretty,' enabling them to engage in a transgressive comedy grounded in the female body—its looks, its race and sexuality, and its relationship to ideal versions of femininity" (2017, 19). That Midge can be both "pretty" and "funny" is initially baffling to other (male) comics and agents, who routinely mistake her for a singer due to her appearance. Midge eventually capitalizes on her looks as part of her performance, and the chic black cocktail dress becomes a hallmark of "Mrs. Maisel's" persona, challenging the notion that femininity and "prettiness" must be satirized in order for her to succeed. In this way, Midge is also challenging feminist critiques concerning the oppressive aspects of conventional femininity in her embracing of her feminine attributes in her stage performances. As Hannah McCann articulates in her discussion of feminist negotiations of the feminine signifiers of fashion and beauty,

> [t]o presume that fashion and beauty are simply oppressive regimes is to overlook several factors: how femininity is embodied and experienced in dynamic

74 *Chapter Three*

ways through fashion and beauty practices; the pleasures these practices might afford; the potential for these arenas to present opportunities to challenge rather than reify gender norms; and the limits of appearance in resisting forces of culture more broadly. (2018, 36)

By embracing instead of disavowing her femininity, Midge complicates traditional notions of the "male gaze," which have positioned women as "objects" for the visual consumption and entertainment of male audiences (Mulvey 1989). Instead, she is distinctively a subject on the stage who actively retaliates against and comments on her male hecklers, thereby denying Sophie Lennon's assertion that she is merely able to access the stage due to her physical appearance. However, her display of femininity simultaneously defies and bolsters traditional norms pertaining to femininity and physical appearance in that her attractiveness works to neutralize the anger and abrasiveness in her stage act. The unintentionally revealing publicity photograph that is used for her hotel club tour in the third season attests to how Midge's appearance cannot be overlooked as a factor in her appeal, thereby failing to inhibit the objectification she castigates in her performances ("Panty Pose," Season 3, Episode 3).

Yet, positioning Midge and detailing her success on the stand-up circuit reflects *The Marvelous Mrs. Maisel's* undertaking to present a female protagonist who penetrates the barriers of a male-dominated space and flourishes within it. As she becomes more comfortable onstage, her ambitions equivalently grow and she recognizes that comedy is a craft that she must

Figure 3.1. Mrs. Maisel (Rachel Brosnahan) on stage at the Gaslight. *The Marvelous Mrs. Maisel,* **"Thank You and Good Night," Season 1, Episode 8.** *Screenshot captured by author.*

hone—"I just, I want to be really, really good at this. I want to be the best" ("The Disappointment of the Dionne Quintuplets," Season 1, Episode 4). By the third season, she has surpassed her initial anticipations for her career and is traveling the country as the opening act for an acclaimed musician. Midge's transgression into conventionally male spaces is further underlined in the fourth season, as her stand-up act is relocated to the Wolford, a burlesque club, a space normally associated with female performances explicitly catered toward the "male gaze." Midge's performances ultimately become so successful that they end up attracting a larger female audience to the club, or "the wrong kind of people," as described by the manager of the Wolford ("Maisel vs. Lennon: The Cut Contest," Season 4, Episode 6), again destabilizing preconceived notions of gendered spaces. This is another demonstration of the series' conspicuous feminism as her stage performances determinately dispute the social (dis)order, in addition to repudiating the domestic role.

Sherman-Palladino pronounces with regard to Midge's accomplishments, "When you see a woman up onstage, talking in a certain way, it can make you feel like, all right, she's up there, so maybe it's not going to be *The Handmaid's Tale*" (Paskin 2017). The contrasting reference to the Hulu series reinforces the charm and vibrancy that characterizes Sherman-Palladino's approach to depicting feminist themes and the overall sanguine quality of *The Marvelous Mrs. Maisel*. However, the effervescence that construes the series often elides the limitations of its portrayal of feminism, obscuring the various points of privilege that Midge possesses, an element that begins to be addressed in the third season.

REMEDYING "WHITE FEMINISM"

The "white feminism" critique that has been attributed to Sherman-Palladino's characters is addressed in the conspicuous feminism portrayed in *The Marvelous Mrs. Maisel*. In their deliberation on the 2016 reboot of Sherman-Palladino's other well-known series, *Gilmore Girls: A Year In The Life* (Netflix, 2016), Aaron Kappel and Jessica Friday state that the miniseries revival of the original 2000–2007 series is "stuck in a white feminism bubble that blithely ignores the realities of our current world" (Kappel and Friday 2016). The perceptions of "white feminism" that have been related to Sherman-Palladino's productions persist in *The Marvelous Mrs. Maisel*, even as the series seeks to feature diversity in terms of race, class, and sexuality. The characters purporting to depict this diversity, including Midge's manager Susie Myerson, are largely relegated to the sidelines of Midge's narrative or merely serve as sources of amusement, which is reminiscent of the diversity incorporated in the *Gilmore Girls'* experiences. As Kappel and Friday ascertain:

> Sherman-Palladino only appears to afford true empathy to characters that resemble her most—white, cisgender, able-bodied, and heterosexual. Anyone not Gilmore enough—meaning mentally ill, slow on the uptake, fat, not white, not English-speaking, not gender-conforming—is ejected from the inner circle. (Kappel and Friday 2016)

Sherman-Palladino reproduces this paradigm in *The Marvelous Mrs. Maisel* by including difference and diversity that do not challenge Midge's dominant perspective, although there are indications of her presumed privilege being questioned in the third season as the narrative undertakes to confront issues of race and class more purposely than in previous seasons.

Several feminist writers have argued for integrating and considering elements of difference and intersectionality in representations of feminism (Butler 2013; Gill 2007a; Tasker and Negra 2007). Gill specifies the need to distinguish the complexities involved in constructions of diversity, arguing that it is not sufficient to merely include portrayals of difference and diversity but imperative to acknowledge the complications entangled in their presence (2007a, 67). This pertains to *The Marvelous Mrs. Maisel*'s ostensible incorporation of race, class, and sexual difference in that it largely fails to confront the inequity that contains these differences. However, the series attempts to engage more comprehensively with these issues in the third and fourth seasons by compelling Midge to recognize her privilege in contrast to other characters, whose struggles she is often ignorant of.

The most explicit foil to Midge's various privileges is manager Susie Myerson, whose ambitions in entertainment management mirror those of Midge's for the comedy stage. Apart from their shared aspirations to succeed in traditionally male-dominated professions, Susie and Midge are distinct opposites, as evidenced by how Midge's conventional beauty and refinement are offset by Susie's masculine, unkempt appearance and insolent persona. The series makes numerous references to Susie's androgynous presentation, with characters addressing her as "young man" on several occasions to humorous effect. In spite of her disruption of conventional gendered attributes, her character is deprived of complexity and subjectivity in terms of her personal life and sexual identity, as her sexuality has not as yet been alluded to on the series. In this way, she is typically rendered as a comic complement and paradox to Midge, particularly in the first two seasons, even though her enterprising spirit and nonconformity to gendered norms are examples of the series' conspicuous feminism.

The disparities in Midge and Susie's class positions are largely addressed through humor, such as in their assorted mutually stunned reactions to the drastic differences in their lifestyles. Upon entering Midge's apartment for the first time, Susie exclaims, "Jesus Christ, what is this, a landing strip? Where is your airplane, in the bathroom? I had no idea you were such an important person" ("Ya Shivu v Bolshom Dome Na Kholme," Season 1, Episode 2), while the extreme crampedness of Susie's tiny basement apartment is an operative joke throughout the series. Similarly, Susie is able to infiltrate Midge's annual family summer vacation in the Catskills by masquerading as a staff member at the upscale resort they stay at. It is only in the third season that Midge genuinely considers Susie's financial position when she eventually accedes to her manager taking on Sophie Lennon as an additional client, which she was initially furiously opposed to due to their competition. After realizing Susie's scarcity, Midge confers her consent to Susie and Sophie's partnership:

> Susie, I want you to have "Associates." I want you to have a suite of offices and windows with views and a sign out front and someone fetching your coffee. I want you to have your own car and a driver 'cause you are a bad fucking driver. I want you to have a big apartment with hot water and a closet full of blazers. I want you to have a bank account. I can deal with Sophie Lennon. ("It's The Sixties, Man!" Season 3, Episode 2)

This is the first time Midge has contemplated Susie's wishes apart from her own ambitions, allowing her to appreciate her own comparative privilege as well. The exchange occurs outside a house party hosted by the musician Shy Baldwin, where Midge and Susie are the only white attendees, prompting Midge to quip, "We are the whitest people in the world," an allusion to the "white feminism" charged to Sherman-Palladino and a suggestion of the series' self-reflexive attempt to redress it.

Midge's own identity as a Jewish woman is frequently referenced throughout the series, but this does not mitigate the privilege of her class and race position. The Maisel and Weisman families' Jewishness provides sources of amusement for the series and draws on traditions of wit and satire in Jewish humor (Rosenberg 2015; Ziv 1998), such as in Midge and Rose's shared glee in procuring the presence of the rabbi at their annual Yom Kippur dinner ("Pilot," Season 1, Episode 1) and the dinner the following year at which Midge discloses her stand-up career to the family ("Look, She Made a Hat," Season 2, Episode 7). However, they are never shown to experience discrimination due to their background and the affluence of both families is established. Instead, Jewishness is satirically celebrated in the series as Midge playfully embraces her Jewish identity, particularly onstage, such as

Figure 3.2. Susie (Alex Borstein) discloses her financial concerns and personal ambitions to Midge (Rachel Brosnahan). *The Marvelous Mrs. Maisel*, "It's The Sixties, Man!" Season 3, Episode 2. *Screenshot captured by author.*

in her retort to a heckler who urges her to return to the domestic space, "Go home and clean the kitchen!" "Oh sir, I'm Jewish. I pay people to do that" ("Thank You and Good Night," Season 1, Episode 8). Midge's repudiation of domesticity in favor of a career outside the home also challenge the "Jewish American Princess" (JAP) and "Jewish American Mother" (JAM) stereotypes that the series alludes to in her positioning as an upper-class Jewish woman (Siegel 1986). Though mother Rose frequently embodies characteristics associated with the stereotype of the overbearing and meddling "JAM," Midge herself eschews the dependence and frivolousness typically assigned to the stereotypes.

The third season features a more diverse supporting cast than in previous seasons and tackles issues of race more adequately in its depiction of Shy Baldwin and his entourage, whom Midge and Susie are on tour with. However, much of Shy and the musician's appearances manifest in the context of the musical performances that follow Midge's comedy set, and while these productions are intricate and captivating, they typically serve as interludes that install racial diversity as a backdrop, rather than as an element to engage with and investigate. There are inferences to aspects of racial inequality, such as Susie assuming Shy must have a white manager, Lou (Ned Eisenberg), who in actuality only handles matters that might require white representation, as explained to Susie by his de facto manager Reggie (Sterling K. Brown):

Reggie: Lou's the white guy that record labels are willing to deal with. Lou's the white guy that Nabisco likes to talk to when they want Shy to front for 'em. Lou is the white guy that glad-hands mayors when they want my man to get a key to the city. Lou's—

Susie: White ("It's The Sixties, Man!" Season 3, Episode 2).

This exchange is indicative of the series' intent to exhibit and critique the prevalent racial attitudes of the time period, particularly with regard to the entertainment industry. Although Shy enjoys fame as a performer, elements of racial bias are upheld in order to sanction his celebrity status. Another incident that illuminates this occurs when Midge is informed by Shy that the black entertainers cannot stay at the Fontainebleau Hotel where they are performing, as prohibited by Florida law, a fact that Midge had blissfully been unaware of ("Kind Of Bleau," Season 3, Episode 6). Her ignorance of segregation laws demonstrates the naivete that belies her savvy disposition and the privilege that has shielded her from these realities. Though these and other examples indicate a consciousness of racial inequities within the series, they are generally depicted as secondary to Midge's central narrative and do not deeply engage with the aspects of prejudice being portrayed.

The revelation that Shy is a closeted homosexual toward the end of the season after Midge discovers him hiding in his private yacht after an encounter with an abusive partner demonstrates the series' effort to acknowledge discrimination related to sexual difference ("Kind Of Bleau," Season 3, Episode 6). Midge's knowledge of Shy's sexuality has profound ramifications in the season's final episode, which depicts Midge realizing her dream of performing at The Apollo Theatre in New York, as the opening act for Shy. The venue of The Apollo is notable for its significance to black performers after its remodeling in the 1930s and subsequent accommodation to the black community of Harlem (Charles 2019), in contrast to the previous "Whites Only" policy that the building invoked in its former incarnation as a burlesque club. Midge's aspiration to perform at the venue is somewhat unexpected for a white woman and another suggestion of the series' venturing to incorporate racial dynamics through her naivete toward race relations, as evidenced in the episode's title "A Jewish Girl Walks Into The Apollo" (Season 3, Episode 8). After a conversation with celebrated black comedienne Moms Mabley (Wanda Sykes), whom she has attained higher billing from by virtue of her whiteness, Midge performs a routine that she has tailored specifically for the predominantly black audience, making definitive references to Shy's sexuality, which she mistakenly assumes is known to the audience due to their shared racial background. The consequences of her mistaken assumption are clear upon Reggie's refusal to allow Midge and Susie to board the plane to the next tour stop:

> Reggie: Midge, Shy is my boy. I'm supposed to protect him. I'm not gonna tell him I sent some girl up there to tell the world that he's what he is.
>
> Midge: What is he?!—Please, they were jokes.
>
> Reggie: "Judy Garland shoes"?
>
> Midge: Oh. Oh shit! Reggie, this can't happen. I mean, me and Shy, we're friends.
>
> Reggie: You are not friends. You were on tour together, and now you're not. ("A Jewish Girl Walks Into The Apollo," Season 3, Episode 8)

Midge is summarily fired as Shy's opening act and the closing moments of the season leave her grappling with the consequences of her obliviousness to the reality of bias and discrimination, signifying the series' first extensive indictment of her disregard for her racial and class privilege. This delineates an uncommon reversal of the power dynamics that have typically enabled Midge to triumph and is suggestive of an intersectional sensibility that further explored in the following season.

Elsewhere in seasons three and four, there are efforts to include diversity, such as in locating Joel's nightclub venture in Chinatown, enabling representation of Chinese people that largely conform to Orientalist patterns of exotic foods, gambling dens, and translation difficulties. Joel's love interest, Mei Lin (Stephanie Hsu) also embodies the clichéd characteristics of mystery and allure stereotypically attributed to Asian women, despite the fact that Mei attends medical school and like Midge searches for fulfillment beyond the traditional environs of femininity and domesticity. Aspects of class privilege and renewed social awareness are also explored through the economic downfall of Midge's parents. Abe Weissman leaves his secure employment with the technology firm Bell Labs and as a tenured mathematics professor at Columbia University when he becomes frustrated at their interference in his personal affairs and rekindles his latent social activism. Inspired by Marxism, he is offered a job as a theatre critic with the *Village Voice*, the alternative weekly newspaper launched in Greenwich Village in 1955, after his article is published by the *New York Times* in defense of a playwright friend being blacklisted for Communist Party connections ("A Jewish Girl Walks Into The Apollo," Season 3, Episode 8). Meanwhile, wife Rose refutes financial aid from her family due to the gender imparity governing the family trust fund, which incites her own feminist enlivening ("It's The Sixties, Man!" Season 3, Episode 2), which is further explored in season four in her efforts to launch her own career as a matchmaker. These developments signify a departure from both parents' characterizations in the first two seasons, which were considerably marked by their gratification in their class and financial privilege. Susie's development of a gambling habit in the third season and instigation of the burning of her deceased mother's home in order to collect the insurance are also indicators of the series' enlarged attention to class and financial inequality. These instances suggest that *The Marvelous Mrs. Maisel* is acknowledging and making some movement toward redressing the "white feminism" designation. By alluding to elements of class, race, and sexual difference, the series is illustrating an awareness of various intersectional factors in order to cultivate a more comprehensive and equitable appreciation of women's roles and experiences.

The features of conspicuous feminism clearly operate in the representation of female empowerment in *The Marvelous Mrs. Maisel*, particularly in its querying of the traditional correlation between female identity and motherhood and domesticity in the series' portrayal of protagonist Midge Maisel's pursuit of success and realization outside of the domestic space. Her aspirations in the male-dominated field of stand-up comedy further reinforce the series' incorporation of themes of resistance toward misogynistic social and cultural structures, as instigated by #MeToo. Midge's tirades against gendered norms and inequality in her stand-up routines and her rejection of conventional female roles render an illustration of female strength and empowerment that is particularly remarkable in the series' 1950s setting and a reminder of the feminist work that remains in the contemporary era.

Much of the series' marketing has also appropriated its 1950s setting with contemporary feminist references, such as the pink poster advertising "The Maisel" pastrami sandwich at the pop-up themed restaurant based on the legendary Carnegie Deli (Leeds 2019). The poster's text proclaims that the sandwich is suitable "For Women Who Eat, Not Women Who Lunch," alluding to traditional connotations between women's eating habits and expectations to maintain particular standards of beauty and body image. Other promotional methods also capitalize on feminist motifs that characterize the themes of empowerment and independence on *The Marvelous Mrs. Maisel*. The pink colors that epitomize the series' logo and Midge Maisel's personal style dominate Prime Video's campaigns for the series, emphasizing pink's association with femininity and female identities. In November 2018, the Empire State Building was lit in pink in order to celebrate the launch of *The Marvelous Mrs. Maisel*'s second season. The event also observed its partnership with Girls Inc., a nonprofit organization aiming to empower and inspire girls and young women through advocacy, research, and educational and health services, enlarging the series' identification with and celebration of female strength. Other "Maisel"-inspired merchandise includes cosmetics and accessories (Robin 2019), reinforcing conventional signifiers of femininity alongside the series' feminist directives, as well as evoking the postfeminist correspondence between femininity and empowerment. The calculated marketing strategies employed by the series firmly exhibit conspicuous feminism's motivation to endorse female empowerment, while also shaping it as a concept to be consumed and displayed.

The field of stand-up comedy itself has been impacted by #MeToo as more female comedians are reflecting aspects of conspicuous feminism and incorporating themes of misogyny into their performances. Like Midge, Krefting's "charged humor" has constituted Amy Schumer and Ali Wong's droll observations on motherhood and pregnancy, as expressed in their respective television specials *Growing* (Netflix 2019) and *Ali Wong: Baby Cobra* (Netflix 2016), which both performed in while pregnant. Australian Hannah Gadsby's show *Nanette* (Netflix, 2018) forcibly confronts the movement in a set detailing her own experiences with assault and homophobia, while anger similarly characterizes the humor showcased in Cameron Esposito's 2018 stand-up special *Rape Jokes*. #MeToo has propelled female comedians to reclaim the "rape joke" in their performances, employing the theme of rape to denounce the crime, rather than to provide unsettling punchlines that rely on mocking ironic constructs of masculinity, as has been executed by male comics, including George Carlin and Louis C. K. (Lockyer and Savigny 2020). In her article on how #MeToo has reconstituted the delineation of the "rape joke," Beth Anne Cooke-Cornell contends that it has derived from "an irony-dependent, male-generated critique of rape culture, to a literal, woman-generated critique foregrounding the comedian's body as the site of sexual assault" (Cooke-Cornell 2018), profoundly shifting the contours of the "rape joke" to the female comedian's own experience. Allegations of sexual misconduct against C. K. and other male comedians, notably Aziz Ansari and Bill Cosby, have also contributed to comedy's association with #MeToo in their exposure of instances of assault within the field.

The Marvelous Mrs. Maisel's representation of a housewife attempting to redefine herself and to access a male-dominated field resonates with the tenets of #MeToo that have shaped its embodiment of conspicuous feminism. As Sherman-Palladino expresses,

> [w]hen we started the series, we didn't want it to feel political, rather relevant to a young woman today. We didn't want it to feel like, "Oh, it's my grandma's story," but that it could be their story. Then it became time to take the gargantuans down [in the #MeToo movement], and it brought a different view to our show that wasn't necessarily intended. It worked in an odd way, freakishly

and also, boo, it shows how far we have not come since the 1950s. (quoted in D'Alessandro 2018b)

The various challenges Midge faces in pursuing her goals, particularly in relation to inverting patriarchal notions of femininity that restrict women's advancements in male-dominated spaces, reflect the endeavors of women to reclaim their subjectivity in spheres that have frequently objectified them, such as in comedy and the entertainment industries. Midge's efforts to forge an identity outside of the prescribed roles of wife and mother and to overcome obstacles in achieving her goals as a female stand-up comic have resounded with #MeToo's advocacy for female empowerment. The fourth season expands on the theme of women positioning themselves outside of the domestic space, in its chronicling of other characters' (including Susie, Rose, and Mei) attempts to prosper in their chosen careers. Despite the series' 1950s setting, its themes of female strength and gender bias, particularly in the workplace, have remained significant in the contemporary era. The third season onwards obliges Midge Maisel to identify and confront the significance of the privilege that was previously unexamined throughout the series, and it is intriguing to appraise how her pursuit of self-realization outside of "something other than a mother or housewife" will progress and evolve.

Chapter Four

Incorporating Intersectionality and Inclusivity

Insecure

The opening moments of the HBO series *Insecure* (2016–2021) immediately hone in on the insecurities of protagonist Issa Dee (Issa Rae) as she attempts to respond to the barrage of questions bluntly aimed at her by the middle school students she is addressing at a classroom visit by the nonprofit organization We Got Y'All. Ranging from "Why you talk like a white girl?" and "What's up with your hair?" to "Are you single?" and "Why ain't you married?" the students are clearly more concerned with Issa's personal life than with the mentoring opportunities that she and the organization are offering. *Insecure* immediately confronts common perceptions of black culture and black womanhood in this opening scene as Issa finds herself having to disclaim one student's comment about "nobody checkin' for bitter-ass black women anymore" with the justification that "black women aren't bitter. They're just tired of being expected to settle for less." The awkwardness and uneasiness of the scene construct the series' premise of single women navigating the chaotic and insecure terrain of relationships, love, and careers and Issa's attestation concerning black women establishes *Insecure*'s particular embodiment of female empowerment and conspicuous feminism on television that is informed by racial dynamics.

Partly based on Rae's lauded web series *Awkward Black Girl*, which had two seasons that premiered on YouTube in 2011, *Insecure* chronicles the experiences of protagonist Issa Dee and her best friend Molly Carter (Yvonne Orji) as they attempt to achieve personal and professional contentment in Los Angeles. With black female protagonists, *Insecure* enlarges television discourses of feminism by reflecting and interrogating structural racial inequalities and prejudices about race and ethnicity, while illustrating the personal predicaments regarding romantic relationships and friendships that the women face. This contrasts with the depictions of an earlier prominent comedic series, *The Mindy Project* (2012–2017), which also featured a woman of color as its protagonist (Mindy Kaling who, like Rae, was also the series' showrunner). Although the series dealt with similar themes relating to career, relationships, and motherhood, issues of race largely did not factor into its narratives and there was critical scrutiny as to its predominantly white cast undermining the significance of a non-white lead (Mora 2013). Across broadcast and streaming platforms in the 2020–2021 season, 22% of female characters on television were black (Lauzen 2021), but black female protagonists remain relatively uncommon.

In its portrayal of Issa and Molly's experiences, *Insecure* has been applauded for its efforts to refigure prevailing stereotypes relating to black womanhood and to depict black female identities that do not conform to paradigms that have contributed to their definition in the media and popular culture (Davies 2018; Welang 2018). The characters resist the "controlling images" and stereotypes that have commonly designated black women on television (Collins 2000). The series' exploration of elements of racial dynamics and inequity, particularly in the workplace, also produces a rare example of intersectionality being incorporated into the depiction of conspicuous feminism and single black women in their pursuit of romantic and professional fulfillment.

The comparative infrequency of black female protagonists on television mirrors the concerns over #MeToo's deficiency in addressing intersectional issues. Although the movement was originated by a black woman in 2006 in response to the abuse of underprivileged and minority women, the incidents highlighted by the media have predominantly focused on the experiences of high-profile white women and have largely not considered aspects of race and class. In their article on #MeToo and intersectionality, which examines the media coverage and public response to the numerous allegations of sexual abuse made against the singer R. Kelly, Rebecca Leung and Robert Williams (2019) assert that it was not until the airing of the documentary *Surviving R. Kelly* in 2019 foregrounding the stories of Kelly's various accusers that allegations made by black women became more visible in the media.

Other social movements have since attempted to redress the relative invisibility of media coverage toward injustices perpetrated on black women, notably the #SayHerName movement, which was established in 2015 by the African American Policy Forum to foster wider awareness of the violence and police brutality committed against black women that is often overshadowed by the media attention granted to anti-black violence toward black men (Workneh 2015). #SayHerName stresses the importance of recognizing the intersectional distinctions that can impact victims of violence, in contrast to the perceived lack of intersectional awareness accorded to media constructions of #MeToo. As Boyle notes on the necessity of incorporating an intersectional perspective into the movement in order to encompass the varying circumstances of the women affected:

> Tarana Burke's Me Too movement originated in the experiences of multiply marginalised victim/survivors who were young, urban, women of colour. However, whilst some multiply marginalised women have had a relatively mainstream platform in the #MeToo moment, this has not necessarily had the effect of shifting either [white] feminist or media practices overall. (2019, 9)

The #MeToo movement that expanded after the Weinstein allegations has broadly concentrated on the accounts with higher media and cultural visibility, echoing conceptions of popular feminism that are generally configured around whiteness and economic privilege. Conspicuous feminism is thus differentiated by a sensibility toward recognizing and exhibiting intersectional perspectives, recalling Jennifer C. Nash's suggestion that "Perhaps it is [intersectionality's] irresistible visuality, its ability to be represented" (2019, 11) that enables intersectional differences to be embodied across and beyond academic disciplines, including in media representations. *Insecure*'s black female protagonists produce an opportunity for the stories of black women to be foregrounded as a notable example of conspicuous feminism and for their experiences of discrimination to be depicted in an effort to reposition feminist and media practices that have dominantly centered on whiteness.

Since its debut in 2016, the HBO series has received critical acclaim, notably for Rae's performance, with two Golden Globe nominations for Best Actress in a Television Series Comedy (2017 and 2018), and a Primetime Emmy Award nomination for Outstanding Lead Actress in a Comedy Series in 2017. The series was also named one of the Top Ten Television Programs of the year by the American Film Institute in 2017. The first two seasons largely focus on the various insecurities that Issa encounters in her career and her relationships, while the last three seasons picture her confronting these challenges as she takes a more proactive role in both her professional and personal ventures. Issa and Molly's friendship fluctuates considerably during these five seasons due to frustrations generated by their respective dilemmas, but their relationship is the most pivotal throughout the series. The depiction of Issa's continued connection with her main love interest Lawrence Walker (Jay Ellis), despite vacillations in their relationship, is also significant to her development as the series progresses. Other key supporting characters include Issa and Molly's friends Kelli Prenny (Natasha Rothwell) and Tiffany DuBois (Amanda Seales), whose recurring narratives concerning dating, marriage, pregnancy, and motherhood also apply to the facets of conspicuous feminism that the series illustrates.

As its title suggests, the series presents Issa's pursuit of personal and professional fulfillment in terms of insecurity, indecision, and oftentimes purposelessness as she struggles to determine what her goals are. The various setbacks and disappointments encountered by Issa and Molly in their romantic and professional endeavors are central to *Insecure*, yet the depiction of these struggles, as well as the triumphs attained in their midst, contributes to the conceptions of empowerment of black female identities that are associated with the series. Yomi Adegoke describes the impact of the series' unconventional representations, which are relieved of preconceived perceptions and characterizations that have commonly characterized black women:

> I thought it was massively important, not just for African Americans but just generally black women all over the world, to see ourselves portrayed so normally. *Insecure* shows the humdrum experiences that all black millennial women go through, but also puts them at the centre of the story. It just hits this sweet spot that quite a lot of predominantly white shows allow their characters to exist in, which is to be realistic, complex and live outside of the stereotypes. (quoted in Davies 2018)

Insecure's nuanced and complex portrayal of black women does not rely on racial stereotypes that have been prevalent in popular culture but affords them a sense of commonality that they have seldom been granted in media representations.

In this regard, *Insecure* has also been commended for its attempts to depart from prevailing stereotypes of black women and to present a perspective of black womanhood that does not conform to these persisting images. Patricia Hill Collins's identification in 1990 of the "controlling images" that have defined black women in popular culture is a key criticism of popular representations of black women. Citing Collins and Julia Jordan-Zachery, Rachel Alicia Griffin lists some of these controlling images, which include "the mammy, jezebel, sapphire, amazon, matriarch, welfare queen, gold digger, Black bitch, superwoman, freak, hoe and hoodrat," stressing that "they all necessitate culturally deficient representations of black femininity in that each is characterized by at least one trait that naturalizes Black female inferiority, deviance, and/or contemptibility" (2015, 36). In this way, these depictions of black women have reproduced negative connotations of black womanhood and sustained intersecting frameworks of inequality in the process.

The "controlling images" specified by Collins have been revised to produce revamped versions of the abiding stereotypes (Griffin 2015; Springer 2007). Kimberley Springer designates "Divas, Black Bitches and Bitter Black Women" as "not so new manifestations of racism and sexism impacting black women in popular culture" (2007, 249). These configurations render black women as perpetually difficult, conniving, and angry, as mainly evidenced in popular reality television series that frequently characterize their black female cast members as contentious, covetous, and rancorous. Notable examples include Omarosa Manigault Newman on *The Apprentice* (NBC, 2004–2015) and Kenya Moore and Porsha Williams on *The Real Housewives of Atlanta* (Bravo, 2008–present). Cookie Lyon (Taraji P. Henson) on *Empire* (Fox, 2015–present), Renee Perry and Wilhemina Slater (both played by Vanessa Williams) on *Desperate Housewives* (ABC, 2004–2012), and *Ugly Betty* (ABC, 2006–2010) are other prominent television characters that conform to this pattern. In relation to these constructions, Springer queries

> black feminism's progress in dismantling images of "the black bitch," "the loud black woman," "the sistah with attitude," and a host of other stereotypes if these cues are still considered easily recognizable. There is also the notable failure of societal transformation in eradicating these images. (2007, 267)

These images still retain their visibility and significance and this has largely been attributed to their potential for entertainment and audience appeal, echoing Banet-Weiser's conjecture that "race is produced as a particular commodity more than a traditional kind of engaged politics" (2007, 215). The inclusion of racial diversity in these instances suggests an integration of race for recognizable traits that viewers can derive amusement or fascination from, rather than an undertaking to address racial dynamics.

Insecure's concern for intersectionality and for the revision of black female stereotypes evokes key paradigms of black feminist critique that stress the importance of employing an intersectional lens when engaging with issues of gender and feminism. The black feminist organization Combahee River Collective's 1977 manifesto declared that

> we are actively committed to struggling against racial, sexual, heterosexual, and class oppression, and see as our particular task the development of integrated analysis and practice based upon the fact that the major systems of oppression are interlocking. (1977, 16)

Other notable black feminist works that have accented the necessity of acknowledging the intersecting forms of oppression imposed on black women include Angela Davis's (1981) work on the convergences of inequality regarding gender, race, and class; Audre Lorde's (1984) notions on the overlapping tenets of racism and patriarchy; and Frances Beal's (2008) concept of the "double jeopardy" of race and gender that inflicts the experiences of black women. *Insecure*'s depiction of black women and the intersectional concerns that significantly comprise their everyday experiences reflects black feminist themes of intersectionality in the series' expression of conspicuous feminism.

Insecure is the most recent manifestation of HBO's acclaimed comedy series centering on single women, paralleling the themes and popularity of *Sex and the City* (1998–2004) and *Girls* (2012–2017). Series creator Lena Dunham and *Girls*' feminist agenda garnered critical acclaim, as well as criticism due to perceived limitations of Dunham's perspectives in constructing and dispensing a feminist position. Nicola Rivers's assertion that Dunham and *Girls* are possibly "promoting a singular, white vision of feminism as universal" (2017, 65) is one of the conflicting factors that popular media constructions of feminism have invariably contended with. Following similar critiques of *Sex and the City*, *Girls* has been charged with envisioning feminist identities that only conform to white, heterosexual, and economically privileged standards (Adriaens and Van Bauwel 2014; Nash and Grant 2017). Nash and Grant note that, "the cultural conversations about the lack of racial diversity in *Sex and the City* in the late 1990s and now *Girls* flags the complex terrain of contemporary post-feminism and the relations of power that produce post-feminist discourses for women" (2017, 981), emphasizing the lack of racial diversity that has defined discourses of femininity on popular television, particularly in relation to narratives focusing on themes of empowerment and independence for single women. *Insecure* is thus notable for its explicit undertaking of racial issues in its portrayal of single black women grappling with issues of self-determination and fulfillment in career, relationships, and romance that were similarly fundamental to both *Sex and the City* and *Girls*. In its depiction of structural racism in the workplace and its celebration of black culture, the series' handling of feminist themes emphasizes race as key to how Issa and Molly experience and navigate elements of choice and empowerment in contrast to reflections of conspicuous feminism on other prolific series.

Thus, *Insecure* addresses the criticisms of feminist television series regarding their lack of engagement with racial issues and the lack of subjectivity typically afforded to female characters of color. As Springer specifies:

> studies of postfeminism have studiously noted that many of its icons are white and cited the absence of women of color, but the analysis seems to stop there. Whiteness studies . . . appears to have dwindled to a whimper when it comes to thinking about how, say, Miranda, Carrie, Samantha, and Charlotte exact racial privilege while they have their sex in the city. The arrival of postfeminist discourse in popular culture, especially, needs to be interrogated about how race is always present. Even when they are not on screen, women of color are present as the counterpart against which white women's ways of being—from Bridget Jones to Ally McBeal to Carrie Bradshaw—are defined and refined. (2007, 249)

The presence of a black female protagonist on *Insecure* diverges from the typical postfeminist model and defines and refines a black woman's "way of being" instead. The racial privilege that is not examined in *Sex and the City* or *Girls* can be explored through the representation of Issa and Molly's precarious circumstances as they seek to attain empowerment in their respective careers and relationships, thereby producing depictions of conspicuous feminism and images of black women that are more thoroughly informed by intersectional frameworks.

RESISTING "CONTROLLING IMAGES"

The character of Issa Dee defies the "controlling images" and stereotypes that have frequently demarcated black women on television. She is not bitter, angry, difficult, or aggressive personally or professionally but instead embodies an ordinariness and self-doubt that is accessible in comparison to earlier archetypes. Rae herself addresses the restrictive stereotypes associated with black femininity in an article she contributed to the *Huffington Post*, stating that "in the end, I have to ask: Who is to say what we do and don't do? What we can and can't do? The very definition of 'blackness' is as broad as that of 'whiteness,' yet we're seemingly always trying to find a specific, limited definition" (Rae 2017). Her commitment to portraying characters that don't comply with established definitions of "blackness" signals a determination to challenge racial paradigms and archetypes pertaining to black women.

Insecure presents an example of the "new kind of female antihero" that Gillian Silverman and Sarah Hagelin suggest is becoming more commonplace on popular television. Silverman and Hagelin describe this antihero as

> narcissistic, failure prone, and uninterested in pursuing likeability. Characters like Amy Jellicoe of *Enlightened*, Ilana Wexler and Abbi Abrams of *Broad City*, Maria Bamford of *Lady Dynamite*, and Issa Dee of *Insecure* present a new kind of female protagonist, frequently frustrated in both romance and work, motivated neither by the marriage plot nor the traditional career trajectory. Their character arcs read a bit like reverse bildungsromans—instead of being educated toward growth and personal development, their life experiences tend toward disappointment and failure. Theirs are narratives of unbecoming, both because they trace the protagonists' undoing and because they usually involve portraits that are deeply unflattering. (2018, 878)

In this way, Issa is reminiscent of Rebecca Wanzo's (2016) classification of the "precarious" female protagonist, who is largely defined by her humiliations and failures in that she does not aspire to any specific personal or professional goals in contrast to Midge Maisel on *The Marvelous Mrs. Maisel* or the protagonists of *Big Little Lies*, who are distinctively construed by their respective career and relationship objectives. Instead, *Insecure* constructs Issa as indeterminate and struggling to designate a sense of purpose for herself, particularly in the earlier seasons of the series and in comparison to the characterization of Molly.

Issa's various insecurities are disclosed in the pilot episode, which establishes that she is discontent in both her occupation at the nonprofit organization and in her long-term relationship with boyfriend Lawrence. The opening scene featuring the awkward questioning by the middle school students is shortly followed by a brief interaction between Issa and her all-white co-workers, who plainly look to her for insights on "people of color" in her status as "the token with all the answers." Later in the episode, Issa imagines her white colleague and friend Frieda (Lisa Joyce) expounding to her on her relationship prospects as a black woman:

> Educated black women are highly unlikely to get married the more education they have. On the bright side, many black women are work-focused and find happiness in their careers. But, then, there is a small percentage of pathetic women who have neither. They are purposeless. ("Insecure as F**k," Season 1, Episode 1)

The various assumptions regarding black women are directly and critically undertaken, establishing the series' imperative to expose and scrutinize them through illustrating Issa's challenges in navigating these expectations in her everyday experiences.

Issa's subjectivity and reflections on her circumstances are largely delivered through voiceover and direct camera addresses, a technique utilized in other series focusing on the narratives of the single woman, including *Sex and the City* and BBC's *Fleabag* (2016–present). Faye Woods proposes that this form of address "establishes a privileged relationship between protagonist and viewer as the women break their connection with narrative action and turn to speak to us. This direct address evokes whispered feminine confidences, a shared intimacy, although [the] women speak with a comic bluntness" (2019, 195). On *Insecure*, the camera address is implemented via the freestyle raps that Issa performs to herself in front of the mirror. The intimacy granted via the direct address is thus heightened as the fourth wall is not merely broken, but allows the viewer further access to Issa's interiority as she confers with her own image in the mirror. This device enables the viewer to witness Issa in her private moments where she attempts to confront her insecurities through her improvised raps. The content of these raps typically centers on the hopes and frustrations she cannot express in public and they generally serve to shore up a sense of confidence to deflect her various uncertainties, such as her relationship woes: "Do you want your man or not? Do you know your plans or not? You gonna go back home or not? You gonna claim your throne or not? Is you Khaleesi or that other bitch . . ." ("Messy as F**k," Season 1, Episode 2) and instances in which she instills encouragement in herself, as when she moves into a new apartment in the third season: "Hey, mirror bitch, you're lookin' real clean. You lookin' real bad, you lookin' like a queen. It's been a long time I shouldn't'a left you, but I got a new spot. It's brand-new, brand-new" ("Fresh-like" Season 3, Episode 4). Although the raps themselves are often awkwardly constructed and delivered, her "mirror bitch" persona provides Issa with an outlet to vent and to contemplate, while also employing the conventions of rap and hip hop, acknowledging their rich and long-established associations with black narratives and culture.

Issa's utilization of rap to manifest her interiority can be discerned as a feminist reclaiming of the rap and hip hop genre that has typically been associated with black masculinity (Collins 2006a; Morgan 2009). As Nahum Welang professes on the gendered properties of the genre, "While hip hop has arguably uplifted the black community, it also functions as a black patriarchal practice that physically, metaphorically and rhetorically marginalizes black womanhood" (2018, 299). Since its establishment in the 1970s, rap and hip hop has functioned as a genre in which black (male) culture has been able to describe the economic and social hardships, as well as the violence, faced by black urban communities (Boyd 2004; Price 2006; Rose 2008). As such, hip hop has conceived a recognizable black identity that was commodified as the genre entered and subsequently dominated mainstream popular music

Figure 4.1. Issa (Issa Rae) raps to her "mirror bitch." *Insecure*, "Messy As F**k," Season 1, Episode 2. *Screenshot captured by author.*

(Collins 2006b). Allan Watson declares that "hip hop has provided one of the few significant employment and wealth-generating opportunities for African Americans" (2016, 182), validating the genre as a source of identification and influence for black culture.

However, black women have not traditionally been able to occupy space in hip hop culture and their presence has typically conformed to misogynistic and objectifying "controlling images" in (male) hip hop lyrics and music videos (Balaji 2010; Kistler and Lee 2009). Although there have been notable examples of black women triumphing in rap and hip hop such as Cardi B, Missy Elliot, and Nicki Minaj, the genre remains a prodigiously masculine space that subordinates and fetishizes black female identities (Balaji 2010). Issa's usage of rap to express her doubts and frustrations thus reproduces black women's aspirations for empowerment within hip hop culture, while also appropriating the genre's style and language to articulate her own specifically female desires and vulnerabilities. In this way, *Insecure* utilizes hip hop to reflect its indebtedness to black culture, as well as to enhance black women's generally delimited presence within it, displaying conspicuous feminism's intentions to give expression to diverse female subjectivities.

Issa's insecurities are set alongside her best friend Molly, whose confident and polished exterior masks insecurities of her own. A corporate lawyer, Molly is more professionally assured than Issa and is attuned to the conventions appropriate to racially specific settings and interactions. As Issa states in her voiceover introduction of Molly in the pilot episode, "White people looove Molly. Black people also looove Molly"; this dialogue is interspersed with juxtaposing scenes of Molly impressing at a business meeting and playing dominoes, respectively. In this way, Molly evokes elements of the "black lady" construction, which has been noted as a more refined counterpart to the fiery and aggressive black female stereotypes (Collins 2000; Griffin 2015; Springer 2007; Wisseh 2019). This image has typically been linked to representations of professional black women, which Springer speculates is "designed to counter accusations of black female licentiousness and one that can accommodate the ascension to middle-class status through work outside the home" (2007, 258). Thus, the "black lady" has been affiliated with notions of sophistication, respectability, and class (Collins 2000) as manifested in venerated television working mothers such as Clair Huxtable (Phylicia Rashad) on *The Cosby Show* (NBC, 1984–1992) and Vivian Banks (Janet Hubert-Whitten and Daphne Maxwell Reid) on *The Fresh Prince of Bel-Air* (NBC, 1990–1996). More recent embodiments have included Olivia Pope (Kerry Washington) on *Scandal* (ABC, 2012–2018) and Annalise Keating (Viola Davis) on *How to Get Away with Murder* (ABC, 2014–present), who are often lauded for their professional competence and fortitude, as well as their elegance and charisma.

In spite of these affirming characteristics, the "black lady" retains conventional elements of the "controlling images," such as her propinquity to the classic "mammy" caricature, which Assatu N. Wisseh describes as "the protective and nurturing Black woman who happily serves Whites" (2019, 4). Although the "mammy" stereotype largely functioned as a symbol of black women's caretaking role during slavery (Collins 2000; Davis 1981), Griffin argues that "Black female characters are still replete with servitude, obedience, self-sacrifice, care-taking, domesticity, and allegiance to White people and White culture" (2015, 36). *Scandal*'s Olivia Pope in particular has been implicated with an amenability toward White culture in her position as a political fixer in Washington, DC (Griffin 2015). The "black lady's" professional ambitions have also been correlated with Daniel Patrick Moynihan's (1965) "matriarchy thesis—Black ladies have jobs that are so all consuming that they have no time for men or have forgotten how to treat them" (Collins 2000, 81), thus deviating from habitual norms of femininity and gendered roles. The "black lady" is still subjugated to prevailing tropes of black womanhood that personify the "racial and gender stereotypes [that] are the commodity and discourse that make difference legible in popular culture" (Springer 2007, 258). In this way, Molly conforms to the "black lady" figuration as the demands of her career, as well as her often improbable expectations, are frequently depicted as hampering her romantic relationships. However, *Insecure* also enables Molly to transcend the stereotype as the series explores the dilemmas and uncertainties she faces in her personal and professional life, while considering how systemic racial dynamics contribute to them.

Both Issa and Molly present images of black womanhood that resist common media stereotypes in the series' regular depiction of their ambitions, frustrations, and relationships. Their navigation of these typical experiences and emotions grants them a sense of normality and accessibility that has rarely been afforded to black women on television. This genuineness extends to the representation of their friendship, which Janice Williams proclaims in an article on *Newsweek* to be one of the "great black female friendships" (Williams 2017) ever to be featured on television. Despite the differences in their aims and professions, their support for each other is evident and sharing their corresponding insecurities is a definitive source of their bond. In this way, Issa and Molly's relationship evokes bell hooks and Cornel West's conception of "critical affirmation," which Cynthia B. Dillard describes: "It pushes and pulls, it critiques and lifts up, it falls apart and puts back together again only to fall apart differently" (2019, 116). The friendship is tested throughout the five seasons of the series as both women respectively critique and support each other's choices and actions. The ways in which the relationship consequently evolves contributes to *Insecure*'s intersectional examination and its representation of conspicuous feminism with regard to the female empowerment and solidarity derived from Issa and Molly's friendship, as well as in their precarious experiences in the realms of work and romance.

INSECURE IN THE WORKPLACE

The setting of the workplace frames much of *Insecure*'s deliberations on racial issues, and is where both Issa and Molly encounter various lingering misconstructions and prejudices. In the first two seasons, Issa's work for "We Got Y'all," the nonprofit organization and after-school program that enables her to aid disadvantaged and minority youth. However, as she is the only employee of color, her standpoints and ideas are often misunderstood or disregarded and she is invariably frustrated by her co-workers' often unintentional misappropriation of elements of black culture. This satire of the microagressions committed by her co-workers in their attempts to demonstrate their racial consciousness produces humor but also emphasizes their obliviousness and even insensitivity toward racial issues. Examples include the brainstorming of ideas for possible after-school activities, with suggestions ranging from "hip hop Shakespeare" to a "drum circle" to watching "*Lemonade* and then we go to Lemonade and we eat" ("Messy as F**k," Season 1, Episode 2) in reference to Beyoncé's 2016 visual album, renowned for its heralding of black culture in its visual and lyrical references to slavery, police violence, and the marginalization of black women, among other themes (McFadden 2016). Issa's boss Joanne (Catherine Curtin), a woman who favors Kenyan proverbs and wearing dashikis, also functions as a satire of white liberal feminism, as she fails to understand how the organization's logo of "a white hand scooping up black kids" is problematic ("Familiar-like," Season 3, Episode 2).

In the same episode, Issa has a conversation with her colleague Ken (Mason McCulley) regarding her unease with the logo, where she alludes to her grievances over being the token person of color in the organization:

> Ken: Well, if it's an issue for some people, maybe those people who it's an issue for should have spoken up.
>
> Issa: Really? I have to speak up about every issue. Do you know how awkward that is? "Hi, I'm Issa, and I'm black and angry!" We should all be angry.
>
> Ken: What's the problem? I represent the gays, and you represent black people.
>
> Issa: I don't want to be the voice of all black people.
>
> Ken: Well, it is what it is. ("Familiar-like," Season 3, Episode 2)

In directly referring to the implied obligation Issa feels to be a representative for her race and how her white colleagues have correspondingly assigned this function to her, *Insecure* illustrates and explores the dilemmas of fitting into the dominant white culture, where structural racism might not be overt but is still occurring. The obliviousness of Issa's co-workers to their own biases serves to perpetuate the racial power dynamics that We Got Y'All assumes to be inapplicable in its outreach mission to disadvantaged youth.

The vexations Issa experiences at We Got Y'All are indicative of critiques and parodies of "woke" culture, which typically refers to the discernible awareness of various elements of racial and social inequality. In discussing *Stay Woke*, the 2016 documentary on the Black Lives Matter movement, with the *International Business Times*, Alex Garofalo states that "the term is commonly used to refer to an awareness about the persistence of racism in America, especially systemic racism, as well as to mockingly refer to people, especially white people, who have newly educated themselves on those social realities" (Garofalo 2016). Issa's co-workers' professed knowledge and awareness of facets of black culture obscure the fact that her own ideas and contributions are often unacknowledged and that she is unable to assert her perspective in the dominantly white workplace. Issa's token positioning in the organization recalls Sara Ahmed's claim that "diversity pride becomes a technology for reproducing whiteness: adding color to the white face of the organization confirms the whiteness of that face" (2012, 151). In the case of We Got Y'All, the "white hand" of the organization is able to retain and even benefit from its' privileged condition, while it incorporates and

Figure 4.2. Issa (Issa Rae) listens to feedback from her co-workers at We Got Y'All. *Insecure*, "Insecure as F**k," Season 1, Episode 1. *Screenshot captured by author.*

simultaneously erases the diversity Issa represents and maintains racial power structures in the process.

The complexities surrounding race and privilege are further interrogated as Issa's own racial partialities are challenged when We Got Y'all is assigned to a school with a substantial Latinx staff and student body in the second season. Issa is initially inclined to acquiesce in the black vice principal's propensity to overlook the needs of the Latinx students and to disregard the occasional racially motivated joke, as long as the black students are being sufficiently accommodated. When her white colleague and friend Frieda (Lisa Joyce) suggests that the vice principal Gaines (A. Russell Andrews) is being discriminatory and that all of the students should benefit from We Got Y'all's services, Issa balks at Frieda's assessment made from her particular racial standpoint:

> Frieda: I still feel weird about just going along with Gaines.
>
> Issa: Still? I was just trying to make the best out of the situation.
>
> Frieda: It seemed like you were trying to help yourself more than—
>
> Issa: Do you know how many racist-ass Gaines types there are out there? And, truthfully, black people can't really be racist like that, so.
>
> Frieda: Yes, they can. Racism is about having the power to manipulate a situation against someone.
>
> Issa: Oh, so you're just gonna be literal?
>
> Frieda: Yes.
>
> Issa: It must be nice to have the privilege to choose to be upset over this.
>
> Frieda: So, you're saying I can never call out when someone of color's doing something wrong?
>
> Issa: Kinda.
>
> Frieda: That's not fair.
>
> Issa: Well, that's the world we live in.
>
> Frieda: Maybe it is. I just expected more from you. ("Hella Shook," Season 2, Episode 5)

This exchange obliges Issa to address her own prejudices, even as she herself strives to elevate black identity. Her antagonism toward Frieda's well-intentioned comments also illustrates *Insecure*'s commitment to depicting the failure to recognize white privilege when evaluating issues of race and inequality. The issue is not resolved and Issa's eventual attempt to encourage the vice principal to be more inclusive toward the Latinx students is summarily dismissed as "some All Lives Matter" ("Hella Disrespectful," Season 2, Episode 7). Issa and Frieda's inability to advocate for the Latinx students, as well as Frieda's disregard of how her own white privilege impacts her views on the issue, delineates the persisting difficulties of repairing misconceptions and inequities in racial communications and perceptions, even as those misconceptions and inequities are increasingly being articulated.

Issa's insecurities regarding her career and ambitions gradually attenuate in the midst of the third season. After becoming increasingly disillusioned and demoralized with her situation at We Got Y'All, she resigns from the organization and is compelled to determine her goals and passions. Her desire to promote black culture and aid the black community drive her to organize an event for the Inglewood community with the aim of celebrating and showcasing black performers and artists as a response to the increasing white gentrification of the area. The process and the resultant success of the block party are prominently featured in the fourth season, signifying a corrective to the professional "insecurity" that had plagued Issa thus far. Her new career as a "cultural curator" ("Lowkey Done," Season 4, Episode 6) provides her with confidence and a sense of purpose, while also enabling the proud presentation of black culture that *Insecure* itself endeavors for.

Issa's journey toward the discovery and realization of her professional goals is set against Molly's apparent secure and accomplished career as a corporate lawyer. Even Molly's sophisticated wardrobe and perfectly blown out hairstyles suggest a more high-maintenance and privileged lifestyle in contrast to Issa's laid-back clothing choices and partiality to wear her cropped hair naturally. In comparison to Issa's struggles at We Got Y'All, Molly is portrayed as being more flexible in the similarly white-dominated office space she inhabits in the first two seasons. However, Molly's own uneasiness with the racial code switching she performs is demonstrated when a new black female intern is hired at her law firm ("Racist as F**k," Season 1, Episode 3). Initially pleased about having another black woman as a colleague, her enthusiasm is tempered when she realizes that the new intern Rasheeda (Gail Bean) will not easily assimilate to the white office culture that Molly is able to negotiate. In contrast to Molly's savvy and elegance, Rasheeda is raucous and crude, to the point that Molly feels the need to tactfully advise her on the inferred guidelines to working in a white-dominated firm:

Molly: Hey! You know, I just wanted to check in to see how you were acclimating.

Rasheeda: Oh, girl, I'm good. Thanks!

Molly: Good 'cause, you know, I just wanna make sure that no one gets the wrong impression of you.

Rasheeda: Um, why would they? Mark said I was doing great.

Molly: Yeah, and you are. I just you know, sometimes you can be a little Girl, you know how these white people are. If you wanna be successful here, you gotta know when to switch it up a little bit.

Rasheeda: Hmm. I appreciate your feedback.

Molly: Good.

Rasheeda: But I didn't switch it up in my interview with the senior partners and I didn't switch it up when I was named editor of the law review, so I don't think I need to switch it up now. But thank you so much.

Molly: Okay, good. 'Cause I'm just trying to help.

Rasheeda: Okay. ("Racist As F**k," Season 1, Episode 3)

Rasheeda's refusal to "switch it up" ultimately leads to her being openly reproached by senior members of the firm after Molly declines her supervisor's request for her to formally counsel Rasheeda on the appropriate demeanor expected, establishing the firm's racialized power structures in its unspoken presumption that Rasheeda should acclimate to the white office culture. Her refusal to challenge her white coworkers' expectations and to support Rasheeda signify Molly's eliciting of the "black lady" construction's deference to white culture.

However, the series also maintains that Molly's progress at the firm depends on this deference, recalling A. N. Wisseh's assertion of "the ways Black women are complicit in a White supremacist capitalist patriarchal system that simultaneously oppresses them" (2019, 15). Similar to Issa's griping sentiments on being "the voice of all black people" at We Got Y'All, Molly resents having to broker racial distinctions at her firm, deploring that, "I'm not the black translator here to tell the colored folks what 'massa' think they done wrong. Like I'm some 'House Molly'" ("Thirsty As F**k," Season 1, Episode 4). Her glib usage of terms ascribed to slavery further indicates the enduring awareness of racial inequality that *Insecure* is confronting in its depiction of bias and prejudice that both Molly and Issa are unable to defy in the workplace.

Molly's predicament at the firm continues into the second season, where she learns that she is being paid less than her white male peers ("Hella Questions," Season 2, Episode 2) and is unlikely to ever receive equal pay when her attempted negotiations for a salary raise result in a "Rising Star" award instead ("Hella Perspective," Season 2, Episode 8). Just as Issa is unable to challenge the racial microaggressions she experiences at We Got Y'All and resigns, Molly cannot alter the systemic race relations embedded in her firm, so she also opts to leave and moves to a black firm in the third season. However, she promptly realizes that her new work environment presents challenges of its own, particularly in relation to her competitive inclinations. Molly's desire to excel is perceived as aggressiveness by both her female and male co-workers, which Issa queries her friend on:

> Molly: I don't want to be like every woman at my office, stalled out at associate.
>
> Issa: You wanna be partner all by yourself? ("Ghost-like," Season 3, Episode 8)

Molly's ambition is thus classified as alienating, recalling "backlash" constructions of working women and suggesting that her professional dissatisfaction and "insecurities" are not only due to unequal race dynamics in the workplace but also stem from her own perfectionist and individualist tendencies. In this way, Molly exemplifies Beck and Beck-Gernsheim's notion of "the loneliness of the professionally successful woman" (2002, 63), whose professional success is achieved at the cost of her personal happiness.

Molly's single-mindedness and individualism regarding her career are reminiscent of elements of neoliberal feminism, which defines feminism and empowerment in terms of personal success rather than of forging alliances. Although Molly is keenly attuned to racial and gender biases in the workplace, she only reacts to them in relation to her own positioning and not on behalf of her counterparts affected by the same biases, as demonstrated in her rejection of defending Rasheeda in the predominantly white law firm. Upon her move to the black law firm, she recognizes the gendered hierarchy, prompting her to collaborate with male co-worker Taurean (Leonard Robinson) on an important case, forfeiting fellowship with her female colleagues ("Fresh-Like," Season 3, Episode 4). Her intentions ultimately fail as her zealous efforts result in her taking the lead on the case on her own ("Ghost-like," Season 3, Episode 8), and the fourth season sees her settling into the dynamics of the office more graciously.

However, she embodies the tenets of neoliberal feminism in her relentless pursuit of career advancement, as well as in her willingness to take full responsibility for her own gratification and self-care, as evidenced by her luxurious lifestyle. This reflects the objective of the harmonious work-life balance outlined in influential neoliberal feminist texts, notably including then Facebook/Meta Platforms COO Sheryl Sandberg's 2013 *Lean In*. Sandberg's bestseller exhorted women to strive toward their potential in the workplace while simultaneously sustaining fulfillment at home and in their personal lives. Sandberg's book attained cultural prominence upon its publication for its message of female empowerment and leadership but has since been criticized for its individualistic inclinations and lack of intersectional considerations (Gibson 2018). Molly's periodic visits to her therapist are also denotive of the neoliberal feminist's undertaking to maintain well-being and self-care, particularly with regard to working women's efforts to attain equilibrium and happiness in neoliberal constructions (Rottenberg 2018).

Molly's personification of these facets of neoliberal feminism provides a counterpoint to *Insecure*'s representation of intersectional feminism in that her individuated figuration of empowerment does not include racial or gender solidarity, recalling the constructions of conspicuous feminism in *Big Little Lies* and *The Marvelous Mrs. Maisel*. As Rottenberg elucidates:

> The creation of the neoliberal feminist subject thus bolsters the assumption that the struggle for racial equality—just like the feminist revolution—has, in some sense, already occurred, been successful, and is, consequently, a thing of the past. At most, there is a gesturing toward the importance of professional women speaking up in their respective workplaces so as to make targeted or surgical improvements. There is no mention of collective solutions to historic injustices: indeed, the neoliberal feminist subject is divested of any orientation toward the common good. (2018, 71)

The substantial effort Molly invests in her career is mainly depicted as individualistic and self-serving, without obvious concern for collective racial or feminist goals.

In contrast, Issa's work for We Got Y'All and her later coordination of the Inglewood block party clearly intend to benefit and promote minority groups, presenting a perspective on women and work that can be more communal and collaborative. In spite of the differences in their respective careers, both women experience gratification from them and work is evidently central to their sense of purpose and identity. Both the achievements and insecurities that Issa and Molly encounter at work are key to *Insecure*'s negotiation of conspicuous feminism and the distinct ways in which black women are circumscribed by systemic frameworks. That these frameworks were being upheld at both We Got Y'All and the law firm illustrates the series' motivation to illuminate the ways in which racial power dynamics can be unwittingly reproduced, as evidenced through the oblivious perpetuation of structural racism enacted by both Issa and Molly's supervisors and co-workers.

INSECURE IN SEX AND ROMANCE

As illustrated by their diligence and ambitions regarding their work and careers, Issa and Molly are not defined by the pursuit of the traditionally feminine realms of romantic love, but romance and sexuality are significant to their goals of fulfillment and empowerment. Thus, the insecurities detailed in the series also encompass the navigation of their romantic and sexual relationships, which are important to both women's sense of identity. The representation of sexuality has strongly been identified with television series featuring single women, particularly after *Sex and the City* sharply challenged conventional portrayals by positioning its female protagonists as active and assertive sexual subjects. Sexuality has since been a key focus in other prominent series reflecting feminist themes and single women such as *Girls*, *The Bold Type* (Freeform, 2017–2021), and *Fleabag*. In this regard, *Insecure*'s delineation of the sexual and romantic lives of its protagonists is fundamental to its representation of conspicuous feminism as it deconstructs elements of the "controlling images" that have demarcated black women and their sexuality.

The beginning of the series establishes that both women are feeling uncertain in their romantic relations. Issa is discontented with Lawrence, whose loss of motivation due to his extended unemployment has made her anxious over the absence of direction in their relationship as she expresses to him, "Because maybe I didn't know it before, but I know it now, and I don't wanna just sit on the couch with you for the rest of my life and wait for something to happen" ("Insecure As F**k," Season 1, Episode 1). Her agitation over Lawrence's listlessness prompts her revived interest in former love interest Daniel (Y'lan Noel), who is progressing in his career as a music producer. Meanwhile, Molly is distressed over her apparent inability to sustain a relationship as she frets to Issa:

> It's, like, it doesn't matter what I do, Issa. If I'm into them, then I'm too smothering. If I take my time or try to give them space, "Oh, I didn't think you were into me." Fine. Sex right away. Lose interest. Wait to have sex. Lose interest. If I don't have sex at all . . . motherfucker, no! I'm a grown-ass woman. I did not sign up for that bullshit. ("Insecure As F**k," Season 1, Episode 1)

Molly's despair inspires Issa to comment on her friend's "broken pussy," which Issa attributes to Molly's chronic efforts to adhere to behaviors determined by the expectations of her partners in her dating life, rather than focusing on her own desires. The phrase becomes thematic throughout the first season as it leads to the first argument on the series between the friends after Issa performs an open mic freestyle rap about Molly's misery that has been engendered by her "broken pussy." This performance will later instigate Issa's affair with Daniel and ultimately her separation from Lawrence at the end of the season. Though Issa employs "broken pussy" for comedy and amusement in her performance, it is symbolic of *Insecure*'s manifestation of sexuality as essential to both Molly and Issa's sense of identity and empowerment as they strive to surmount their apprehensions in their romantic and sexual lives. The phrase serves to underscore how their ideals for romantic and sexual fulfillment have been defined and subsequently "broken" by the men they have been involved with, rather than focusing on their own expectations and desires, as they both attempt to do as the series progresses.

The "controlling images" of black women defined by Collins (2000) that have rendered black women in terms of sexualization have typically been countered with representations that nullified black women's sexuality and concentrated on their maternal and professional attributes instead, such as *The Cosby Show*'s Clair Huxtable (Smith-Shomade 2002). This has produced black female representations whose sexual subjectivity is repressed, thus dehumanizing them in this respect, as their sexuality has considerably been denied (Levy 2021). The 2010s have observed more complex representations of black women's sexuality that do not conform to the conventional archetypes, notably in Shonda Rhimes's heroines Olivia Pope on *Scandal* and Annelise Keating on *How to Get Away with Murder*. *Insecure* likewise constructs sexuality as an integral component of its protagonists' identities and revises stereotypes of black female sexuality in the process.

Both Issa and Molly are assertive sexual subjects, even if their sexual encounters and relationships are at times awkward and disappointing. In the second season, Issa attempts to rebound from her breakup with Lawrence by setting up a "ho-tation" of men to date. Early in the season, she laments to Molly about the absence of a "ho phase" in her dating experiences:

Issa: But it's not like I don't want somebody.

Molly: Then, girl, get yours.

Issa: I should. We should. I mean, we were supposed to do this ho shit together. Girl, I always wanted to have a ho phase. But then I met Lawrence and he made me fall in love with him and shit.

Molly: Tsk, yeah, y'all did get boo'd up real quick.

Issa: You know what? Fuck love, okay? Fuck getting to know these niggas. Fuck feeling feelings. I just wanna be on my Halle Berry shit, okay? I just wanna feel good.

Molly: Cool, cool, cool. Well, can you fuck with my bookshelf, though?

Issa: Yeah, yeah. Hey let's go somewhere tonight. Can you teach me how to ho?

Molly: Bitch, that's rude. And, yes. ("Hella Open," Season 2, Episode 3)

In this exchange, the connotations traditionally associated with the term and figuration of the "ho" are redacted to signify sexual satisfaction and confidence. Issa's inclination for a "ho phase" is denoted as a desire for sexual empowerment and to "feel good," thereby resisting the negative affiliations the phrase has sustained in constructions of black women's sexuality. As Yael Levy states, *Insecure* "does not ignore the fact that labels and stereotypes still rule cultural representations of black women, but it insists on making racial discourse present so as to challenge it" (2021, 1214). Therefore, the series acknowledges the "controlling images" and stereotypes that have denigrated black women but insists on claiming and regenerating them to signify assertiveness and empowerment instead.

Molly's frustration at her inability to achieve the elements required of the conventional romance script are made clear with the identification of her "broken pussy" at the beginning of the series. Where she is successful in her professional life, it is apparent that she is not experiencing the same fulfilment in her romantic enterprises. As she does with her work, Molly expects perfection in her romantic relationships and is continually embittered when she fails to attain it. At one of their sessions, her therapist refers to the particular pressures faced by black women to prosper, both professionally and personally, "Listen, Molly, I know as black women it can feel like there's a lot of things stacked against us. We feel invisible at work, we feel the need to have the perfect relationship" ("Hella Questions," Season 2, Episode 2). Molly's ideals for the quintessential relationship lead her to discontinue potential connections with men who don't meet her educational standards ("Racist as F**k," Season 1, Episode 3) or who are from a different racial background ("Ready-Like," Season 3, Episode 6). Her aspirations toward romantic perfection are further disintegrated upon the discovery of her father's previous infidelity after believing that her parents embodied the flawless marriage ("Hella Disrespectful," Season 2, Episode 7). Her disenchantment compels her to embark on an affair with a married friend, reinforcing her disillusion with the conventional romance script.

Molly's unhappiness due to her relationship failures also reflects neoliberal feminist discourses that ascertain individual responsibility for one's fulfillment, including in aspects of sex and romance (Gill 2007b; Ringrose 2007). As Claire Moran notes of constructions of female heterosexuality in neoliberal and postfeminist culture:

> Neoliberalism assumes that all individuals have, and should exercise, choice, freedom and personal responsibility. This results in a cultural narrative of free choice and autonomy, and a denial of structural constraints, context or external influence. Structural inequities and relative (dis)advantage defined by race, class and gender are rendered invisible, and social structures are no longer regarded as having an impact. As such, negative outcomes, for example, engaging in unwanted sex, are positioned as personal failings, and the individual positioned as fully responsible for her own actions. (2017, 124)

Similarly, Molly's inability to attain romantic contentment is mainly characterized in terms of her own deficiencies in flexibility and pragmatic expectations, rather than by the structural and external factors that have impacted her decisions, such as the gendered power structures underlying her parents' marriage. Until the final season, Molly's romantic trajectory is largely characterized by disappointment through her own self-sabotaging tendencies, as specified by Issa: "It seems like you always finding a problem. Sometimes I'm like, do you want to be happy?" ("Lowkey Distant," Season 4, Episode 2), underscoring the insecurity Molly suffers due to her own perfectionist ideals.

The insecurity experienced by both Issa and Molly is often depicted in the various sex scenes exhibited throughout the series. As in other prominent series concerned with female sexuality and relationships, such as *Sex and the City* and *Girls*, the scenes are typically explicit and function as a device that furthers aspects of the protagonists' characterization and narrative. A range of approaches is employed to portray the sexual encounters on *Insecure*, including those that are sensuous and romantic, but also those that emphasize awkwardness and embarrassment, such as Issa's first rendezvous via a dating app after her break-up ("Hella Great," Season 2, Episode 1) and a blundering episode with her younger neighbor Eddie (Leon Thomas) ("Hella Open," Season 2, Episode 3). As Levy suggests, the realism conveyed in *Insecure*'s sex scenes "are not inserted merely to signify erotic intimacy, but rather function as a narrative feature for its own sake, encapsulating multifaceted dynamics that may include power with passion, trepidation with attraction" (2021, 1217). In this way, the series recognizes and affirms black women's sexuality without reverting to the traditional tropes and stereotypes that have encompassed the "controlling images," while enacting the explicit visuality fundamental to constructions of conspicuous feminism.

In addition, the male nudity that is often employed in these scenes also reverses the female objectification that has typically occurred in film and television, furthering *Insecure*'s motivation to reassert black women's female subjectivity and control in portrayals of sexuality. The candor in the representation of intimacy also confronts the relative lack of contemplation of black romantic relationships in popular culture. As media history professor Ellen C. Scott recounts:

> Often Black romantic relationships onscreen existed primarily by implication rather than any case in point—and were not, unlike white romances, tied to a marriage trajectory. Often this marriage trajectory was abandoned or impossible because of the stereotypical assumption that Black men were always "good-for-nothings" when it came to many things—hard work, keeping a job, and staying with a woman. (McDonald 2017)

The depictions of sexuality on *Insecure* thus exhibit the explicitness of conspicuous feminism and remodel traditional notions of black romance and sexuality, instilling layers of depth and acuity that they are not usually afforded. In doing so, the series also revises gendered stereotypes of both black women and men in the process.

In relation to *Insecure*'s depiction of romance and sexuality, traditional constructions of black masculinity are also examined in terms of the self-doubt similarly experienced by the female protagonists. The stereotype of hypermasculinity that has conventionally defined black men in the media and popular culture (Benson 2014; hooks 2015; Welang 2018) is dismantled and interrogated in the delineation of Issa and Molly's love interests. In particular, the character of Lawrence is imbued with an awareness of the influence of the hypermasculine archetype, which impacts his own initiatives as well as his relationship with Issa. His unemployment, lack of career objectives, and the discovery of Issa's infidelity in the first season threaten his sense of identity and his insecurity displays a sensitivity not typically afforded to representations of black masculinity. As demonstrated in a discussion during a night out with his friends shortly after his discovery of Issa's affair, the notion of classic gender roles within relationships still maintains influence:

> Mike: You know what it is? These women today, they wanna be the woman and the man in the relationship. That's why they ass ain't never satisfied. They some "never happy" bitches.
>
> Lawrence: Issa was like that all the fucking time, man. It was either some shit about work or some shit about me. It was like, fuck! Just chill.
>
> Brandon: Hey, they don't make black women like they used to. ("Broken As F**k," Season 1, Episode 8)

This exchange occurs in the setting of a strip club, attesting to Lawrence's persistence toward conventional constructions of masculine dominance, which he continues to attempt to revalidate in his subsequent relationships. Lawrence regains his confidence as the series develops and he establishes a career in the IT field, but the portrayal of his continuing insecurity in his relationships and ambitions produces a construction of black masculinity that is not characterized by conceptions of hypermasculinity.

Other instances that complicate perceptions of black masculinity include the bisexuality of Jared (Langston Kerman), whom Molly dates in the first season, and the mental health struggles of Nathan (Kendrick Sampson), Issa's other significant love interest on the series. *Insecure*'s destabilization of prevailing gender roles addresses Welang's contention of the "correlation thereupon exist[ing] between black hypermasculinity and the marginalization of black female voices in black spaces. Contemporary popular culture is crowded with instances of the erasure of black women in influential black spaces often commandeered by black men" (2018, 298). *Insecure*'s representation of the delicacy and complexity in its male characters typically absent in the hypermasculine stereotype thus contributes to rectifying the marginalization of black female perspectives as it further complicates the gendered dynamics that have regulated depictions of black women's sexuality and subjectivity.

However, elements of traditional femininity in the heterosexual romance narrative are alluded to on *Insecure,* even as the series aims to deconstruct established ideals of female identity and romance. Despite her pursuit of a "ho phase" after their separation, Issa's relationship with Lawrence remains the principal romance on the series, recalling the oscillating relations between Carrie and Mr. Big on *Sex and the City* and Hannah and Adam on *Girls*. After their break-up at the end of the first season due to Issa's infidelity with Daniel, Lawrence remains a fixture, allowing for the possibility of a reconciliation, which is explored in the fourth season. The fantasy sequence that closes the second season pictures Lawrence proposing to Issa in their formerly shared apartment, followed by blissful scenes of marriage, pregnancy, and a child. This "happily ever after" vignette is abruptly shattered by the reality of Lawrence walking away and leaving Issa alone in the apartment ("Hella Perspective," Season 2, Episode 8). This second season conclusion illustrates *Insecure*'s acknowledgment of and general adherence to the dominance of the conventional romance script in its candid portrayal of both Issa and Molly's romantic experiences. As Francesca Sobande observes on the heteronormative dispositions that the series projects:

> The normativity of heterosexual coupledom in *Insecure* may be identified as a particularly post-feminist trait, given the implicitness of compulsory heterosexuality within much post-feminist discourse, as opposed to the rich contributions of queer and lesbian Black women mobilised by Black feminist thought, which more firmly foregrounds the experiences of Black women who do not identify as heterosexual. (2019, 443)

Insecure's replication of the heterosexual romance narrative thus posits the series more closely to the (white) postfeminist narratives in *Sex and the City* and *Girls* that largely picture their protagonists in pursuit of conventional (heterosexual) romantic ideals. The relationship between Issa and Lawrence is consistently deferred throughout the series, resembling Tania Modleski's (1994) supposition of the deferred goals and desires afforded to protagonists in the soap opera genre, a characteristic common to series such as *Sex and the*

City, which keeps viewers similarly expectant and invested in the protagonist's quest for fulfilment.

Insecure's parallels to these narratives concerning romance thus mitigate the possibilities for a more specifically black feminist perspective to be integrated into its embodiment of conspicuous feminism. Black feminism is typically intent on foregrounding aspects of difference in terms of sexuality, which *Insecure* neutralizes in its heterosexual focus. Though queer identities are included in the depiction of supporting characters such as Issa's brother Ahmal (Jean Elie) and Molly's bisexual love interest Jared, their presence largely consists of supporting the main narrative and queer sexuality has not been explored in depth in the series thus far. *Insecure*'s reproduction of the heterosexual romance narrative thus reinforces certain traditional elements relating to femininity and sexuality, even as its delineation of black women's sexuality challenges others and manifests the boldness of conspicuous feminism.

CENTERING RACE AND BLACK CULTURE

The use of Kendrick's Lamar's "Alright," widely regarded as the unofficial anthem of the Black Lives Matter movement (Limbong 2019) in the opening moments of the pilot episode indicates *Insecure*'s engagement with racial injustice. Released on Lamar's studio album *To Pimp a Butterfly* in 2015, "Alright" gained cultural prominence when its chorus became a rallying refrain at numerous Black Lives Matter protests that year and its lyrics advocating peace and justice in the face of inequality engendered its anthem status for the movement's mobilizing against police brutality toward black people in particular. The simultaneous recognition of injustice and hope for change that the song encompasses and that has become identified with the movement can also be affiliated with *Insecure*'s engagement with and celebration of black lives. Various cultural references are drawn from and celebrate African American culture. From the hip hop soundtrack scored and curated by renowned Soul and R&B artist Raphael Saddiq to the unequivocal use of the black vernacular, the series accentuates and uplifts black popular culture.

The series' embodiment of black identities and black culture has also contributed to its associations with the Black Lives Matter movement, particularly after its revived impact following the public outrage in response to the release of video footage of George Floyd, a black man, being killed by a white police officer in May 2020. The incident triggered renewed support for the movement, which was originally founded in 2013 after George Zimmerman was acquitted in the shooting of black teenager Trayvon Martin in 2012. The fourth season of *Insecure* aired in April 2020 and the series' concentration on black culture became closely identified with the protests and calls for activism that followed Floyd's death in May 2020 (Meara 2020). Rae and her co-stars have all been outspoken in their advocacy for the movement, most notably Kendrick Sampson, who has been prominent in the nationwide protests against police brutality and anti-black violence that ensued after Floyd's death (Galuppo 2020). Although established by three black women (Patrice Cullors, Alicia Garza, and Opal Tometti), the movement has chiefly been identified with black men and their experiences of racism, particularly with regard to police violence. In this way, the movement has similarly struggled to sufficiently comprise the experiences of black women, as has been applied to the #MeToo movement. However, both movements share pertinent concerns in their goals to resist systemic racism and sexism, respectively. As Linda Greene observes on the affinities between their objectives:

> Both movements challenge the current allocation of power to white patriarchy in society. Black Lives Matter seeks to stop the explicit or implicit racial bias that results in the discriminatory deployment of deadly force. #MeToo focuses on the gendered power structures in the workplace that sustain a gender subordination conducive to sexual harassment, an abuse of that power. (2019, 12)

In its depiction of black female identities, *Insecure* reflects the considerations of both movements in its distinct reflection of black culture and the exclusive experiences of black women, which have not commonly been accentuated on television.

Although it abstains from overt confrontation with political issues, *Insecure* highlights discrimination and racial inequities in its narrative. From Lawrence's uncomfortable encounter when being pulled over by a white policeman ("Hella LA," Season 2, Episode 4), to Molly's altercation with a hotel employee over preferential treatment toward white guests ("Lowkey Trippin," Season 4, Episode 7), the series illustrates how systemic racism impacts the daily experiences of its protagonists. Racial inequality is also alluded to in the faux television series featured on *Insecure*. In the second season, the characters are captivated by the antebellum South parody "Due North," which incorporated a dark satire of the power dynamics within slavery, and in the fourth season, several episodes depicted the characters avidly viewing "Looking For Latoya," a crime series focusing on the mystery of a missing black woman. Rae explains the inclusion of the fabricated series as a means to comment on racial disparity, as in the racial dynamics encompassing the sensibility toward missing women cases:

And I think the conversation was just about, these are always about missing white girls and what would it look like if there were a podcast centered around trying to find a black girl? Because people don't necessarily care when black girls go missing. There have been documentaries about how people don't care. I think about the Craigslist Killer who killed like 100 black women before anybody cared. And so that was the dark humor that went into "Looking for LaToya." (Maas 2020)

The focus on missing black women in the faux series evokes the #SayHerName movement, and this referencing of the relative anonymity of violent crimes against black women further demonstrates *Insecure*'s appeal toward intersectionality and a reconception of black women's representation. In conjunction with the assorted microaggressions endured by both Issa and Molly in the workplace, these instances accentuate racial prejudices without overwhelming key narrative and character developments.

Instead of centering on details of bias and discrimination, *Insecure* also uplifts blackness in its exhibition of its cultural specificities in its negotiation of racial dynamics. The accomplishment of Issa's block party in the fourth season exemplifies the series' conviction to honor black culture in its exuberant promotion and featuring of black artists ("Lowkey Movin' On," Season 4, Episode 5). The final episode of the season also acknowledges the deaths of revered black public figures such as rapper Nipsey Hussle and basketball star Kobe Bryant and his daughter Gianna through location shots featuring murals dedicated to them ("Lowkey Lost," Season 4, Episode 10). The empowerment and celebration of black culture extends to the representation of black women on *Insecure*. The series demonstrates its discernment of black feminism, with characters referencing seminal black feminist bell hooks, filmmaker Ava DuVernay, and even *How to Get Away with Murder*'s Annalise Keating in relation to aspects of femininity and womanhood.

Insecure's blatant celebration of black culture coalesces with the main trajectory of the fifth and final season, which finds both Issa and Molly ultimately attaining the "security" they have pursued throughout the series. The final episode features Molly's wedding to co-worker Taurean and shows Issa blissfully reunited with Lawrence. Both women have also continued to prosper in their respective careers, indicating that they are "secure" in both their romantic and professional lives. Molly's reference to her "broken pussy" on her honeymoon in the closing moments of the episode firmly accentuates the full circle that the series has encompassed ("Everything Gonna Be, Okay?" Season 5, Episode 10). In this way, the finale of *Insecure* echoes the "happily ever after" conclusions reminiscent of postfeminist series such as *Sex and the City*, delivering a satisfying closure for the characters after all the insecurity witnessed throughout the series. In the final episode, Issa muses that "no one was doubting me, except for me," displaying the affirmative and inspirational tenets of neoliberal feminist discourses. The gratifying conclusion to the series definitively repairs the insecure status of the characters and illustrates how conspicuous feminism often adapts to conventional television narratives and constructions while simultaneously interrogating them in the process.

HBO's promotion of *Insecure* has relied heavily on viewer participation that relates to the series' content and signification of conspicuous feminism. Each season has been launched with a block party for fans in honor of the series' celebration of music and community, growing in scale each year as *Insecure*'s popularity increased, with over 2,500 fans attending Insecure Fest at Banc of California Stadium to launch the third season. The fourth season's launch in April 2020 took place in the form of a virtual block party due to mass gathering restrictions imposed by the COVID-19 pandemic, featuring a live Twitter watch party hosted by Issa Rae, as well as live musical performances and cast interviews on Rae's Instagram Live account (Fuster 2020). Following the virtual event, which had particular resonance with the series' narrative with regard to Issa's endeavours to organize her own block party in season four, *Insecure* maintained its considerable social media presence and viewer interaction with its "Insecuritea" podcasts recapping each week's episode and "Lowkey Live" Q&A sessions for fans and the series' stars. These discussions largely concentrated on feminist issues of female friendship, particularly in relation to the conflict between Issa and Molly, the struggles to attain professional and romantic fulfillment as experienced by both protagonists, and the challenges of motherhood as depicted in the character Tiffany's experience of postpartum depression.

The promotional and viewer focus on women's issues shifted after the death of George Floyd in May 2020, and the series' media and cultural presence became identified with the revived visibility of the Black Lives Matter movement that proceeded it. *Insecure*'s representation of black lives and culture acquired a marked resonance with the movement's goals to expose and amend systemic racism, particularly in relation to police brutality and anti-black violence. The fourth season finale was preceded by another virtual event featuring musical performances and the series' stars in support of Act Blue charities, one of the nonprofit organizations aiding the Black Lives Matter movement. *Insecure* was also featured in HBO's curation of programming specifically focusing on race and civil rights issues in response to the movement's renewed prominence. The series' deliberation of conspicuous feminism has been inadvertently refitted by its association with Black Lives Matter, underscoring the intersectional factors and racial dynamics within the series' examination of female empowerment more distinctly.

Insecure considerably enlarges the scope of investigation in its representation of single women by closely considering the racial dynamics relevant to the circumstances of its black protagonists. Similar to other series focusing on the experiences of the single woman, Issa and Molly are also managing issues of love, relationships, and career objectives but the added components of racial specificity allow for an observance of black life that is not commonly presented on television. As Angelica Jade Bastien reflects on the series' impact during a time of cultural reckoning with racial discrimination and bias:

> Perhaps that's why *Insecure* feels like such a balm. The HBO series.... lingers on the joys of blackness, giving us a succor that is often missing in depictions of black life. There's something moving about being able to escape into a vibrant series populated by beautiful and beautifully rendered black and brown folks that allows them to just be. (Bastien 2020)

In this way, *Insecure* differs from other series that similarly accent and interrogate race and culture such as *Atlanta* (FX, 2016–2022) and *Dear White People* (Netflix, 2017–2021) in that its deliberation of racial inequity is not as explicit, though no less piercing. Rather, its approach toward racial concerns is embedded in its sensitive rendering of black women and the regular issues they navigate in their personal and professional lives.

Female empowerment on *Insecure* is also defined through conspicuous feminism's explicit presentation of and capitalization on feminist issues. Additionally, the series exemplifies an intersectional perspective on conspicuous feminism in its foregrounding of elements of black culture, in contrast to the other three series discussed in this study. The presence of black female protagonists enables a more comprehensive and incisive examination of the impact of race on mediations of feminism and the series attempts to challenge conventional stereotypes of black women in its examination. The series' observations on systemic racism, particularly in the workplace, invoke #MeToo's endeavors for a more intersectional approach to confronting gendered inequality. By emphasizing the various and intersecting prejudices that beset Issa and Molly, as well as affirming their triumphs and satisfactions, the series is keenly intent on eclipsing archetypes of black women, thereby expanding the possibilities for configurations of conspicuous feminism and gendered identities on popular television.

Chapter Five

Resistance and Retaliation
The Handmaid's Tale

In the third season of Hulu's *The Handmaid's Tale* (2017–present), protagonist June Osborne's (Elisabeth Moss) recollections of the time before Gilead, the setting for the dystopian drama, precisely illustrate the feminist themes that characterize the series. Her delineations of a place where women are free to pursue their own goals and desires are what women and girls, such as ten-year-old Kiki (Kate Moyer) can anticipate outside of the Republic of Gilead, a fundamentalist dictatorship that has severely deprived women of their rights:

> Kiki: Do you know what it's like? Out.
>
> June: Well, it's like things were before Gilead.
>
> Kiki: I don't remember before.
>
> June: You'll be free. You can wear whatever you want. No one's gonna hurt you for reading. Or tell you what to think, or who to love, or what to believe in. And, you know, you don't have to be a wife. Or a mother, if you don't want to.
>
> Kiki: Then what would I be?
>
> June: You. ("MayDay," Season 3, Episode 13)

Kiki has been conditioned to believe that there are no alternatives for her future apart from the roles of wife and mother that women in Gilead have been constrained to. June is a handmaid, one of the remaining fertile women culled for her reproductive capacities amidst Gilead's efforts to combat the declining fertility rates that have resulted from environmental factors, radiation, and sexually transmitted diseases. Handmaids are posted to the homes of Gilead's elite families in order to procreate for them, submitting to sanctified rapes by their masters at the monthly "Ceremony" in which the Wife is also present, typically holding the handmaid down during the assault. By the end of the series' third season, June has experienced and witnessed a spectrum of cruelties and has determined to facilitate the escape of as many children as possible, including Kiki, to neighboring Canada in order to liberate them from Gilead's brutal regime and to grant them individuality and agency.

The Handmaid's Tale evokes the issues of sexual violence and gendered power structures that are being interrogated in the era of #MeToo, and Hulu's critically acclaimed adaptation of Margaret Atwood's 1985 dystopian novel has been notable in the resurgence of women's narratives and perspectives on television. Created by Bruce Miller, the series won eight Primetime Emmy Awards for its first season (including Best Drama Series, Best Actress for Moss, and Best Supporting Actress for Lydia Dowd), as well as the Golden Globe awards for Best Television Drama and Best Actress for Moss. While the first season is broadly based on Atwood's novel, the following seasons expand on the events, characters, and settings that Atwood conceived. The series centers on the adversity June suffers in Gilead in her position as a handmaid and her efforts to survive it and be reunited with her family. The first season establishes Gilead's regime, portraying the systems that maintain its specific gender roles and power dynamics, while focusing on June's predicament. In the second season, June is pregnant with a child she is expected to give up to Commander Waterford (Joseph Fiennes) and his wife, whose household she is serving. The season thus continues to illustrate June's endurance of her conditions in Gilead in order to sustain her unborn child and to preserve her hope of reconciling with her family. Season three concentrates on June's involvement with the underground resistance movement MayDay and delineates the potential of overcoming Gilead's regime, culminating in the escape of a number of Gilead's children to Canada at the end of the season. Season four finds June herself finally acquiring her own freedom and being reunited with Luke in Canada, while grappling with the aftermath of the abuse and trauma she sustained in Gilead.

The opening scenes of the pilot episode depict June and daughter Hannah (Jordana Blake) attempting to run and hide from Gilead's armed forces, the Guardians, before being caught and separated. Husband Luke (O. T. Fagbenle) is able to elude the Guardians and eventually succeeds in reaching Canada, where the family had been attempting to escape. Throughout the series, flashbacks provide the viewer with glimpses of the happiness June experienced with her husband and daughter, as well as the gradual disintegration of female rights and agency as the "new Republic" took power.

In Gilead, June has been renamed Offred to literally signify that she is "Of Fred" Waterford (Joseph Fiennes), the Commander to whom she now belongs. Other handmaids are similarly renamed "Ofglen," "Ofwarren," "Ofsteven," etc., to indicate who their male masters are. Like the handmaids who are instantly recognizable in their red uniforms, other women in Gilead are similarly classed and recognized through the color of their attire. The elite Wives are dressed in blue, EconoWives married to lower-class men wear gray, Marthas who serve the households as cooks and housekeepers wear green, and Aunts who train and oversee the handmaids wear brown. Two other groups of women, Jezebels and Unwomen, are prostitutes and prisoners, respectively, who do not reside in Gilead. The Jezebels are maintained in the illicit men's club of the same name while Unwomen who have no useful function in Gilead society as they are older, infertile, and/or dissident are exiled to the Colonies, where they are made to work cleaning toxic waste until their deaths. Regardless of their status, there is no space for agency or individuality for any of the women, and they must all conform to the parameters of their respective roles.

It is noteworthy that in the midst of the severe privation for women in Gilead, *The Handmaid's Tale* offers a sense of resistance to patriarchal oppression. The red uniform that the handmaids are conscripted to wear has become an iconic symbol of feminist protest and women's rights. Donning the red cloaks and white bonnets inspired by the series' costume designer Ane Crabtree, handmaids have appeared to silently protest at circumstances such as the Republican Senate health care bill that portended to reduce funding for birth control and abortions in June 2017, US President Donald Trump's visit to Warsaw, Poland, for the G8 summit in July 2017, and Christine Blasey Ford's allegations of sexual assault against then Supreme Court nominee Brett Kavanaugh in September 2017. These instances and others have been notable in regard to their threat to women's rights and the presence of the handmaids has served as a symbolic reminder of patriarchal oppression, as well as resistance to it. The phenomenon of the series has thus correspondingly developed amidst a renewed cognizance of women's experience of sexism and gendered power relations, demonstrated by the surge in activist movements, such as #MeToo and #TimesUp. The conspicuous feminism of the series is apparent in its stark focus on the extremely gendered power imbalances that uphold Gilead society and its harsh depictions of misogyny and abuse.

RESISTANCE AND RESILIENCE TOWARD ABUSE AND OPPRESSION

The conspicuous feminism integrated into the series is evident in its portrayal of the absence of female autonomy and the brutality inflicted on women in Gilead. Flashbacks to "the time before Gilead" depict June and all the other women in her office being summarily fired from their jobs without warning, and women are suddenly no longer allowed to own property and have their bank accounts frozen ("Late," Season 1, Episode 3). These measures are mere precursors to women's existence in Gilead, where they have become entirely subordinate to men, no matter the role they occupy. As June plainly states in one of the voiceovers that are frequently utilized to illustrate the rich interior consciousness that is central to the narrative, "There's only women who are fruitful and women who are barren" ("Nolite Te Bastardes Carborundorum," Season 1, Episode 4), with no alternatives in between. During a routine medical checkup, the doctor follows up his examination with an offer to "help" impregnate June, who is not yet pregnant at this point in the series:

> Doctor: I can help you. It could be the only way for you. If Waterford can't get you pregnant, they won't blame him. It'll be your fault. It'll only take a few minutes, honey.
>
> June: I can't. It's too dangerous. Thank you. ("Nolite Te Bastardes Carborundorum," Season 1, Episode 4)

The doctor's insinuation that June would still get the blame even if her Commander was sterile is just one example of the disenfranchisement that handmaids, and indeed all women in Gilead, are subjected to.

The misogyny inherent in *The Handmaid's Tale* corresponds to Kate Manne's definition of the structural properties of a patriarchal society:

> a social milieu counts as patriarchal insofar as certain kinds of institutions or social structures both proliferate and enjoy widespread support within it—from, for example, the state, as well as broader cultural sources, such as material resources, communal values, cultural narratives, media and artistic depictions, and so on. These patriarchal institutions will vary widely in their material and structural, as well as their social, features. But they will be such that all or most women are positioned as subordinate in relation to some man or men therein, the latter of whom are thereby (by the same token) dominant over the former, on the basis of their genders (among other relevant intersecting factors). (2018, 45)

In Gilead, all women are positioned as subordinate, with the explicit utilization of fear and retribution for those who dare to question their position, and the various forms of cruelty inflicted on the women is a testament to the series' enactment of female oppression.

Several episodes in the series illustrate the penalties doled out to any women who dare to challenge their circumstances. In addition to the monthly Ceremonies, handmaids are routinely subjected to beatings, electrocution with cattle prods, and even the loss of body parts for transgressions ranging from speaking back to attempting escape. A Martha is hanged for engaging in a lesbian affair with a handmaid whose punishment is having her clitoris removed ("Late," Season 1, Episode 3), while an Econowife is sentenced to death by drowning along with the guard she has attempted to run away with ("Postpartum," Season 2, Episode 12). Even the elite Wives are not immune to these punitive measures—upon the discovery that she has forged and written documents using her husband's name while he is recuperating in hospital due to injuries sustained in a rebel bombing, Serena Waterford is whipped by Commander Waterford ("Women's Work," Season 2, Episode 8) and later loses a finger after daring to suggest to the Gilead council that girls be allowed to learn to read the Bible ("The Word," Season 2, Episode 13).

The graphic depiction of these and other instances of female persecution is key to the integration of conspicuous feminism on the series. These depictions have generated controversy as to whether these severe representations are necessary to communicate its themes of oppression, indicating the commercial facets to conspicuous feminism and reiterating concerns over the increase of graphic violence in quality television series overall. A number of quality television series, notably *Breaking Bad*, *Game of Thrones*, and *The Sopranos* have been noted for the amount of explicit violence featured (Lawler 2016). In her article on the increase of violent imagery in the second season, Fiona Sturges claims that "*The Handmaid's Tale* has stripped away all hope, swallowed its fury, abandoned Atwood's social commentary and descended into cynical, pointless cruelty. It has left us as mere rubberneckers, peering stupidly at the carnage" (Sturges 2018). However, creator and writer Bruce Miller asserts that the violence enables the viewer to fully empathize with the characters' experiences and to be cognizant of the real-life horrors that exist for women in particular societies. As he expounds on the motivations for the graphic scenes:

> I really try to show only the things that if you didn't see, you wouldn't understand the story or the characters. You have to go through it with June in order to understand her. To take that away is to take away what June is fighting against. Also, there's the cautionary part of the tale. We don't ever make up cruelties, because that just seems like pornography. We unfortunately have plenty of material that exists in the world. (Stanford 2019)

Miller's repudiation of the term "pornography" in relation to the violence depicted on the series suggests the explicitness and commodification that distinguishes representations of conspicuous feminism, and indeed, the violent images are significant to the series' exhibition of abuse and injustice toward women. In this way, women in Gilead are subject to Manne's denotation of misogyny in that it "ought to be understood as the system that operates within a patriarchal social order to police and enforce women's subordination and to uphold male dominance" (2018, 33), and Gilead's dystopia can be likened to a most extreme rendering of Manne's description in that women's subordination is explicitly "enforced."

Protagonist June most keenly manifests conspicuous feminism on the series as she refuses to accept a fate of subjugation and forced reproduction from the outset. At the end of the pilot episode, June informs the viewer of her intention to resist through voiceover: "I intend to survive for her. Her name is Hannah. My husband was Luke. My name is June" ("Offred" Season 1, Episode 1). This declaration is symbolic of the assertion of her own subjectivity and her will to persevere as the series progresses. The affirmation is followed by the use of Lesley Gore's "You Don't Own Me" as a soundtrack over the end credits, cementing that in spite of her present circumscription as a handmaid, she still maintains hope for the happy and fulfilling life she had before Gilead.

When she discovers the mock Latin phrase "Nolite te bastardes carborundorum" carved by her predecessor in the Waterford household at the bottom of the closet in her room, it becomes one of the catalysts of her survival and resistance. Though it "is a gibberish phrase of broken Latin described by Atwood as a middle-school joke" (Bayne 2018, 601), its translation, "Don't let the bastards grind you down" becomes a mantra for June in her struggle for survival and symbolic to the feminist resistance associated with *The Handmaid's Tale* itself, as she professes: "There was an Offred before me. She helped me find my way out. She's dead. She's alive. She is me. We are Handmaids. Nolite te bastardes carborundorum, bitches" ("Nolite Te Bastardes Carborundorum," Season 1, Episode 4). Though the former Offred hung herself in that room, June is determined to survive the suffering and abuse and becomes a figure of resistance that triggers the insurgency that develops throughout the series.

The utilization of her voiceover narrative is one manner in which June's resilience is portrayed, giving the viewer access to the rich and irreverent inner thoughts that she cannot outwardly state in Gilead. Restrained by a regime that does not allow personal expression, her voiceover enables the viewer to share in her insights and emotions. As Jan Alber notes in her discussion of the use of interior monologue in film, voiceover techniques can "convey a character's thoughts, feelings or motivations at the auditory level" (2017, 277), and June's vibrant narrative provides an intimate perspective on the circumstances depicted in Gilead. Her wry observations on the nature and status of her position as handmaid are jarringly paradoxical to the rote phrases commonly employed in Gilead greetings, such as "Blessed be the fruit" and "We've been sent good weather." In contrast, June's candid commentary grants an impression on the rituals of Gilead:

A bath is required before the Ceremony. I am to make myself clean. Washed and brushed like a prized pig. ("Offred," Season 1, Episode 1)

It's forbidden for us to be alone with the Commanders. We aren't concubines. We're two-legged wombs. ("Birth Day," Season 1, Episode 2)

The vigor and audacity of June's thoughts strikingly contrast with the placid demeanor that she must outwardly present, suggesting a divided sense of self that mirrors the partition between her previous life as June and her enforced situation as Offred. In her examination of the construction of "split selves" in both fiction and nonfiction, Catherine Emmott denotes that such characters typically experience their identity as "split" due to "a transitory sense of experiential discontinuity or because of a traumatic life change" (2002, 170). In illuminating the distinctions between her inner psyche and her outer countenance, June's voiceovers evidence a split in her sense of self that functions as a response to the distress of her imposed confinement in Gilead, and that endow her with the resilience to survive and surmount it.

The Handmaid's Tale's constant employment of close-ups of June's face also enables the viewer to perceive her staunch resilience. These close-ups underline the array of facial expressions executed by the actress Moss, as well as heightening the emotional impact for the viewer. As Chloe Harrison observes on the effect of the close-ups in the series, they "allow the audience greater emotional connection to a character but also increase the sense of claustrophobia generated by such an arrangement, and the close alignment of a character perspective (both literally and figuratively) can become, at times, uncomfortable" (2020, 28). Indeed, the close-up is often used to evoke June's hardship and elicit disquiet in the viewer, as in the fixated shots on her face that frequently comprise scenes of the Ceremony, including the viewer in her forced submission. Voiceover often combines with these instances to emphasize her attempts at disengagement and disembodiment: "You treat it like a job. One detaches oneself. No. No more to you than a bee is to a flower. Not me. Not my flesh. I'm not here" ("The Last Ceremony," Season 2, Episode 10). Close-ups also oblige the viewer to witness her pain in childbirth ("Holly," Season 2, Episode 11) and her agony at seeing her daughter through the window of a locked car and being unable to hold or speak to her ("Night," Season 1, Episode 10). The employment of lingering tight shots on Moss's anguished expressions in these two scenes are accompanied by the primal groans emitted in the process of childbirth in the former and by eerie silence in the latter, as her desperate screams are inaudible through the locked car door. The willful use of close-ups in both scenes cogently enables the viewer to perceive the varying layers of pain that June experiences in motherhood—one viscerally accentuating the physical pain of birthing a child and the other harrowingly demonstrating the emotional pain of forced separation from her daughter. Apart from illustrating her adversity, the close-ups can also emphasize June's fortitude, as in exhibiting her resoluteness at the close of the second season as she walks back toward Gilead after giving up an opportunity to escape, as she cannot leave without her daughter ("The Word," Season 2, Episode 13).

The close-up is used to exceptional effect during June's powerful testimony against the Waterfords and crimes of Gilead in the fourth season. Her testimony begins in a long shot with the camera gradually zooming in closer as it progresses, eventually ending in the established close-up, forcefully accenting her demand for justice:

> mine is just one voice. Countless others will remain unheard, imprisoned by men like Fred Waterford. Women . . . my friends . . . who lost their lives and can never be heard. It is for those women that I ask the International Criminal Court to confirm the charges against this man and put him on trial. I ask for the maximum possible sentence. I ask for justice. ("Testimony," Season 4, Episode 8)

These and other examples of the close-up provide a palpability to the various instances of pain and suffering that June undergoes, as well as illustrate her fierce determination and tenacity.

June's survival mechanisms recall Sarah Bracke's suggestion that resilience can incorporate specifically gendered qualities:

> Resilience is not merely about bending without breaking; it is also about bouncing back in shape, possibly stronger than one was before. . . . Resilience here

Figure 5.1. June's (Elisabeth Moss) testimony against the Waterfords and Gilead begins in a long shot. *The Handmaid's Tale,* **"Testimony," Season 4, Episode 8.** *Screenshot captured by author.*

Figure 5.2. And ends in a close-up. *The Handmaid's Tale,* "Testimony," Season 4, Episode 8. *Screenshot captured by author.*

implies efficient action—that is the opposite of [her] current state of being paralyzed. It also captures the toughness and relentlessness that come with bouncing back, which are commonly connotated as masculine.... This renders the gendered politics of resilience more complex, and beyond the connotation of resilience with [traditional] femininity, we might want to consider the gendered dimension of resilience as a particular reconfiguration of qualities commonly considered as feminine or masculine. (2016, 66)

While the concept of resilience is often associated with the traditional feminine quality of endurance in suffering, Bracke also imbues it with action and the ability to overcome. These qualities of toughness and relentlessness are more commonly associated with notions of masculine strength, which June embodies not only in her struggle to survive her imprisonment and conditions in Gilead, but also in her resolve to overcome them and be reunited with her daughter.

As she contends with her situation, June further displays Bracke's construction of resilience in suffering by "adapting to a new situation through adjustment, negotiation, and compromise, and finally by seizing on the occasion by 'creatively' responding to the challenge of the shock or trauma" (2020, 55). These "creative" responses enable her to navigate her relationship with Commander Waterford, from their clandestine games of Scrabble, which she prudently allows him to win and in which she herself finds gratification, participating in a board game prohibited to women in Gilead due to its forbidden components of reading and writing. This "creative" resilience enables her to embark on a romance with the Waterfords' driver Nick (Max Minghella), a pairing that was originally engineered by the Commander's Wife Serena in the hopes of utilizing another means of impregnating Offred due to the Commander's sterility. These instances illustrate how June not only passively survives her conditions but actively attempts to defeat them as well.

In addition to her own survival, her "creative resilience" is ultimately able to precipitate collective resistance to the Gilead regime. By manipulating the Commander in their illicit visits to the Jezebel's club, she is able to secure the delivery of a package from the resistance group MayDay with the help of best friend Moira (Samira Wiley), who has been assigned to Jezebel's after being brought back to Gilead following a failed escape attempt. The package is revealed to contain letters written by various women enslaved in Gilead, which has the potential to sever Gilead's relationships with international trade partners if they were ever released ("Night," Season 1, Episode 10). This eventually occurs toward the end of the second season during the Waterfords' diplomatic visit to Canada, where Nick is able to pass them on to June's husband's Luke, who immediately posts them online ("Smart Power," Season 2, Episode 9). The letters instigate immense public outrage, resulting in Canada withdrawing their negotiations with Gilead and producing a sense of accomplishment for the women in Gilead. As Howell comments, "To be heard, to be believed, and to prompt a political response is a striking victory for the women, for the MayDay resistance, and for the protesters who support them in Canada" (2019, 9). Giving the women an outlet to express their experiences on *The Handmaid's Tale* draws parallels to the fundamental aims of the #MeToo movement to enable survivors of abuse to disclose and seek redress for the violations. The movement had gained significant momentum by the time the second season was filmed in its depiction of concern "with the intersection of sex and power and . . . its concerns in terms of justice" (Orgad and Gill 2018, 1318).

June's resilience and collusion with the MayDay resistance movement advances through to the final episode of the second season, where she is poised to escape Gilead with newborn baby daughter Holly ("The Word," Season 2, Episode 13). After handing the baby over to handmaid Emily (Alexis Bledel), who is already sitting in the back of the van that will escort them out of Gilead, June abruptly pivots and begins walking back, signifying that she will return to Gilead and will not leave until she is able to do so with Hannah. In this way, June is illustrating Bracke's notion of gendered resilience by embodying the "individual woman, who might have suffered structural disadvantage and has the damage to show for it, now has the means at her disposal to overcome such disadvantage" (2020, 67). The scene as she walks determinedly back toward Gilead, to the spirited musical accompaniment of the Talking Heads' "Burning Down the House," echoes the scene toward the final episode of the first season, when the handmaids collectively march back toward their homes to the triumphant strains of Nina Simone's

"Feeling Good." This occurs after the handmaids are dismissed by their formidable overseer and trainer Aunt Lydia (Ann Dowd) on their collective refusal, led by June, to stone handmaid Janine (Madeline Brewer) to death as her punishment for attempting her own suicide after running away with the baby she has been forced to give up to her assigned family. The image of June marching defiantly, alone or with the other handmaids, at the close of both of the first two seasons evokes the resilience and solidarity spurred by #MeToo and which is important to conspicuous feminism.

EXPANDING RESISTANCE

The third season expands on June's resilience in her resolve to aid in the escape of Gilead's children, indicating that her concerns have extended beyond her own individual circumstances and toward all others who have been afflicted by Gilead's regime. This development manifests the collective constitution of #MeToo and the militant qualities of conspicuous feminism. As such, her resistance has broadened to undertaking to dismantle the establishment itself, instead of solely overcoming her individual subjugation. In doing so, this season in particular reflects an awareness of the limitations in circumscribing the series' focus to June's predicament and endeavors to further the efforts of the second season in more comprehensively portraying the experiences of other characters in Gilead and beyond. While the first season was predominantly set in Gilead, apart from flashbacks to "the time before," the second season ventures beyond its perimeters to depict the "unwomen" laboring in the Colonies and Luke and Moira's adaptation to life in Canada as refugees. The third season extends this expansion with its concentration on Emily's difficulties in adjusting to freedom in Canada, as well as on Gilead's diplomatic relationship with Canada, largely connoted through the relentless undertakings of the Waterfords to attain ownership of baby Nichole/Holly.

The series' venturing to invest in the narratives of other characters simultaneously allows for June to become more conscious of the hardships faced by others in Gilead, such as the children, the Marthas, and her fellow handmaids. For the first half of the third season, June remains mired in her individual concerns for her own situation and that of her children, of which Janine pointedly accuses her, "When did you get to be so selfish? Everything is always about you; your problems" ("Heroic," Season 3, Episode 9). Shortly after this, June encounters a teenaged girl at the hospital who is being examined for her reproductive capacities, a harsh reminder to her of the future awaiting all of Gilead's children, including her daughter Hannah, and this galvanizes her determination to "get out as many children as I can. I don't really know how yet, but I swear to you, I'm gonna get them out. Because Gilead should know how this feels. It's their turn to hurt" ("Heroic," Season 3, Episode 9). June's resistance thus takes on a more collective function as it encapsulates more than her own circumstances and aspires to destabilize the regime of Gilead itself.

June's intent to enable the children's escape embodies the feminist concern to shift the focus from the individual's circumstances to a more consolidated awareness of mutually oppressed groups. Barbara Tomlinson articulates that "Feminism is a collective oppositional social movement and a critical intellectual practice, but it is also an entity that holds power inside institutions that parcel out individual rewards and promote interpersonal competition" (2019, 1), summoning June's centrality and singularity to the greater part of the feminist incentives of *The Handmaid's Tale*. In her objective to take the children out of Gilead, she exhibits a mode of feminism that transcends her individual condition, as illuminated in her voiceover at the beginning of the final episode of the third season:

> To the ruthless go the spoils. Fifty-two kids will be brought to the Lawrence house after sunset. We will move in darkness. We can hide in the dark at least. We have a chance at least. If there is actually a Martha network. If this all isn't a trap set by the eyes, I will get the children to the airport. The plane leaves at midnight. Because I am ruthless. ("MayDay," Season 3, Episode 13)

June's ruthlessness takes on a more expansive dimension than that illustrated in the first two seasons, where the series' depiction of resistance largely concentrated on her own adversity.

Her undertaking is ultimately successful and the third season closes with the emotional arrival of the plane of children and Marthas in Canada. June has meanwhile has been shot and wounded in her efforts to divert attention from the Guardians during the operation, and the final scene of the season pictures her being rescued and carried out of the woods by her fellow handmaids. Though the season similarly ends with the close-up of June that has exemplified the conclusion of the previous two seasons, she is not pictured alone on this occasion, and the musical accompaniment of Mazzy Star's "Into Dust" is also a more somber selection in contrast to the defiant anthems that have been employed to close the prior seasons. This signifies the possibility of the series continuing to move in the more divergent direction that has been instituted. Constance Grady speculates on the prospects of amplifying the capacity of the resistance in Gilead without relying solely on June's efforts:

> If June is going to be a resistance leader, that's the kind of resistance I want to see: one based not in June's unique specialness, but in class solidarity, in groups of people working together to overcome an oppressive state. That's the kind of

grounding that can help move *The Handmaid's Tale* out of the realm of fantasy and back toward thinking about how power works and travels, how it can be abused, and how it can be resisted—even just by ordinary people who are working together and don't have any kind of destiny or special plot armor to protect them. (VanDerWerff and Grady 2019)

Moving beyond June's particular resilience and circumstances would allow the series to explore the shared struggles of other characters in more depth and allow them to persist in the resistance against Gilead more synchronously.

The combative elements of conspicuous feminism are absolutely apparent in the fourth season as the theme of resistance is further expanded to incorporate explicit facets of justice and vengeance. The season details June's eventual escape to Canada and processing of the trauma she has endured in Gilead. Her jarring return to the world outside of Gilead is disconcertingly underscored by the audio accompaniment of Etta James's "At Last," and she is pictured walking through the luxurious surroundings of the hotel she has been escorted to upon her arrival in Montreal where the glittering chandeliers and the sumptuous array of food and alcohol in the hotel suite are in stark disaccord with her dazed countenance ("Home," Season 4, Episode 7). In the same episode, the physical and emotional scope of her trauma is depicted through scenes such as a routine supermarket trip, where the sight of women clad in burquas recollects images of handmaids and induces a panic attack. The physical wounds she has sustained are literally exposed during her first shower outside of captivity, as the running water flows relentlessly across the bruises and welts covering her body.

Her mental scars are further manifested in her struggles to restore intimacy with Luke, culminating in a controversial and disquieting sex scene that divided viewers as to whether it constituted June's assault of her husband (Romero 2021). Toward the end of the episode depicting June's "homecoming" ("Home," Season 4, Episode 7), June affronts Serena Waterford, who is being held in jail while awaiting a trial for the crimes she and Fred Waterford have committed in Gilead. During this encounter, June vigorously unleashes her fury at Serena, condemning her to "a fraction of the pain that you caused us when you tore our children from our arms!" leaving Serena kneeling and sobbing in front of June, who stands ferociously above her, denoting a blunt reversal of power. June carries this fervor into her return to bed with Luke, who she awakens and has sex with, subduing his demurrals by forcefully pinning his hand down and covering his mouth. The scene is intended to disquietingly illustrate the weight of the repercussions of the abuse inflicted on June in Gilead and to suggest a contorted reclaiming of the power and agency she had lost there. As episode writer Yahlin Chang reflects on the motivations of the scene:

> Is it realistic, given what this particular character has gone through ... given her years in Gilead and all the trauma and violence that has infused her life there (and some of which she has been forced to inflict), that on this particular day right after she left Gilead that she could instantly snap into a super healthy and tender intimate relationship with Luke? ... Is it more honest to the character that issues of power and dominance along with just the thrill of escapism have creeped into her relationship to sex ... and that sex might be more enmeshed with some of those issues rather than being about an intimate loving connection with the husband you haven't seen in years? (Romero 2021)

The indeterminate and disconcerting air persists in the following scene, which pictures June and Luke in a cheerful family tableau playing with baby Nicole in the snow, a perturbed expression crossing Luke's face as he observes his wife. June's dubious adaptation of gender and power is a compelling example of the series' intention to probe the impacts of trauma and abuse, but its' lack of consideration thus far toward the effects of the assault on Luke is problematic. Apart from his admission to Moira that June has become "like a stranger half the time.... I mean, it's like ... when we talk about Hannah ... and ... in bed" ("Testimony," Season 4, Episode 8), the incident is not specified again. Moira's response to him that "Getting over trauma is a bumpy fucking road.... You need to be patient till June gets where she's going" again stresses the significance of June's trauma, while seeming to disregard his. The series' persistence in concentrating on June's adversity, while sidelining that of other characters including Luke, is evocative of the way in which particular #MeToo narratives have been privileged over others, particularly in relation to the low visibility of male survivors of sexual abuse (Boyle 2019; Clark-Parsons 2021). This is also suggestive of how representations of conspicuous feminism have tended to focus on constructions of gender and power that are more recognizable and coherent to audiences (i.e., the abuse of women vs. men). These constructions can be expanded to reflect the more inscrutable facets of gendered power structures that are commonly omitted in popular cultural texts.

Conspicuous feminism's determination to resist and challenge gendered inequality is most distinctly illustrated in June's taking justice into her own hands upon discovering that Fred Waterford has struck a deal with the US government, enabling his freedom in exchange for classified information on Gilead. June's desire for vengeance is inferred soon after her arrival in Montreal, as evinced in the "group meetings" attended by former handmaids. In one of these sessions, she unequivocally expresses her need to channel her rage in a concrete form, "Why does healing have to be the only goal? Why can't we be as furious as we feel? Don't we have that right?" ("Testimony," Season 4, Episode 8), reflecting conspicuous feminism's aspiration to act against injustice and inequality. June's retribution is ultimately realized when she conspires with Joseph Lawrence to have Fred Waterford taken into the woods, where he is savagely beaten and killed by June and a group of handmaids in the season finale. The season thus ends as it customarily does by featuring the handmaids as a collective, brutally attacking Fred to the soundtrack of Lesley Gore's "You Don't Own Me," an acknowledgment of the song's use in the pilot episode, to more chilling effect in this context. Unlike previous seasons, the closing image is not of June but of Fred hanging on the wall under the inscription, "Nolite te bastardes carborundorum," plainly reiterating the theme of retribution that characterized the season as a whole ("The Wilderness," Season 4, Episode 10).

Thus far, the series' focus on June has also prompted some feminist writers to question whether its commitment to reflecting its feminist motives is for all women or if it is simply privileging the white, heterosexual female protagonist conventionally pictured in popular television's representations of feminism, despite featuring diversity in the casting of key characters. As Karen Crawley asserts, "the show's explicit focus on gender, sexuality and resistance at the expense of race, politics and history invites its viewers to keep our eyes shut to the ongoing reproduction of whiteness in contemporary (neo)liberal configurations of legal subjectivity and state authority" (2018, 336). Characters such as Moira, Luke, Rita, and handmaid Natalie (Ashleigh LaThrop) have not been given the same degree of depth and background as some of their white counterparts, namely Janine and Emily, among others. As a result, there is apprehension as to certain elements of feminist incentives being elided in *The Handmaid's Tale* and in constructions of conspicuous feminism in general, namely with regard to their disavowal to engage in the dynamics of race, particularly in relation to concerns of reproductive justice, which has largely and historically been denied to women marginalized by race, class, and sexuality (Fixmer-Oraiz 2020; Ross and Solinger 2017).

Although the dystopian circumstances chronicled in Atwood's novel and presented in the series are fictional, numerous critics have commented on their relevance to contemporary issues that women are contending with and that have been amplified by #MeToo. As Jessica Valenti notes:

> What the show does so well—especially now, under the Trump administration—is make its shocking dystopia feel so terrifyingly possible. We see that before the US government has been overthrown by Gilead, its misogynist tenets have already slowly made their way into state law: June must get her husband's written permission for birth control pills, and when her daughter gets sick in school, June undergoes formal questioning about her parental fitness because she works full-time. In other flashbacks from Alexis Bledel's character, Emily,

the lesbian professor is sidelined from teaching because of the increasing anti-LGBT cultural sentiment, and is later prevented from leaving the country with her wife and child because their marriage is deemed illegal. That slippery slope sure seems familiar. Teachers are still fired for being gay in this country, working mothers are still looked at askance (and sometimes punished in custody battles), and multiple states have tried to pass laws that would mandate women have written spousal permission before getting abortions. (Valenti 2018)

The themes being reflected on the series reverberate with the contemporary struggles for rights relating to abortion and reproduction, such as the laws imposing restrictions on abortions in nine US states in 2019 (Lai 2019) and the July 2020 Supreme Court upholding of a regulation limiting women's access to birth control coverage under employers' religious or moral objections (Liptack 2020). Ongoing legislation regarding the discrimination against the LGBTQ community in the workplace (Liptack 2020) and lack of support frameworks for working mothers (Shellenbarger 2020), among other issues, also reiterates the timeliness of the series' subject matter with the cultural preoccupation with matters of gender and power.

However, the series restriction of its portrayal of gender and power in Gilead to June's perspective also resounds with concerns leveled at the #MeToo movement's sidelining of narratives that require intersectional scrutiny. As Boyle states:

The extent to which women's experiences of violence are inflected by race, location and economic privilege in particular have been recurring themes in the wider #MeToo discourse. As noted above, Tarana Burke's Me Too movement originated in the experiences of multiple marginalised victim/survivors who were young, urban, women of colour. However, whilst some multiply marginalised women have had a relatively mainstream platform in the #MeToo moment, this has not necessarily had the effect of shifting either [white] feminist or media practices overall. (2019, 9)

Similarly, *The Handmaid's Tale*'s concentration on June's specific resilience and struggles to resist Gilead's domination impedes the narrative possibilities for the trials of other characters, particularly those embodying positions of racial, class, or sexual marginality, to be collectively explored and confronted.

The series corresponds to the depictions of conspicuous feminism generated by the influence of #MeToo in its vivid depiction of patriarchal power and female oppression. The themes of resistance and vengeance are pointedly utilized as key factors in protagonist June Osborne's struggle against a fundamentalist and misogynist regime, while the potential for the narratives of other characters to be more fully explored opens up the possibilities for more diversified conceptions of feminism and empowerment to be incorporated.

This could be significant to the development of the resistance movement and the theme of retribution in the fifth season, as *The Handmaid's Tale* continues to grapple with the themes of resilience and resistance that have come to inform the image of the handmaid itself.

Chapter Six

Conclusion

Advocating and Commodifying Female Empowerment in Conspicuous Feminism

In July 2022, Margaret Atwood posted a photograph of herself holding a coffee mug with the slogan "I Told You So," an eerie allusion to the parallels between the overturning of *Roe vs. Wade* in June 2022 and the fictional disciplining of female autonomy and reproductive rights illustrated in *The Handmaid's Tale*. Following the ruling, comments regarding the possibility of reconsidering LGBTQ rights and rights to contraception made by Supreme Court Justice Clarence Thomas (Durkee 2022) have contributed to the increasingly fraught atmosphere surrounding issues of gender and power. As witnessed by the numerous protests and rallies that have taken place across the United States since the Supreme Court's decision was announced, the feminist activism and consciousness sparked by #MeToo has apparently been regenerated, potentially enlarging the scope for reflections of conspicuous feminism.

The impact of #MeToo continues to be perceived into the 2020s with television series persisting in representing narratives incorporating conspicuous feminism. Notable examples include the eight episodes in *Roar* (Apple TV, 2022), based on Cecilia Ahern's 2018 short story collection, which are promoted by the streaming channel as "darkly comedic feminist fables that take unexpected approaches to subjects like gender roles, autonomy, and identity," indicating the persevering inclination for television narratives to incorporate themes relating to gender and power. The limited series features acclaimed actors strongly associated with constructions of conspicuous feminism on television, including Nicole Kidman and Issa Rae, further denoting the iconographic and performative elements that signify conspicuous feminism itself. Hulu's *Mrs. America* (2020) depicts the feminist movement to ratify the Equal Rights Amendment (ERA) in the early 1970s and is a distinct illustration of how feminism has become central to representations of women on television. The miniseries' picturing of real-life issues and events encompassing second-wave feminism indicates the progressions and specificities that have come to characterize television reflections of feminism. *I May Destroy You* (BBC One/HBO, 2020) features an unusually acute and complex depiction of sexual violence based on the real-life experience of creator and star Micaela Cole, emphasizing the propensity of television narratives to address the trauma of sexual assault in the #MeToo era. The series' interrogation of how race, class, and sexuality affects the actions of and responses to survivors suggests the future potential of more intersectional approaches to portraying themes of abuse and misogyny.

Conspicuous feminism's incorporation of resistance, perceptibility, and commodification can be correlated with the cultural presence of #MeToo. The large-scale media coverage generated by the movement enabled a more extensive awareness of the extent to which systemic misogyny is operating within society, instigating structural changes in the entertainment industry and beyond. A notable example is the "Time's Up," initiative which was launched in January 2018 to provide financial and legal support to victims of assault and harassment and to endorse transformations in laws, policies, and workplace cultures (Hillstrom 2019). The expanse of the movement also encouraged a wider expression of experiences of abuse, with the Rape, Abuse and Incest National Network (RAINN) reporting a 23% increase in calls to their crisis hotline in October–December 2017 (after the media pervasiveness of the Weinstein allegations) in comparison to the same period two years prior (Boyle 2019). The guilty verdicts delivered to Weinstein on one count of third degree rape and another of a first degree criminal sexual act in February 2020 were viewed as victories for the #MeToo movement (Twohey and Kantor 2020), following high-profile convictions for sexual assault against comedian Bill Cosby and US gymnastics team doctor Larry Nasser in 2018, among others.

However, the release of Bill Cosby in June 2021 upon the overturning of his conviction by a Pennsylvania court due to violations of his due process rights was a stark indication that the goals of #MeToo and its appeals for justice have not been realized. Other criticisms of the movement such as incidents of false accusations, the privileging of particular abuse narratives over others, and the perceived lack of definition in its agenda have contributed to pronouncements of the failure of #MeToo (Doyle 2017; Stephens 2017). In 2022, the highly publicized trial over the actor Johnny Depp's 2019 defamation lawsuit against his ex-wife Amber Heard's allegations of abuse heightened the perceived collapse of #MeToo. The livestreaming of the trial attracted considerable public interest, with viewers overwhelmingly supportive of Depp and derisive of Heard as evidenced by the abundant posts and comments on various social media platforms that mocked Heard and implied that she was lying. Upon the eventual favorable ruling for Depp, Heard stated that the verdict, "sets back the clock to a time when a woman who spoke up and spoke out could be publicly shamed and humiliated. It sets back the idea that violence against women is to be taken seriously" (Flannery 2022). The outcome and the spectacle surrounding the trial has prompted concern that women will become even more wary of speaking out about their experiences of abuse, essentially decelerating the principles of #MeToo.

The changes and awareness provoked by #MeToo have occurred alongside the intense visibility of the movement, which has largely emerged on social media. The hashtag activism of #MeToo ensued from previously circulating hashtags denoting sexual abuse and gendered injustice, such as #BeenRapedNeverReported and #YesAllWomen (Mendes et al. 2019; Serisier 2018). In his discussion of the mobilizing properties of hashtag activism, Simon Lindgren contends that "Hashtags are therefore not pure referents but can also be conceived of as tools of activating certain interpretive frames" (2019, 421), indicating its transformative potential, as evidenced by the structural changes stimulated by the movement. Conversely, this form of activism has frequently been associated with notions of "virtue signalling," which are often deemed superficial for their conspicuous indications of support for political and social issues, such as feminism, without any substantial action being taken. Though #MeToo has effected genuine structural change and awareness of the prevalence of systemic misogyny, its cultural presence has also facilitated its corporate co-optation, as evidenced by the range of merchandise, from apparel to homeware, that emblematizes feminism and the movement (Bond 2019). The representations of conspicuous feminism on quality television series similarly assimilate these components of commodification, directness, and activism in their portrayals of misogyny and gendered power dynamics.

Paralleling #MeToo's cultural visibility, the conspicuous feminism reflected in the series examined in this book extends to their considerable prominence in the media and popular culture, particularly on social media. Unlike earlier television series featuring feminist themes, these series have developed amidst the proliferation of social media platforms, generating opportunities for the use of #hashtivism in their presentation of conspicuous feminism. The official Facebook and Instagram accounts affiliated with each series feature promotional content that stresses themes of female empowerment and raises awareness of the issues relating to gender inequality that each show is concerned with. For instance, *Big Little Lies'* Instagram account @biglittlelies advertises HBO merchandise such as wine glasses that incorporate the series taglines (e.g., "Secrets Always Surface," "I Want More") and petitions for donations to organizations such as Safe House, which supports survivors of domestic violence. @maiseltv showcases cosmetics collections inspired by Midge Maisel, launched by brands such as Revlon, and posts from the series of Midge and Suzie emphasizing female solidarity and friendship. @Insecurehbo regularly includes posts endorsing the Black Lives Matter movement, while @handmaidsonhulu encourages the creativity of its fans to produce artwork exhibiting themes of resistance and empowerment in its #fanartchallenges. Such posts appear alongside episode clips and publicity photographs of the series' stars, demonstrating the simultaneous feminist advocacy and commercialization that encompasses the series' embodiment of conspicuous feminism.

The expression of conspicuous feminism is also determined by the varying timelines, settings, and genres that constitute each series. As a dystopian drama, *The Handmaid's Tale* yields the opportunity for counterfactualism to be incorporated from a feminist perspective—although the narrative is concerned with genuine facets of misogyny and abuse, the speculative depictions that arise from the setting and specifications of Atwood's novel allow for the intensely visual and visceral manifestation of conspicuous feminism that the series evinces. *The Marvelous Mrs. Maisel* similarly invokes counterfactualism in its feminist envisaging of a 1950s housewife attempting to defy gender norms outside of the domestic space. The comedy genre and Midge's stand-up routines also enable conspicuous feminism to be displayed in a whimsical and performative manner. In contrast, *Big Little Lies'* dramatic contemporary setting accords a more synchronic reflection of misogyny and abuse that is plainly influenced by #MeToo, while the topical concerns of intersectionality and discrimination similarly inform the embodiment of conspicuous feminism within the comedic structures of *Insecure*. These distinctions illustrate how the characteristics of conspicuous feminism have been specifically refitted across these series in order to correspond to their respective contexts and generic frameworks.

Apart from *Insecure*, the designation of conspicuous feminism across the series discussed in this book does not fundamentally interrogate intersectional elements and their implications for the construction of female identities and perceptions of female empowerment. The protagonists are predominantly white and economically privileged, and though racially diverse characters are included in all the series, their racial backgrounds are either mostly unacknowledged (*The Handmaid's Tale* and *Big Little Lies*) or serve to facilitate the narrative of the main protagonist (*The Marvelous Mrs. Maisel*). The issue of class is generally muted in all four series, suggesting that representations of conspicuous feminism depend on the financial ability to consume in its denotation of female empowerment. On *Insecure*, Issa and Molly are frequently depicted in upscale stores and fashionable restaurants, indicating that empowerment via consumerism is a postfeminist factor that transcends race and is key to conspicuous feminism's visibility and appeal. As Francesca Sobande notes, "the qualities of potentially post-feminist contemporary media texts do not simply disappear when the protagonist is a Black woman" (2019, 445), complicating *Insecure*'s embodiment of intersectional feminism. In this way, the relative lack of racial and class diversity in the series' presentation of conspicuous feminism summons the criticisms regarding the insufficient intersectional consideration leveled at the cultural salience of the #MeToo movement (Leung and Williams 2019; Williams 2021).

Several studies have referred to #MeToo's identification with the experiences of racially and economically privileged women, particularly in media coverage of the movement (Boyle 2019; Leung and Williams 2019; Gill and Orgad 2018). As Gill and Orgad claim, #MeToo's "politics and aesthetics are exclusionary in various problematical ways" (2018, 1319), referring to the marginalization of the experiences of women of color, as well as the lack of media attention afforded to the narratives of queer women (Fournier 2017). The omission of the accounts of disabled women has also been noted as deficient in the movement's scope (Flores 2018). The portrayals of conspicuous feminism on television largely share this lack of inclusivity in their depictions of female empowerment, inclining instead to reproduce images that conform to modes with commercial appeal.

Both the commodifying and advocating elements to conspicuous feminism indicate the burgeoning cultural concernment toward issues of gender and power. The conspicuous feminism reflected on the quality television series examined in this book have been influenced and facilitated by the prominence of #MeToo. The scrutiny of feminist concerns relating to the exposure of sexual abuse, challenging traditional gender expectations concerning domesticity and the public space, and the revisioning of racial stereotypes and resistance against gendered inequality is undertaken on these series in a way that builds upon and expands feminist discourse of previous eras. This shift has been prompted by #MeToo's exposure and dissemination of systemic misogyny that has raised awareness of women's experiences of abuse, harassment, and discrimination and is reflected in the series' complex discernment of both the trauma and resilience of its protagonists. The commodifying features that underlie these series' delineation of female empowerment demonstrate quality television's capitalization of the feminist themes amplified by #MeToo, producing representations of conspicuous feminism that integrate both feminist advocacy and commodification in their confrontation of misogyny and sexism. These constructs are crucial to advancing awareness of and endeavoring resistance toward issues of gender inequality, but care should be taken to ensure that the sheer volume and compelling attributes of such images do not obscure their complexity.

Bibliography

Adegoke, Yomi. 2019. "We're in a Golden Age of Feminist TV, and Don't Need the Bechdel Test to Prove It." *The Guardian*, May 9, 2019. https://www.theguardian.com/commentisfree/2019/may/09/golden-age-feminist-tv-bechdel-test.

Adriaens, Fien, and Sofie Van Bauwel. 2014. "Sex and the City: A Postfeminist Point of View? Or How Popular Culture Functions as a Channel for Feminist Discourse." *Journal of Popular Culture*, 47, no. 1: 174–195. https://doi.org/10.1111/j.1540-5931.2011.00869.x.

Ahmed, Sara. 2012. *On Being Included: rRcism and Diversity in Institutional Life*. Durham, NC: Duke University Press.

Alber, Jan. 2017. "The Representation of Character Interiority in Film: Cinematic Versions of Psychonarration, Free Indirect Discourse and Direct Thought." In *Emerging Vectors of Narratology*, edited by P. K. Hansen et al., 265–283. Berlin: De Gruyter.

Allen, Robert C. 1992. *Channels of Discourse, Reassembled Television and Contemporary Criticism*. 2nd ed. Chapel Hill: University of North Carolina Press.

Antler, Joyce. 2010. "One Clove away from a Pomander Ball: The Subversive Tradition of Jewish Female Comedians." *Studies in American Jewish Literature*, 29: 123–138. https://link-gale-com.eproxy.lib.hku.hk/apps/doc/A252385139/LitRC?u=hku&sid=LitRC&xid=4af195d3.

Assiter, Alison. 1996. *Enlightened Women: Modernist Feminism in a Postmodern Age*. London: Routledge.

Atwood, Margaret Eleanor. 1998. *The Handmaid's Tale*. 1st Anchor Books ed. New York: Anchor Books.

Bakhtin, Mikhail. (1965) 1984. *Rabelais and His World*. Translated by Helene Iswolsky. Bloomington: Indiana University Press.

Balaji, Murali. 2010. "'Vixen Resistin': Redefining Black Womanhood in Hip-Hop Music Videos." *Journal of Black Studies* 41, no. 1: 5–20. https://doi.org/10.1177/0021934708325377.

Banet-Weiser, Sarah. 2018. *Empowered: Popular Feminism and Popular Misogyny*. Durham, NC: Duke University Press.

———. 2007. "What's Your Flava? Race and Postfeminism in Media Culture." In *Interrogating Postfeminism: Gender and the Politics of Popular Culture*, edited by Yvonne Tasker and Diane Negra, 201–226. Durham, NC: Duke University Press.

Bartky, Sandra Lee. 1990. *Femininity and Domination: Studies in the Phenomenology of Oppression*. New York: Routledge.

Bastien, Angelica Jade. 2020. "*Insecure* Is a Balm, Even When It Fails." *Vulture*, June 15, 2020. https://www.vulture.com/2020/06/insecure-season-4-finale-review.html.

Bathrick, Serafina. 2003. "*The Mary Tyler Moore Show*: Women at Home and at Work." In *Critiquing the Sitcom: A Reader*, edited by Joanne Morreale, 155–186. Syracuse, NY: Syracuse University Press.

Bayne, Caroline N. 2018. "#nolitetebastardescarborundorum: Self-Publishing, Hashtag Activism, and Feminist Resistance." *Communication, Culture & Critique* 11, no.1: 201–205. https://doi.org/10.1093/ccc/tcx016.

Beail, Linda, and Lilly J. Goren. 2009. "Introduction: Feminism, Front and Center." In *You've Come a Long Way, Baby: Women, Politics and Popular Culture*, edited by Lilly J. Goren, 1–14. Lexington: University Press of Kentucky.

Beal, Frances M. 2008. "Double Jeopardy: To Be Black and Female." *Meridians* 8, no. 2: 166–176.

Beale, Lewis. 1992. "Maude's Abortion Fades Into History." *Chicago Tribune*, November 13, 1992. https://www.chicagotribune.com/news/ct-xpm-1992-11-13-9204130017-story.html.

Beauvoir, Simone de. 1972. *The Second Sex*. Harmondsworth, UK: Penguin Books.

Beck, Ulrich, and Elisabeth Beck-Gernsheim. 2002. *Individualization: Institutionalized Individualism and Its social and Political Consequences*. Thousand Oaks, CA: SAGE.

Benson, Josef. 2014. *Hypermasculinities in the Contemporary Novel: Cormac McCarthy, Toni Morrison, and James Baldwin*. Lanham, MD: Rowman & Littlefield.

Bentham, Jeremy. (1748–1832) 1791. *Panopticon: Postscript Part I: Containing further particulars and alterations relative to the plan of construction originally proposed; principally adapted to the purpose of a panopticon penitentiary-house*. London: Printed for T. Payne.

Bergson, Henri. 1911. *Laughter: An Essay on the Meaning of the Comic*. Translated by Cloudesley Brereton and Fred Rothwell. New York: Macmillan.

Bignell, Jonathan. 2004. *An Introduction to Television Studies*. New York: Routledge.

Boddy, William. 2004. *New Media and Popular Imagination: Launching Radio, Television and Digital Media in the United States*. Oxford: Oxford University Press.

Bodroghkozy, Aniko. 2003. "'Is This What You Mean by Color TV?' Race, Gender, and Contested Meanings in Julia." In *Critiquing the Sitcom: A Reader*, edited by Joanne Morreale, 129–150. Syracuse, NY: Syracuse University Press.

Bond, Casey. 2019. "Does Your Favorite Feminist Merchandise Actually Support Women's Causes?" *The Huffington Post*, October 31, 2019. https://www.huffpost.com/entry/feminist-clothing-harm-women_l_5db9debde4b0bb1ea373e237.

Bordo, Susan. 1993. *Unbearable Weight: Feminism, Western Culture and the Body*. Berkeley: University of California Press.
Boyd, Todd. 2004. "Intergenerational Culture Wars: Civil Rights vs Hip Hop." *Socialism and Democracy: Hip Hop, Race, and Cultural Politics* 18, no. 2: 51–69. https://doi.org/10.1080/08854300408428398.
Boyle, Karen. 2019. *#MeToo, Weinstein and Feminism*. Cham, Switzerland: Palgrave Macmillan.
Bracke, Sarah. 2016. "Bouncing Back: Vulnerability and Resistance in Times of Resilience." In *Vulnerability in Resistance*, edited by Judith Butler, Zeynep Gambetti, and Leticia Sabsay, 52–75. Durham, NC: Duke University Press.
Brooks, Ann. 1997. *Postfeminisms: Feminism, Cultural Theory and Cultural Forms*. New York: Routledge.
Brownmiller, Susan. 1984. *Femininity*. New York: Simon & Schuster.
Brunsdon, Charlotte. 2000. *The Feminist, the Housewife, and the Soap Opera*. Oxford: Oxford University Press.
Buchbinder, Eli, and Zvi Eiskovits. 2003. "Battered Women's Entrapment in Shame: A Phenomenological Study." *American Journal of Orthopsychology* 73, no. 4: 355–366. https://doi.org/10.1037/0002-9432.73.4.355.
Budgeon, Shelley. 2011. *Third-Wave Feminism and the Politics of Gender in Late Modernity*. Basingstoke, UK: Palgrave Macmillan.
Buonanno, Milly, ed. 2017. *Television Antiheroines: Women Behaving Badly in Crime and Prison Drama*. Bristol, UK; Chicago, USA: Intellect.
Busch, Elizabeth Kaufer. 2009. "*Ally McBeal* to *Desperate Housewives*: A Brief History of the Postfeminist Heroine." *Perspectives on Political Science* 38, no. 2: 87–98. https://doi.org/10.3200/PPSC.38.2.87-98.
Butler, Jessalyn. 2013. "For White Girls Only: Postfeminism and the Politics of Inclusion." *Feminist Formations* 25, no. 1: 35–58. https://doi.org/10.1353/ff.2013.0009.
Butler, Judith. 1990. *Gender Trouble: Feminism and the Subversion of Identity*. New York: Routledge.
Carastathis, Anna. 2016. *Intersectionality: Origins, Contestations, Horizons*. Lincoln: University of Nebraska Press.
Carbin, Maria, and Sara Edenheim. 2013. "The Intersectional Turn in Feminist Theory: A Dream of a Common Language?" *European Journal of Women's Studies* 20, no. 3: 233–248. https://doi.org/10.1177/1350506813484723.
Center for the Study of Women in Television & Film. 2018. https://womenintvfilm.sdsu.edu.
Chamberlain, Prudence. 2017. *The Feminist Fourth Wave: Affective Temporality*. Cham, Switzerland: Palgrave Macmillan.
Charles, Nick. 2019. "The Apollo: A National Stage for a Generation of Black Performers." *NBC News*, November 27, 2019. https://www.nbcnews.com/news/nbcblk/apollo-national-stage-generation-black-entertainers-n1086086.
Christian, Aymar Jean. 2020. "Beyond Branding: The Value of Intersectionality on Streaming TV Channels." *Television and New Media* 21, no. 5: 457–474. https://doi.org/10.1177/1527476419852241.

Clark-Parsons, Rosemary. 2021. "I SEE YOU, I BELIEVE YOU, I STAND WITH YOU: #MeToo and the Performance of Networked Feminist Visibility." *Feminist Media Studies* 21, no. 3: 362–380. https://doi.org/10.1080/14680777.2019.1628797.

Cochrane, Kira. 2013. *All the Rebel Women: The Rise of the Fourth Wave Feminist*. Guardian Books.

Collins, Patricia Hill. 2013. "Defining Black Feminist Thought." In *Feminist Theory Reader: Local and Global Perspectives*, 3rd ed., edited by Carole R. McCann and Seung-Kyung Kim, 379–394. New York: Routledge.

———. 2006a. *From Black Power to Hip Hop: Racism, Nationalism, and Feminism*. Philadelphia: Temple University Press.

———. 2006b. "New Commodities, New Consumers: Selling Blackness in a Global Marketplace." *Ethnicities* 6, no. 3: 297–317.

———. 2000. *Black Feminist Thought: Knowledge, Consciousness, and the Politics of Empowerment*. 2nd ed. New York: Routledge.

Combahee River Collective. 1982. "A Black Feminist Statement." In *All the Women Are White, All the Blacks Are Men, but Some of Us Are Brave: Black Women's Studies*, edited by Gloria T. Hull, Patricia Bell-Scott, and Barbara Smith, 13–22. Old Westbury, NY: Feminist Press.

Cooke-Cornell, Beth Anne. 2018. "Rape Jokes in the Era of #MeToo." *Response: The Journal of Popular and American Culture* 3, no. 2. https://responsejournal.net/issue/2018-11/article/rape-jokes-era-metoo.

Conklin, Audrey. 2020. "Streaming Services by the Numbers." *Fox Business*, May 4, 2020. https://www.foxbusiness.com/lifestyle/streaming-services-cost-users.

Corry, Kristen. 2022. "'And Just Like That' Is Desperately Trying to Prove It Has Black Friends." *Vice*, January 14, 2022. https://www.vice.com/en/article/g5qjb9/and-just-like-that-sex-and-the-city-is-trying-to-prove-it-has-black-friends.

Crawley, Karen. 2018. "Reproducing Whiteness: Feminist Genres, Legal Subjectivity and the Post-Racial Dystopia of *The Handmaid's Tale* (1970–)." *Law and Critique* 29, no. 3, 2018: 333–358. https://doi.org/10.1007/s10978-018-9229-8.

Crenshaw, Kimberlé Williams. 1989. "Demarginalizing the Intersection of Race and Sex: A Black Feminist Critique of Antidiscrimination Doctrine, Feminist Theory and Antiracist Politics." *University of Chicago Legal Forum* 1: 139–167. https://heinonline.org/HOL/P?h=hein.journals/uchclf1989&i=143.

Cuklanz, Lisa M. 2000. *Rape on Prime Time: Television, Masculinity, and Sexual Violence*. Philadelphia: University of Pennsylvania Press.

Curry, Ramona. 1995. "Mae West and Film Censorship." In *Classical Hollywood Comedy*, edited by Kristine Brunovska Karnick and Henry Jenkins, 227–230. New York: Routledge.

D'Acci, Julie. 1994. *Defining Women: Television and the Case of* Cagney & Lacey. Chapel Hill, NC: University of North Carolina Press.

D'Alessandro, Anthony. 2018a. "'Big Little Lies' Even More Resonant in #MeToo Times—Golden Globes Backstage." *Deadline*, January 7, 2018. https://deadline.com/2018/01/nicole-kidman-reese-witherspoon-big-little-lies-golden-globe-metoo-1202238030/.

———. 2018b. "She is 'Maisel,' Hear Her Roar: Amazon Series Creators and Stars on #MeToo Timing & Blazing a New Trail." *Deadline*, August 15, 2018. https://deadline.com/2018/08/the-marvelous-mrs-maisel-metoo-times-up-rachel-brosnahan-emmy-nominations-1202444659/.

Davies, Hannah. J. 2018. "'It Was Important for Black Women to See Ourselves Normally': How *Insecure* Changed TV." *The Guardian*, July 31, 2018. https://www.theguardian.com/tv-and-radio/2018/jul/31/issa-rae-insecure.

Davis, Angela Yvonne. 1981. *Women, Race and Class*. New York: Vintage Books.

Davis, Natalie Zemon. 1975. *Society and Culture in Early Modern France*. Stanford, CA: Stanford University Press.

Dejmanee, Tisha. 2016. "Consumption in the City: The Turn to Interiority in Contemporary Postfeminist Television." *European Journal of Cultural Studies* 19, no. 2: 119–136. https://doi.org/10.1177/1367549415585555.

Dicker, Rory Cooke. 2016. *A History of U.S. Feminisms*. Berkeley, CA: Seal Press.

Dillard, Cynthia B. 2019. "To Experience Joy: Musings on Endarkened Feminisms, Friendship, and Scholarship." *International Journal of Qualitative Studies in Education* 32, no. 2: 112–117. https://doi.org/10.1080/09518398.2018.1533149.

Dillaway, Heather, and Elizabeth Pare. 2008. "Locating Mothers: How Cultural Debates about Stay-at-Home versus Working Mothers Define Women and Home." *Journal of Family Issues* 29, no. 4: 437–464. https://doi.org/10.1177/0192513X07310309.

Dobson, Amy Shields, and Akane Kanai. 2019. "From 'Can-Do' Girls to Insecure and Angry: Affective Dissonances in Young Women's Post-Recessional Media." *Feminist Media Studies* 19, no. 6: 771–786. https://doi.org/http://dx.doi.org/10.1080/14680777.2018.1546206.

Donahue, Anne T. 2018. "Midge Maisel Isn't the Feminist Hero You're Looking For—and That's Okay." *Marie-Claire*, December 6, 2018. https://www.marieclaire.com/culture/a25415662/marvelous-mrs-maisel-season-2-feminism/.

Douglas, Susan J. 2010. *Enlightened Sexism: The Seductive Message That Feminism's Work Is Done*. New York: Time's Books.

Dow, Bonnie J. 1996. *Prime-Time Feminism: Television, Media Culture, and the Women's Movement since 1970*. Philadelphia: University of Pennsylvania Press.

Doyle, Jude Ellison Sady. 2017. "Despite What You May Have Heard, 'Believe Women' Has Never Meant 'Ignore Facts.'" *Elle*, November 29, 2017. https://www.elle.com/culture/career-politics/a13977980/me-too-movement-false-accusations-believe-women/.

Durkee, Alison. 2022. "Clarence Thomas: Court Should Reconsider Gay Marriage, Birth Control Decisions next after Overturning Roe." *Forbes*, June 24, 2022. https://www.forbes.com/sites/alisondurkee/2022/06/24/clarence-thomas-court-should-reconsider-gay-marriage-birth-control-decisions-next-after-overturning-roe/?sh=575487076097.

Eckhardt, Stephanie. 2017. "Does *The Handmaid's Tale*'s Aggressively IRL Marketing Campaign Go Too Far?" *W*, June 13, 2017. https://www.wmagazine.com/story/the-handmaids-tales-real-life-marketing/.

Emmott, Catherine. 2002. "'Split Selves' in Fiction and in Medical 'Life Stories': Cognitive Linguistic Theory and Narrative Practice." In *Cognitive Stylistics: Language and Cognition in Text Analysis*, edited by Elena Semino and Jonathan Culpepper, 153–182. Philadelphia: J. Benjamins Publishing Co.

Epstein, Adam. 2020. "Thanks to Streaming, We May Never Reach the Peak of 'Peak TV.'" *Quartz*, January 11, 2020. https://qz.com/1783165/thanks-to-streaming-we-may-never-reach-the-peak-of-peak-tv/.

Faludi, Susan. 1992. *Backlash: The Undeclared War against American Women*. New York: Doubleday.

Farrow, Ronan. 2017. "From Aggressive Overtures to Sexual Assault: Harvey Weinstein's Accusers Tell Their Stories." *The New Yorker*, October 10, 2017. https://www.newyorker.com/news/news-desk/from-aggressive-overtures-to-sexual-assault-harvey-weinsteins-accusers-tell-their-stories.

Feasey, Rebecca. 2012. *From Happy Homemaker to Desperate Housewives: Motherhood and Popular Television*. New York: Anthem Press.

Feuer, Jane, Paul Kerr, and Tise Vihamangi, eds. 1984. *MTM: "Quality Television."* London: BFI Publishing.

Fixmer-Oraiz, Natalie. 2020. "Motherhood and the Struggle for Reproductive Justice." In *The Routledge Companion to Motherhood*, edited by Lynn O'Brien Hallstein et al., 510–519. New York, NY: Routledge.

Flanery, Amanda. 2022. "Amber Heard Issues Statement Following Defamation Verdict." *FM104*, June 1, 2022. https://www.fm104.ie/news/buzz/amber-heard-issues-statement-following-defamation-verdict/.

Ford, Jessica. 2016. "The 'Smart' Body Politics of Lena Dunham's *Girls*." *Feminist Media Studies* 16, no. 6: 1029–1042. https://doi.org/10.1080/14680777.2016.1162826.

Fortmueller, Kate. 2021. *Hollywood Shutdown: Production, Distribution, and Exhibition in the Time of COVID*. Austin: University of Texas Press.

Foucault, Michel. 1979. *Discipline and Punish: The Birth of the Prison*. New York: Vintage Books.

Fousiannes, Chloe. 2018. "*The Marvelous Mrs. Maisel*'s Real-Life Inspirations: Joan Rivers, Phyllis Diller and More." *Town & Country*, December 16, 2018. https://www.townandcountrymag.com/leisure/arts-and-culture/a25460957/marvelous-mrs-maisel-midge-real-life-inspiration-joan-rivers-phyllis-diller/.

Foy, Jennifer. 2015. "Fooling Around: Female Stand-Ups and Sexual Joking." *Journal of Popular Culture* 48, no. 4: 703–713. https://doi.org/10.1111/jpcu.12222.

Friedan, Betty. 1963. *The Feminine Mystique*. New York: Norton.

Friedlander, Whitney. 2016. "Gilmore Girls Has a Privilege Problem." *Paste*, November 29, 2016. https://www.pastemagazine.com/tv/gilmore-girls/gilmore-girls-has-a-privilege-problem/.

Fung, Katherine. 2021. "Streaming Services Dominate 2021 Emmy Award Nominations." *Newsweek*, July 13, 2021. https://www.newsweek.com/streaming-services-dominate-2021-emmy-award-nominations-1609341.

Fuster, Jeremy. 2020. "Issa Rae Is Launching Season 4 of 'Insecure' with Virtual Block Party." *The Wrap*, April 12, 2020. https://www.thewrap.com/issa-rae-is-launching-season-4-of-insecure-with-virtual-block-party/.

Gagnier, Regenia. 1988. "Between Women: A Cross-Class Analysis of Status and Anarchic Humor." *Women's Studies* 15, no. 1–3: 135–148. https://doi.org/:10.1080/00497878.1988.9978723.

Galuppo, Mia. 2020. "Actor-Organizer Kendrick Sampson Is Putting 'Pressure in the Streets' for Change." *Hollywood Reporter*, July 10, 2020. https://www.hollywoodreporter.com/news/actor-organizer-kendrick-sampson-is-putting-pressure-streets-change-1302116.

Garcia, Sandra E. 2017. "The Woman Who Created #MeToo Long Before Hashtags." *The New York Times*, October 20, 2017. https://www.nytimes.com/2017/10/20/us/me-too-movement-tarana-burke.html.

Garofalo, Alex. 2016. "What Does 'Stay Woke' Mean? BET to Air Documentary on Black Lives Matter Movement." *International Business Times*, May 26, 2016. https://www.ibtimes.com/what-does-stay-woke-mean-bet-air-documentary-black-lives-matter-movement-2374703.

Genz, Stéphanie. 2009a. "'I Am Not a Housewife, But . . .': Postfeminism and the Revival of Domesticity." In *Feminism, Domesticity and Popular Culture*, edited by Stacey Gillis and Joanne Hollows, 49–64. New York: Routledge.

———. 2009b. *Postfemininities in Popular Culture*. Basingstoke, UK: Palgrave Macmillan.

Genz, Stéphanie, and Benjamin A. Brabon. 2009. *Postfeminism*. Edinburgh: Edinburgh University Press.

Gerson, Jeannie Suk. 2018. "Bill Cosby's Crimes and the Impact of #MeToo on the American Legal System." *The New Yorker*, April 27, 2018. https://www.newyorker.com/news/news-desk/bill-cosbys-crimes-and-the-impact-of-metoo-on-the-american-legal-system.

Gibson, Caitlin. 2018. "The End of Leaning In: How Sheryl Sandberg's Message of Empowerment Fully Unraveled." *The Washington Post*, December 21, 2018. https://www.washingtonpost.com/lifestyle/style/the-end-of-lean-in-how-sheryl-sandbergs-message-of-empowerment-fully-unraveled/2018/12/19/9561eb06-fe2e-11e8-862a-b6a6f3ce8199_story.html.

Gilbert, Joanne R. 2004. *Performing Marginality: Humor, Gender and Cultural Critique*. Detroit: Wayne State University Press.

Gilbert, Sophie. 2018. "*The Handmaid's Tale* and the Suffering of Women." *The Atlantic*, April 25, 2018. https://www.theatlantic.com/entertainment/archive/2018/04/the-handmaids-tale-season-two/558809/.

Gill, Rosalind. 2017. "The Affective, Cultural and Psychic Life of Postfeminism: A Postfeminist Sensibility 10 Years On." *European Journal of Cultural Studies* 20, no. 6: 606–626. https://doi.org/10.1177/1367549417733003.

———. 2007a. *Gender and the Media*. Cambridge, UK; Malden, MA, USA: Polity.

———. 2007b. "Postfeminist Media Culture: Elements of a Sensibility." *European Journal of Cultural Studies* 10, no. 2: 147–166. https://doi.org/10.1177/1367549407075898.

Gill, Rosalind, and Shani Orgad. 2018. "The Shifting Terrain of Sex and Power: From the 'Sexualization of Culture' to #MeToo." *Sexualities* 21, no. 8: 1313–1324. https://doi.org/10.1177/1363460718794647.

Gillis, Stacey, and Joanne Hollows. 2009. *Feminism, Domesticity and Popular Culture*. New York: Routledge.

Gilmore, Stephanie. 2008. *Feminist Coalitions: Historical Perspectives on Second-Wave Feminism in the United States*. Champaign: University of Illinois Press.

Gitlin, Todd. 1982. "Prime-Time Ideology: The Hegemonic Process in Television Entertainment." In *Television: The Critical View*, 3rd ed, edited by Horace Newcomb, 426–454. New York: Oxford University Press.

Grant, Ruby, and Meredith Nash. 2017. "From *Sex and the City* to *Girls*: Paving the Way for 'Post?Feminism.'" In *Reading Lena Dunham's Girls*, edited by Meredith Nash and Imelda Whelehan, 61–74. Cham, Switzerland: Palgrave Macmillan.

Greene, Linda S., Lolita Buckner Inniss, and Bridget J. Crawford. 2019. "Talking about Black Lives Matter and #MeToo." *Wisconsin Journal of Law, Gender and Society* 32, no. 2: 109–177.

Greer, Germaine. 1986. *The Female Eunuch*. London: Grafton Books.

Griffin, Penny. 2019. "MeToo, White Feminism and Taking Everyday Politics Seriously in the Global Political Economy." *Australian Journal of Political Science* 54, no. 4: 556–572. https://doi.org/10.1080/10361146.2019.1663399.

Griffin, Rachel Alicia. 2015. "Olivia Pope as Problematic and Paradoxical." In *Feminist Theory and Pop Culture*, edited by Patricia Adrienne Trier-Bienek, 35–48. Rotterdam: SensePublishers.

Haralovich, Mary Beth, and Lauren Rabinovitz, eds. 1999. *Television, History and American Culture: Feminist Critical Essays*. Durham, NC: Duke University Press.

Harrison, Chloe. 2020. "'The Truth Is We're Watching Each Other': Voiceover Narration as 'Split Self' Presentation in *The Handmaid's Tale* TV Series." *Language and Literature* 29, no. 1: 22–38, https://doi.org/10.1177/0963947020905756.

Harp, Dustin. 2019. *Gender in the 2016 US Presidential Election*. New York: Routledge.

Hekman, Susan J. 1992. *Gender and Knowledge: Elements of a Postmodern Feminism*. Boston: Northeastern University Press.

Henry, Astrid. 2004. "Orgasms and Empowerment: *Sex and the City* and the Third Wave Feminism." In *Reading* Sex and the City, edited by Kim Akass and Janet McCabe, 65–82. London; New York: I. B. Tauris.

Hewitt, Nancy A. 2010. *No Permanent Waves: Recasting Histories of U.S. Feminism*. New Brunswick, NJ: Rutgers University Press.

Hillstrom, Laurie Collier. 2019. *The #Metoo Movement*. Santa Barbara, CA: ABC-CLIO.

Hoff, Lee Ann. 2009. *Violence and Abuse Issues: Cross-Cultural Perspectives for Health and Social Service*. London; New York: Routledge.

Hollows, Joanne. 2000. *Feminism, Femininity, and Popular Culture*. Manchester, UK: Manchester University Press.

Home Box Office. n.d. "HBO Amplifies Black Stories with Free Movies and Shows." Accessed November 2, 2019. https://www.hbo.com/hbo-news/watch-black-stories-movies-shows-free.

hooks, bell. 2015. *Feminist Theory: From Margin to Center*. New York: Routledge.

hooks, bell, and Cornel West. 1991. *Breaking Bread: Insurgent Black Intellectual Life*. Boston: South End Press.

Householder, April Kalogeropoulos. 2015. "Girls, Grrrls, Girls: Lena Dunham, *Girls*, and the Contradictions of Fourth Wave Feminism." In *Feminist Theory and Pop Culture*, edited by Patricia Adrienne Trier-Bienek, 21–33. Rotterdam: SensePublishers.

Howell, Amanda. 2019. "Breaking Silence, Bearing Witness and Voicing Defiance: The Resistant Female Voice in the Transmedia Story World of *The Handmaid's Tale*." *Continuum: Journal of Media & Cultural Studies* 33, no. 2: 216–229. https://doi.org/10.1080/10304312.2019.1569392.

Hunt, Grayson. 2017. "Intersectionality: Locating and Critiquing Internal Structures of Oppression within Feminism." *Philosophy: Feminism*, edited by Carol Hay, 121–140. Farmington Hills, MI: Macmillan Reference USA.

James, Meg. 2015. "2015: Year of 'Peak TV' Hits Record with 409 Original Series." *Los Angeles Times*, December 16, 2015. https://www.latimes.com/entertainment/envelope/cotown/la-et-ct-2015-peak-tv-new-record-409-original-series-20151216-story.html.

Jeltsen, Melissa. 2017. "'Big Little Lies' Offers a Rare, Nuanced Portrayal of an Abusive Relationship." *Huffington Post*, March 21, 2017. https://www.huffpost.com/entry/big-little-lies-offers-a-rare-nuanced-portrayal-of-an-abusive-relationship_n_58d01a59e4b00705db518a0d.

Johnson, Jo. 2017. "The Revelatory Relatability of 'Big Little Lies.'" *New America*, April 20, 2017. https://www.newamerica.org/weekly/revelatory-relatability-big-little-lies/.

Johnson, Merri Lisa. 2007. *Third Wave Feminism and Television: Jane Puts It in a Box*. London; New York: I. B. Tauris.

Jones, Ellen E. 2019. "Is *Big Little Lies* Selling Us a Version of Consumer Feminism That's Too Good to Be True?" *The Guardian*, June 8, 2019. https://www.theguardian.com/tv-and-radio/2019/jun/08/big-little-lies-reese-witherspoon-meryl-streep-nicole-kidman-zoe-kravitz-laura-dern.

Kanai, Akane. 2020. "Between the Perfect and the Problematic: Everyday Femininities, Popular Feminism, and the Negotiation of Intersectionality." *Cultural Studies* 34, no. 1: 25–48. https://doi.org/10.1080/09502386.2018.1559869.

Kappel, Aaron, and Jessica Friday. 2016. "'Gilmore Girls: A Year in the Life' Has a White Feminism Problem." *Medium*, November 29, 2016. https://medium.com/the-establishment/gilmore-girls-a-year-in-the-life-has-a-white-feminism-problem-e10693185b96.

Kavka, Misha. 2008. *Reality Television, Affect and Intimacy: Reality Matters*. New York: Palgrave Macmillan.

Keller, Jessalynn, and Maureen E. Ryan, eds. 2018. *Emergent Feminisms: Complicating a Postfeminist Media Culture*. New York: Routledge.

Kelly, Liz. 1988. *Surviving Sexual Violence*. Cambridge, UK: Polity Press.

Kistler, Michelle E., and Moon J. Lee. 2009. "Does Exposure to Sexual Hip-Hop Music Videos Influence the Sexual Attitudes of College Students?" *Mass Communication & Society* 13, no. 1: 67–86, https://doi.org/10.1080/15205430902865336.

Krefting, Rebecca. 2014. *All Joking Aside: American Humor and Its Discontents*. Baltimore, MD: John Hopkins University Press.

Lagerwey, Jorie, and Taylor Nygaard. 2020. *Horrible White People: Gender, Genre, and Television's Precarious Whiteness*. New York: New York University Press.

Lai, K. K. Rebecca. 2019. "Abortion Bans: 9 States Have Passed Bills to Limit the Procedure This Year." *The New York Times*, May 29, 2019. https://www.nytimes.com/interactive/2019/us/abortion-laws-states.html.

Landay, Lori. 1998. *Madcaps, Screwballs, & Con Women: The Female Trickster in American Culture*. Philadelphia: University of Pennsylvania Press.

Lauzen, Martha M. 2021. "Boxed In: Women on Screen and Behind the Scenes on Broadcast and Streaming Television in 2020–21." *Center for the Study of Women in Television & Film*. Accessed March 27, 2022. https://womenintvfilm.sdsu.edu/wp-content/uploads/2021/09/2020-21_Boxed_In_Report.pdf.

Lawler, Kelly. 2016. "Has Violence on TV Finally Gone Too Far?" *USA Today*, December 20, 2016. https://www.usatoday.com/story/life/tv/2016/12/20/violence-on-tv-walking-dead-westworld/94831794/.

Leeds, Sarene. 2019. "Inside the Marvelous Marketing of 'Mrs. Maisel.'" *AdAge*, July 31, 2019. https://adage.com/article/member-content/inside-marvelous-marketing-mrs-maisel/2186606.

Legates, Marlene. 1996. *Making Waves: A History of Feminism in Western Society*. Toronto: Cop Clark.

Lentz, Kirsten Marthe. 2000. "Quality versus Relevance: Feminism, Race, and the Politics of the Sign in 1970s Television." *Camera Obscura* 15, no. 1: 44–93.

Leung, Rebecca, and Robert Williams. 2019. "MeToo and Intersectionality: An Examination of the #MeToo Movement through the R. Kelly Scandal." *The Journal of Communication Inquiry* 43, no. 4: 349–371. https://doi.org/10.1177/0196859919874138.

Levy, Yael. 2021. "A Sexual Subject: Black Women's Sexuality in *Insecure*." *Feminist Media Studies* 21, no. 7: 1209–1221. https://doi.org/10.1080/14680777.2020.1722723.

Li, Shirley. 2019. "How *The Morning Show* Interrogates the #MeToo Debate." *The Atlantic*, November 7, 2019. https://www.theatlantic.com/entertainment/archive/2019/11/morning-show-tries-reflect-messy-reality/601582/.

Limbong, Andrew. 2019. "Kendrick Lamar's 'Alright' Is the Sound of Black Life, Both Party and Protest." *NPR*, August 26, 2019. https://www.npr.org/2019/08/26/753511135/kendrick-lamar-alright-american-anthem-party-protest.

Lindgren, Simon. 2019. "Movement Mobilization in the Age of Hashtag Activism: Examining the Challenge of Noise, Hate, and Disengagement in the #MeToo Campaign." *Policy and Internet* 11, no. 4: 418–438, https://doi.org/10.1002/poi3.212.

Lipsitz, George. 2003. "Why Remember Mama? The Changing Face of a Woman's Narrative." In *Critiquing the Sitcom: A Reader*, edited by Joanne Morreale, 7–24. Syracuse, NY: Syracuse University Press.

Liptak, Adam. 2020. "Civil Rights Law Protects Gay and Transgender Workers, Supreme Court Rules." *The New York Times*, June 15, 2020. https://www.nytimes.com/2020/06/15/us/gay-transgender-workers-supreme-court.html.

Little, Judy. 1983. *Comedy and the Woman Writer: Woolf, Spark, and Feminism*. Lincoln: University of Nebraska Press.

Lobato, Ramon. 2019. *Netflix Nations: The Geography of Digital Distribution*. New York: New York University Press.

Lockyer, Sharon, and Heather Savigny. 2020. "Rape Jokes Aren't Funny: The Mainstreaming of Rape Jokes in Contemporary Newspaper Discourse." *Feminist Media Studies* 20, no. 3, 2020: 434–449. https://doi.org/10.1080/14680777.2019.1577285.

Lorde, Audre. 1984. *Sister Outsider: Essays and Speeches*. Trumansburg, NY: Crossing Press.

Lotz, Amanda D. 2017. *Portals: A Treatise on Internet-Distributed Television*. Michigan Publishing Services. https://doi.org/10.3998/mpub.9699689.

———. 2006. *Redesigning Women: Television after the Network Era*. Champaign: University of Illinois Press.

———. 2001. "Postfeminist Television Criticism: Rehabilitating Critical Terms and Identifying Postfeminist Attributes." *Feminist Media Studies* 1, no. 1: 105–121. https://doi.org/10.1080/14680770120042891.

Lynn, Susan. 1994. "Gender and Progressive Politics: A Bridge to Social Activism of the 1960s." In *Not June Cleaver: Women and Gender in Postwar America, 1945–1960*, edited by Joanne J. Meyerowitz, 103–127. Philadelphia: Temple University Press.

Maas, Jennifer. 2020. "Why Issa Rae Made a Fictional True-Crime Series about a Missing Black Woman for 'Insecure.'" *The Wrap*, June 10, 2020. https://www.thewrap.com/insecure-issa-rae-season-4-looking-for-latoya/.

Manne, Kate. 2018. *Down Girl: The Logic of Misogyny*. New York: Oxford University Press.

Massey, Doreen B. 1994. *Space, Place and Gender*. Cambridge, UK: Polity Press.

Matte, Gerard, and Ian Mcfadyen. 2011. "Can We Talk? The Reframing of Social Permissions in the Comedy of Joan Rivers." *Comedy Studies* 2, no. 2: 161–171. https://doi.org/10.1386/cost.2.2.161_1.

Mbabazi, Donah, and Joan Mbabazi. 2018. "Hashtag Activism: Powerful or Pointless?" *The New Times*, September 27, 2018. https://www.newtimes.co.rw/society/hashtag-activism-powerful-or-pointless.

McCabe, Janet, and Kim Akass, eds. 2007a. *Quality TV: Contemporary American Television and Beyond*. London: I. B. Tauris.

———. 2007b. "Sex, Swearing and Respectability." In *Quality TV: Contemporary American Television and Beyond*, edited by Janet McCabe and Kim Akass, 62–78. London: I. B. Tauris.

———. 2006. *Reading Desperate Housewives: Beyond the White Picket Fence*. London: I. B. Tauris.
McCann, Hannah. 2018. *Queering Femininity: Sexuality, Feminism and the Politics of Presentation*. New York: Routledge.
McDermott, Maeve. 2018. "'Big Little Lies' stars Laura Dern, Nicole Kidman Condemn Abuse in Golden Globe Speeches." *USA Today*, January 7, 2018. https://www.usatoday.com/story/life/entertainthis/2018/01/07/big-little-lies-stars-laura-dern-nicole-kidman-condemn-abuse-golden-globes-speeches-we-can-elicit-ch/1011908001/.
McDonald, Soraya Nadia. 2017. "Why the Hot Black Bodies on 'Insecure' Are More Revolutionary Than You Think." *The Undefeated*, July 28, 2017. https://theundefeated.com/features/hot-black-bodies-on-hbo-insecure-revolutionary/.
McFadden, Syreeta. 2016. "Beyoncé's Formation Reclaims Black America's Narrative from the Margins." *The Guardian*, February 8, 2016. https://www.theguardian.com/commentisfree/2016/feb/08/beyonce-formation-black-american-narrative-the-margins.
McRobbie, Angela. 2004. "Post-Feminism and Popular Culture." *Feminist Media Studies* 4, no. 3: 255–264. https://doi.org/10.1080/1468077042000309937.
Meara, Paul. 2020. "Issa Rae Is Using Her Platform to Demand Radical Change for Black America." BET, July 4, 2020. https://www.bet.com/celebrities/news/2020/07/04/issa-rae-defunding-the-police.html.
Mendes, Kaitlynn, Jessica Ringrose, and Jessalynn Keller. 2019. *Digital Feminist Activism: Girls and Women Fight Back against Rape Culture*. New York: Oxford University Press.
Meyerowitz, Joanne J., ed. 1994. *Not June Cleaver: Women and Gender in Postwar America, 1945–1960*. Philadelphia: Temple University Press.
Miller, Quinlan. 2019. *Camp TV: Trans Gender Queer Sitcom History*. Durham, NC: Duke University Press.
Mills, Brett. 2011. "'A Pleasure Working with You': Humour Theory and Joan Rivers." *Comedy Studies* 2, no. 2: 151–160. https://doi.org/10.1386/cost.2.2.151_1.
Mizejewski, Linda, and Victoria Sturtevant, eds. 2017. *Hysterical!: Women in American Comedy*. Austin: University of Texas Press.
Mock, Roberta. 2019. "Ageing, Temporality and Performance: Joan Rivers' Body of Work." *Performance Research: On Ageing (and Beyond)* 24, no. 3: 144–152. https://doi.org/10.1080/13528165.2019.1579022.
Modleski, Tania. 1994. *Loving with a Vengeance: Mass-Produced Fantasies for Women*. London; New York: Routledge.
Moeggenberg, Zarah, and Samantha Solomon. 2018. "Power, Consent, and the Body: #MeToo and *The Handmaid's Tale*." *Gender Forum* 70: 4–25. https://search-proquest-com.eproxy.lib.hku.hk/docview/2167787956?accountid=14548.
Mora, Celeste. 2013. "Has 'Mindy' Fixed Its Race Problem?" *Bustle*, November 21, 2013. https://www.bustle.com/articles/9309-the-mindy-projects-controversial-episode-on-race-didnt-clear-up-any-concerns.

Moran, Claire. 2017. "Re-Positioning Female Heterosexuality within Postfeminist and Neoliberal Culture." *Sexualities* 20, no. 1–2: 121–139. https://doi.org/10.1177/1363460716649335.

Morgan, Joan. 1999. *When Chickenheads Come Home to Roost: My Life as a Hip-Hop Feminist*. New York: Simon & Schuster.

Moriarty, Liane. 2014. *Big Little Lies*. New York: G. P. Putnam's Sons.

Morreale, Joanne, ed. 2003. *Critiquing the Sitcom: A Reader*. Syracuse, NY: Syracuse University Press.

Moynihan, Daniel P. 1965. *The Negro Family: The Case for National Action*. Office of Policy Planning and Research, U.S. Department of Labor.

Mulvey, Laura. 1989. *Visual and Other Pleasures*. Bloomington: Indiana University Press.

Munford, Rebecca, and Melanie Waters. 2014. *Feminism and Popular Culture: Investigating the Postfeminist Mystique*. New Brunswick, NJ: Rutgers University Press.

Nakamura, Lisa. 2008. *Digitizing Race: Visual Cultures of the Internet*. Minneapolis: University of Minnesota Press.

Nash, Jennifer C. 2019. *Black Feminism Reimagined: After Intersectionality*. Durham, NC: Duke University Press.

Nathanson, Elizabeth. 2013. *Television and Postfeminist Housekeeping: No Time for Mother*. London; New York: Routledge.

Negra, Diane. 2009. *What a Girl Wants?: Fantasizing the Reclamation of Self in Postfeminism*. London; New York: Routledge.

Nicolson, Paula. 2010. *Domestic Violence and Psychology: A Critical Perspective*. New York: Routledge.

Oakley, Ann. *Housewife*. London: Penguin Books.

O'Falt, Chris. 2019. "'Big Little Lies' Season 2 Turmoil: Inside Andrea Arnold's Loss of Creative Control." *IndieWire*, July 12, 2019. https://www.indiewire.com/2019/07/big-little-lies-season-2-andrea-arnold-lost-creative-control-jean-marc-vallee-1202156884/.

Opinde, Walter. 2019. "*Julia* TV Series: The First Portrayal of the Non-Stereotypical Role of an African-American Woman, Diahann Carroll." *BlackThen*, April 23, 2019. https://blackthen.com/julia-tv-series-first-portrayal-non-stereotypical-role-african-american-woman-diahann-carroll/.

Paskin, Willa. 2017. "'Nothing Like a Jew Eating a Pickle and You Put Some Christmas Carols Over It.'" *Vulture*, November 27, 2017. https://www.vulture.com/2017/11/amy-sherman-palladino-the-marvelous-mrs-maisel.html.

Patten, Dominic. 2021. "'And Just Like That' Review: 'Sex & the City' Return Just Not All That as Hard as HBO Max Series Tries." *Deadline*, December 9, 2021. https://deadline.com/video/and-just-like-that-review-sex-the-city-return-sarah-jessica-parker-kim-cattrall-cynthia-nixon-kristin-davis-hbo-max/.

Petruska, Karen, and Faye Woods. 2018. "Traveling without a Passport: 'Original' Streaming Content in the Transatlantic Distribution Ecosystem." In *Transatlantic Television Drama: Industries, Programs and Fans*, edited by Matt Hills, Michele Hilmes, and Roberta Pearson, 49–68. Oxford: Oxford University Press.

Press, Joy. 2018. *Stealing the Show: How Women Are Revolutionizing Television*. New York: Atria Books.
Price, Emmett George. 2006. *Hip Hop Culture*. Santa Barbara, CA: ABC-CLIO.
Probyn, Elspeth. 1995. "Perverts by Choice: Towards an Ethics of Choosing." In *Feminism Beside Itself*, edited by Diane Elam and Robyn Wiegman, New York: Routledge.
Projansky, Sarah. 2001. *Watching Rape: Film and Television in Postfeminist Culture*. New York: New York University Press.
Rabinovitz, Lauren. 1999. "Ms.-Representation: The Politics of Feminist Sitcoms." In *Television, History, and American Culture*, edited by Mary Beth Haralovich and Lauren Rabinovitz, 144–167. Durham, NC: Duke University Press.
Rae, Issa. 2017. "Black Folk Don't Like to Be Told They're Not Black." *Huffington Post*, December 6, 2017. https://www.huffpost.com/entry/black-folk-dont-movie_b_912660.
Ringrose, Jessica. 2007. "Successful Girls? Complicating Post-Feminist, Neoliberal Discourses of Educational Achievement and Gender Equality." *Gender and Education* 19, no. 4: 471–489. https://doi.org/10.1080/09540250701442666.
Rivers, Nicola. 2017. *Postfeminism(S) and the Arrival of the Fourth Wave: Turning Tides*. Cham, Switzerland: Palgrave Macmillan.
Robin, Marci. 2019. "Revlon's New *Marvelous Mrs. Maisel* Lipstick Is Perfect for Lovers of Retro Makeup Looks." *Allure*, July 11, 2019. https://www.allure.com/story/revlon-marvelous-mrs-maisel-lipstick-collection-sets.
Robson, Ruthann. 2020. "The Sexual Misconduct of Donald J. Trump: Toward a Misogyny Report." *Michigan Journal of Gender and Law* 27, no. 1: 81. https://doi.org/10.36641/mjgl.27.1.sexual.
Romanchick, Shane. 2022. "Here's Why You Can't Keep Up with TV Anymore; Over 550 Original Series Aired in 2021." *Collider*, January 15, 2022. https://collider.com/too-many-tv-shows-550-series-2021/.
Romero, Ariana. 2021. "*The Handmaid's Tale's* Latest Sex Scene Is Complicated—& Dark. Let's Talk about It." *Refinery29*, May 27, 2021. https://www.refinery29.com/en-us/2021/05/10474960/june-luke-handmaids-tale-sex-scene-season-4.
Rose, Tricia. 2008. *The Hip Hop Wars: What We Talk about When We Talk about Hip Hop—and Why It Matters*. New York: BasicCivitas.
Rosenberg, Roberta. 2015. "Jewish 'Diasporic Humor' and Contemporary Jewish-American Identity." *Shofar* 33, no. 3: 110–138.
Ross, Loretta, and Rickie Solinger. 2017. *Reproductive Justice: An Introduction*. Berkeley: University of California Press.
Rottenberg, Catherine. 2018. *The Rise of Neoliberal Feminism*. New York: Oxford University Press.
Rowe, Kathleen. 1995. *The Unruly Woman: Gender and the Genres of Laughter*. Austin: University of Texas Press.
Samuel, Lawrence R. 2001. *Postwar Television Advertising and the American Dream*. Austin: University of Texas Press.
Sandberg, Sheryl. 2013. *Lean In: Women, Work and the Will to Lead*. London: W. H. Allen.

Serisier, Tanya. 2018. *Speaking Out: Feminism, Rape and Narrative Politics*. Cham, Switzerland: Palgrave Macmillan.

SheMedia. n.d. Accessed July 26, 2018. https://www.shemedia.com.

Shellenbarger, Sue. 2020. "The Challenges That Working Mothers Still Face." *The Wall Street Journal*, January 3, 2020. https://www.wsj.com/articles/the-challenges-that-working-mothers-still-face-11578067249.

Siegel, Rachel Josefowitz. 1986. "Antisemitism and Sexism in Stereotypes of Jewish Women." *Women & Therapy* 5, no. 2–3: 249–257. https://doi.org/10.1300/J015V05N02_23.

Silverman, Gillian, and Sarah Hagelin. 2018. "Shame TV: Feminist Antiaspirationalism in HBO's *Girls*." *Signs: Journal of Women in Culture and Society* 43, no. 4, 2018: 877–904. https://doi.org/10.1086/696694.

Smith-Shomade, Beretta E. 2002. *Shaded Lives: African American Women and Television*. New Brunswick, NJ: Rutgers University Press.

Sobande, Francesca. 2918. "Awkward Black Girls and Post-Feminist Possibilities: Representing Millennial Black Women on Television in *Chewing Gum* and *Insecure*." *Critical Studies in Television* 14, no. 4: 435–450. https://doi.org/10.1177/1749602019870298.

Spangler, Lynn. 2003. *Television Women from* Lucy *to* Friends: *Fifty Years of Sitcoms and Feminism*. Westport, CT: Praeger.

Spigel, Lynn. 2001. *Welcome to the Dreamhouse: Popular Media and Postwar Suburbs*. Durham, NC: Duke University Press.

Springer, Kimberly. 2007. "Divas, Evil Black Bitches, and Bitter Black Women: African American Women in Postfeminist and Post-Civil-Rights Popular Culture." In *Interrogating Postfeminism: Gender and the Politics of Popular Culture*, edited by Yvonne Tasker and Diane Negra, 249–276. Durham, NC: Duke University Press.

Stanford, Eleanor. 2019. "'The Handmaid's Tale' Wants to Be More Than TV Medicine." *The New York Times*, June 5, 2019. https://www.nytimes.com/2019/06/05/arts/television/the-handmaids-tale-bruce-miller-season-three.html.

Stephens, Bret. 2017. "When #MeToo Goes Too Far." *The New York Times*, December 20, 2017. https://www.nytimes.com/2017/12/20/opinion/metoo-damon-too-far.html.

Strause, Jackie. 2019. "Why Matt Lauer Looms Large over Apple's 'Morning Show.'" *The Hollywood Reporter*, November 2, 2019. https://www.hollywoodreporter.com/live-feed/apples-morning-show-matt-lauer-weinstein-metoo-parallels-1251782.

Strauss Swanson, Charlotte, and Dawn M. Szymanski. 2020. "From Pain to Power: An Exploration of Activism, the #Metoo Movement, and Healing from Sexual Assault Trauma." *Journal of Counseling Psychology* 67, no. 6: 653–668. https://doi.org/10.1037/cou0000429.

Sturges, Fiona. 2018. "Cattleprods! Severed Tongues! Torture Porn! Why I've Stopped Watching *The Handmaid's Tale*." *The Guardian*, June 16, 2018. https://www.theguardian.com/tv-and-radio/2018/jun/16/handmaids-tale-season-2-elisabeth-moss-margaret-atwood.

Tasker, Yvonne, and Diane Negra, eds. 2007. *Interrogating Postfeminism: Gender and the Politics of Popular Culture*. Durham, NC: Duke University Press.

Taylor, Ella. 1989. *Prime-Time Families: Television Culture in Postwar America*. Berkeley: University of California Press.

Thompson, Robert J. 1996. *Television's Second Golden Age: From* Hill Street Blues *to* ER. New York: Continuum.

Thorburn, David. 2008. "*The Sopranos*." In *The Essential HBO Reader*, edited by Gary R. Edgerton and Jeffrey P. Jones, 61–70. Lexington: University Press of Kentucky.

Tomlinson, Barbara. 2019. *Undermining Intersectionality: The Perils of Power Blind Feminism*. Philadelphia: Temple University Press.

Trier-Bieniek, Patricia Adrienne, ed. 2015. *Feminist Theory and Pop Culture*. Rotterdam: SensePublishers.

Twohey, Megan, and Jodi Kantor. 2020. "With Weinstein Conviction, Jury Delivers a Verdict on #MeToo." *The New York Times*, February 24, 2020. https://www.nytimes.com/2020/02/24/us/harvey-weinstein-verdict-metoo.html.

Ullman, Sarah E. 2010. *Talking about Sexual Assault: Society's Response to Survivors*. Washington, DC: American Psychological Association.

Valenti, Jessica. 2018. "Why *The Handmaid's Tale* Is More Relevant One Year after the First Season." *The Guardian*, April 25, 2018. https://www.theguardian.com/commentisfree/2018/apr/25/handmaids-tale-season-2-return-trump-america-2018.

VanDerWerff, Emily Todd, and Constance Grady. 2019. "*The Handmaid's Tale* Closes a Messy Season with a Surprisingly Satisfying Finale." *Vox*, June 14. 2019. https://www.vox.com/culture/2019/8/14/20802862/the-handmaids-tale-season-3-finale-mayday-recap-canada.

Veblen, Thorstein. (1857–1929) 1998. *The Theory of the Leisure Class*. Amherst, NY: Prometheus Books.

Vlassis, Antonios. 2021. "Global Online Platforms, COVID-19, and Culture: The Global Pandemic, an Accelerator towards Which Direction?" *Media, Culture and Society* 43, no. 5: 957–969. https://doi.org/10.1177/0163443721994537.

Waisanen, Don. 2011. "Jokes Inviting More Than Laughter . . . Joan Rivers' Political-Rhetorical World View." *Comedy Studies* 2, no. 2: 139–150. https://doi.org/10.1386/cost.2.2.139_1.

Walker, James R., and Robert V. Bellamy. 1993. *The Remote Control in the New Age of Television*. Westport, CT: Praeger.

Walsh, Megan. 2017. "The Gaslight Café on 'The Marvelous Mrs. Maisel' Has an Impressive History." *Romper*, December 5, 2017. https://www.romper.com/p/is-the-gaslight-cafe-on-the-marvelous-mrs-maisel-a-real-place-it-has-a-long-history-6769120.

Walters, Suzanna Danuta. 2017. "Lesbian Request Approved: Sex, Power and Desire in *Orange Is the New Black*." In *Television Antiheroines: Women Behaving Badly in Crime and Prison Drama*, edited by Milly Buonanno, 199–215. Bristol, UK; Chicago, US: Intellect.

Wanzo, Rebecca. 2016. "Precarious-Girl Comedy: Issa Rae, Lena Dunham, and Abjection Aesthetics." *Camera Obscura: Feminism, Culture, and Media Studies* 31, no. 2: 27–59. https://doi.org/10.1215/02705346-3592565.

Warner, Kristen J. 2017. "In the Time of Plastic Representation." *Film Quarterly* 71, no. 2: 32–37. https://doi.org/10.1525/fq.2017.71.2.32.

———. 2015. "The Racial Logic of *Grey's Anatomy*: Shonda Rhimes and Her 'Post-Civil Rights, Post-Feminist' Series." *Television & New Media* 16, no. 7: 631–647. https://doi.org/10.1177/1527476414550529.

Watson, Allan. 2016. "One Time I'ma Show You How to Get Rich!" Rap Music, Wealth and the Rise of the Hip-Hop Mogul." In *Handbook on Wealth and the Super-Rich*, edited by Iain Hay and Jonathan V. Beaverstock, 178–198. Northampton, MA: Edward Elgar Pub.

Welang, Nahum. 2018. "Triple Consciousness: The Reimagination of Black Female Identities in Contemporary American Culture." *Open Cultural Studies* 2, no. 1: 296–306. https://doi.org10.1515/culture-2018-0027.

Whelehan, Imelda. 2000. *Overloaded: Popular Culture and the Future of Feminism*. London: Women's Press.

White, Rosie. 2017. "Roseanne Barr: Remembering *Roseanne*." In *Hysterical! Women in American Comedy*, edited by Linda Mizejewski and Victoria Sturtevant, 233–250. Austin: University Of Texas Press.

Wilkes, Karen. 2015. "Colluding with Neo-Liberalism: Post-Feminist Subjectivities, Whiteness and Expressions of Entitlement." *Feminist Review* 110, no. 1: 18–33. https://doi.org/10.1057/fr.2015.19.

Williams, Janice. 2017. "Issa Rae's 'Insecure' and the Very Few Shows to Ever Depict 'Great Black Female Friendships' on TV." *Newsweek*, April 11, 2017. https://www.newsweek.com/issa-rae-insecure-girlfriends-living-single-cast-show-black-female-friendships-581819.

Wisseh, Assatu N. 2019. "Mapping Mammy 2.0: *Insecure* and the Middle Class Black Woman's Burden." *Howard Journal of Communications* 30, no. 5: 391–410. https://doi.org/10.1080/10646175.2018.1471755.

Wolf, Naomi. 1990. *The Beauty Myth*. Toronto: Random House.

Woods, Faye. 2019. "Too Close for Comfort: Direct Address and the Affective Pull of the Confessional Comic Woman in *Chewing Gum* and *Fleabag*." *Communication Culture & Critique* 12, no. 2: 194–212. https://doi.org/10.1093/ccc/tcz014.

Workneh, Lilly. 2015. "#SayHerName: Why We Should Declare That Black Women and Girls Matter, Too." *The Huffington Post*, May 10, 2015. https://www.huffpost.com/entry/black-women-matter_n_7363064.

Yang, Rachel. 2019. "'Big Little Lies': HBO Partnering with *The Wing* for Season 2 Launch." *Variety*, May 7, 2019. https://variety.com/2019/tv/news/hbo-the-wing-partnership-big-little-lies-season-2-1203206591/.

Zinoman, Jason. 2012. "Phyllis Diller and Her Comic Craft." *The New York Times*, August 22, 2012. https://artsbeat.blogs.nytimes.com/2012/08/22/phyllis-diller-and-her-comic-craft/?_r=0&mtrref=en.wikipedia.org&gwh=6C50510652FEB80B4016486771940F2F&gwt=pay&assetType=PAYWALL.

Ziv, Avner. 1998. *Jewish Humor*. New Brunswick, NJ; London: Transaction Publishers.

Zuckerman, Esther. 2017. "Corsets and Comedy: Inside Amazon's *The Marvelous Mrs. Maisel*." *Vanity Fair*, November 28, 2017. https://www.vanityfair.com/hollywood/2017/11/marvelous-mrs-maisel-amazon-amy-sherman-palladino-set-visit.

Index

Page references for figures are italicized.

abuse themes: in *Big Little Lies* (TV series), 44–57; domestic violence, 51–53; maternal abuse, 54; race and, 53–57. *See also* sexual abuse
activism, political, conspicuous feminism and, 12–13
Adegoke, Yomi, 33, 88
Adventures of Ozzie and Harriet, 22
advertising: intersectional feminism in, 11. *See also* femvertising

The Affair, 39

African American women. *See* black women
Ahern, Cecilia, 133
Ahmed, Sara, 97
Alber, Jan, 120
Alice, 25
All in the Family, 24–25
Ally McBeal: ambiguous feminism an, 18; postfeminism and, 29–31
Amazon Prime, 19–20
ambiguous feminism, 18
And Just Like That . . . , 38
Ansari, Aziz, 82
Anthony, Susan B., 18

antihero narratives: for female characters, 91; in *Insecure*, 91; for male characters, 35
Antler, Joyce, 71
Apple TV, 3, 17
The Apprentice, 89
Arnaz, Desi, 22–23
Arnold, Andrea, 42, 55–56
Arthur, Beatrice, 25
Atlanta, 113
Atwood, Margaret, 1, 116, 133
Awkward Black Girl, 85

Bakhtin, Mikhail, 60–61
Ball, Lucille, 22–23
Banet-Weiser, Sarah, 11; on female empowerment, 43; on popular feminism, 6–7, 56; on race as commodity, 89
Barr, Roseanne, 28
Bastien, Angelica Jade, 113
Baxter Birney, Meredith, 27
BBC, 3
Beal, Frances, 89
Bean, Gail, 99–100
beauty ideals, in *The Marvelous Mrs. Maisel*, 66–67, 69–70

Bentham, Jeremy, 12
Bergson, Henri, 60–61
Bewitched, 24
Beyoncé, 96; celebrity feminism and, 7, 11; popular feminism and, 6; racial politics of, 11
Bianculli, David, 28
Big Little Lies (book) (Moriarty), 41
Big Little Lies (TV series), 3, 13, 34, 39, *46*, *50*, 136; abuse themes in, 44–57; celebrity feminism and, 56; conspicuous feminism in, 54, 56–57, 102; critical acclaim for, 41–42; domestic violence in, 51–53; female empowerment themes in, 56; feminist gloss and, 43–44, 56; maternal abuse in, 54; #MeToo Movement and, 44–45, 50, 57; patriarchal structures in, 47–48, 55; promotion campaigns for, 56; as quality television, 56; race themes in, 53–57; rape narratives in, 49; sexual violence in, 45–48, 53; traditional ideals of motherhood in, 51; trauma themes in, 44–53; victim blaming in, 53; whiteness as element of, 43
Bignell, Jonathan, 34
Billingsley, Barbara, 22–23
"black lady" trope, 94–95
Black Lives Matter movement, 109–10, 112–13
black masculinity, 107–8
black women: controlling images of, 86, 88–89, 91–96, 104; discrimination towards, as unique experience, 10; "double jeopardy" narratives for, 89; intersectional narratives for, 86; matriarchy thesis, 95; rap music reclaimed by, 93–94; #SayHerName movement, 86–87; sexuality for, 103–9; stereotypes of, 86, 88, 89, 91–96
Blake, Jordana, 116
Bledel, Alexis, 124
Boardwalk Empire, 35

body positivity, in popular feminism, 19
The Bold Type, 103
Borstein, Alex, 59, *78*
Boyle, Karen, 9
Brabon, Benjamin, 29, 61–62
Bracke, Sarah, 122–23
The Brady Bunch, 24
Breaking Bad, 32, 35
Brewer, Madeline, 125
Brice, Fanny, 71
Broad City, 33
Brooks, Ann, 29
Brosnahan, Rachel, 59, 66–67, *74*, *78*
Brown, Sterling K., 78–79
Bruce, Lenny, 69, 71, 73
Bryant, Aidy, 1
Bryant, Kobe, 111
Budgeon, Shelley, 28, 31
Burke, Tarana, 3, 87; erasure from #MeToo Movement, 10. *See also* #MeToo Movement
Busch, Elizabeth Kaufer, 43

cable networks: HBO, 3, 30; during multichannel transition period, 30
Cagney and Lacey, 26–27
Carastathis, Anna, 11
Cardi B., 94
Carlin, George, 82
carnival literary mode, 60–61
Carroll, Diahann, 25
celebrity feminism, 7, 56
Chamberlain, Prudence, 18
Chang, Yahlin, 127–28
charged humor, 70, 82
Cherry, Marc, 32
choice: in *Girls*, 36–37; postfeminism and, 28–29, 36–37
Christian, Aymar Jean, 38–39
Civil Rights Act of 1964, Title VII, 24
C. K., Louis, 82
Cochrane, Kira, 18
code switching, in *Insecure*, 99–100
Cole, Micaela, 19, 134; *I May Destroy You*, 3, 38–39

Collins, Patricia Hill, 88
Combahee River Collective, 89
comedy: charged humor, 70, 82; as gendered space, in *The Marvelous Mrs. Maisel*, 60–61, 69–75; gender parody, 73; Jewish comedy traditions, 71; Jewish women in, 71; as male space, 75; "unruly woman" in, 28, 70; women and, 69–75. *See also* stand-up comedy
commodification: of conspicuous feminism, 136–37; of female independence, 2; of intersectional feminism, 11; of popular feminism, 7
Conroy, Frances, 32
conspicuous consumption, 5–6; economic status and, 6
conspicuous feminism: activist perspective on, 12–13; in *Big Little Lies* (TV series), 54, 56–57, 102; commodification of, 136–37; etymological development of, 5; female resistance and, 134; in *The Handmaid's Tale*, 117, 119–20, 125, 127, 130; in *Insecure*, 102, 107, 113; intersectionality in, 87; in *The Marvelous Mrs. Maisel*, 61, 67, 75, 81–82, 102; #MeToo Movement and, 3–9, 39; neoliberalist principles and, 7–8; quality television era and, 33–40; scope of, 2; sexual assault and harassment and, 12
consumption. *See* conspicuous consumption
controlling images, of black women, 86, 88–89; "black lady" trope, 95; female sexuality and, 104; in *Insecure*, 91–96
Cooke-Cornell, Beth Anne, 82
Cosby, Bill, 4, 82, 134
The Cosby Show, 27, 94, 104
Crabtree, Ane, 117
Crawley, Karen, 129
Crenshaw, Kimberlé, 10
critical affirmation, as concept, 95–96

Cuklanz, Lisa M., 47
Cullors, Patrice, 110
cult of motherhood, 32; "happy housewife" trope, 22–24, 42–43
Curran, Holly, 64
Curtin, Catherine, 96

Daly, Tyne, 27
Danes, Claire, 31
Davis, Angela, 89
Davis, Viola, 31
Dear White People, 113
Depp, Johnny, 134–35
Dern, Laura, 41–42
Designing Women, 26
Desperate Housewives, 32, 42–43, 89
DeYoung, Bailey, 64
The Dick Van Dyke Show, 22–23
Dillard, Cynthia, 95
Diller, Phyllis, 73
disabled women, 137
Disney Plus, 19–20
diversity, female empowerment and, 11
domesticity, home and: as gendered space, 59–60; "happy housewife" trope, 22–24, 42–43; in *The Marvelous Mrs. Maisel*, 62–69; second wave feminism and, 62
domestic violence, in *Big Little Lies* (TV series), 51–53
The Donna Reed Show, 22
Douglas, Susan, 27–28
Dowd, Ann, 116, 125
Dunham, Lena, 19, 31, 36. *See also Girls*
DuVernay, Ava, 111

Eckhardt, Stephanie, 9
economic privilege, in *The Marvelous Mrs. Maisel*, 61–62, 76–77, 80
Ehrens, Kerri, 17
Eisenberg, Ned, 78–79
Elliot, Missy, 94
emergent feminism, in contemporary media culture, 5

Emmott, Catherine, 121
Empire, 89
empowerment. *See* female empowerment
equality. *See* gender equality/inequality
Equal Pay Act (1963), 24
ER, 30
Esposito, Carmen, 82

Facebook, #MeToo Movement on, 4
Fagbenle, O. T., 116
Falco, Edie, 32
Faludi, Susan, 27
Family Ties, 27
Farrow, Ronan, 3–4
Father Knows Best, 22
Feasey, Rebecca, 51
female empowerment: Banet-Weiser on, 43; in *Big Little Lies* (TV series), 56; diversity themes in, 10–11; in *Girls*, 36–37; in *Insecure*, 88, 113; in *The Marvelous Mrs. Maisel*, 82; #MeToo Movement advocacy of, 83; popular feminism and, 6–7, 43
female friendships: in *Insecure*, 95–96. *See also Sex and the City*
female representation, on television: growth and diversity in, 19; women creators and, 19. *See also specific shows*
female resistance: conspicuous feminism and, 134; in *The Handmaid's Tale* (TV series), 8, 117–25
female sexuality: for black women, 102–9; in *The Bold Type*, 103; controlling images of black women and, 104; in *Fleabag*, 103; in *Girls*, 103, 106; in *Insecure*, 102–9; in *Sex and the City*, 103, 106
The Feminine Mystique (Friedan), 23–24, 62–63
femininity, ideals of: Friedan on, 62–63; in *The Marvelous Mrs. Maisel*, 62–69, 72–74, 81–82; postfeminism and, 31; transgression of, 72

feminism: ambiguous, 18; first wave, 17–18; fourth wave, 18–19; intersectionality and, 10–11; neoliberal, 101–2; postfeminism as rewriting of, 29; representational, 102; second wave, 17–18, 20–26; social agenda of, 3; third wave, 18; tropes, 20. *See also* conspicuous feminism; popular feminism; postfeminism; white feminism; *specific topics*
"feminist gloss," 43–44, 56
feminist tropes, 20
femvertising, 7; intersectional feminism and, 11; #MeToo Movement as influence on, 8
Feuer, Jane, 34
Fiennes, Joseph, 116–17
first wave feminism, 17–18; equal access to public sphere as focus of, 17
Fleabag, 3, 33, 92; female sexuality in, 103
Flockhart, Calista, 18
Floyd, George, 109–10
Ford, Christine Blasey, 117
Foucault, Michel, 12
fourth wave feminism, 18–19
Fox, Crystal, 53
Foy, Jennifer, 71–72
Franklin, Bonnie, 25
The Fresh Prince of Bel-Air, 94
Friday, Jessica, 75–76
Friedan, Betty, 18; on feminine mystique, 62–63; *The Feminine Mystique*, 23–24, 62–63; "problem with no name" and, 23–24
friendships. *See* female friendships

Gadsby, Hannah, 82
Gagnier, Regenia, 72
Game of Thrones, 39
Garofalo, Alex, 97
Garza, Alicia, 110

gendered spaces: comedy as, in *The Marvelous Mrs. Maisel*, 60–61, 69–75; home as, 59–60; in *The Marvelous Mrs. Maisel*, 59–83
gender equality/inequality: #MeToo Movement and, 2; second wave feminism's focus on, 17–18
gender identity: postfeminism and, 11. *See also* black masculinity
gender parody, 73
gender roles: "happy housewife" trope and, 22–23; parody of, 23; resilience and, 122
Genz, Stephanie, 29, 61–62
Gilbert, Joanne, 69–70
Gill, Rosalind, 12, 43–44, 56, 137
Gilmore Girls, 31, 60–61
Gilmore Girls: A Year in the Life, 75–76
Girls, 31; choice as theme in, 36–37; empowerment themes in, 36–37; female sexuality in, 103, 106; independence themes in, 36–37; primacy of whiteness in, 90–91
Gless, Sharon, 27
Glow, 33
The Good Fight, 39
Gore, Lesley, 120
Grady, Constance, 126–27
Graham, Lauren, 31
Grant, Ruby, 36
Greene, Linda, 110
Grey's Anatomy, 31, 39
Griffin, Rachel Alicia, 88
Groom, Bill, 63
Growing Pains, 27
Gunn, Anna, 32

Hagelin, Sarah, 91
The Handmaid's Tale (book), 1, 116
The Handmaid's Tale (TV series), 34, *122–23*; cinematography choices in, 121; conspicuous feminism in, 117, 119–20, 125, 127, 130; contemporary social issues reflected in, 130; costume design in, 117; critical acclaim for, 116; economic dynamics in, 129–30; female resistance in, 8, 117–25; feminist incentives of, 126; #MeToo Movement as influence on, 39; misogyny in, 118; music in, 120, 124, 126–27, 129; neoliberal themes in, 129; "Nolite te bastardes carborundorum," 120, 129; parody of, 1–3; patriarchal oppression and power in, 117–18, 130; physical violence in, 118–19; racial dynamics in, 129–30; resilience themes in, 117–31; sexual violence in, 116; voiceovers in, 120–21; white female privilege in, 129
Happy Days, 24
"happy housewife" trope, 22–24; in *Desperate Housewives*, 42–43; "problem with no name" and, 23–24
harassment. *See* sexual assault and harassment
Hargitay, Mariska, 31
Harrison, Chloe, 121
hashtag activism, #MeToo Movement as, 6, 135–36
HBO, 3, 30. *See also specific shows*
HBO Max, 19–20
Heard, Amber, 134–35
HeForShe initiative, 7
Henderson, Florence, 24
Henry, Astrid, 36
Henson, Taraji P., 89
heteronormative narratives, in *Insecure*, 108–9
Higher Act, Title IX (1972), 24
Hillstrom, Laura Collier, 39
Hinkle, Marin, 60
home. *See* domesticity
Homeland, 31
homosexuality, in *The Marvelous Mrs. Maisel*, 79. *See also* LGBTQ identities
hooks, bell, 95, 111
Hope, Bob, 73

How to Get Away with Murder, 31, 94, 104, 111
Hsu, Stephanie, 80
Hulu, 3, 8–9, 19–20. *See also The Handmaid's Tale* (TV series)
Hussle, Nipsey, 111

identity. *See* gender identity
I Love Lucy, 22–23; trans gender queer components in, 23
I May Destroy You, 3, 38–39
independence, as theme, in *Girls*, 36–37
individuality, postfeminism and, 28–29
inequality. *See* gender equality/inequality
Insecure, 31, 34, 38, *97*; black culture in, celebration of, 109–13; black female friendship in, 95–96; "black lady" trope in, 94–95; black masculinity and, 107–8; black prejudicial biases in, 98–99; code switching in, 99–100; conspicuous feminism in, 102, 107, 113; critical acclaim for, 87; critical affirmation concept in, 95–96; female antihero in, 91; female empowerment themes in, 88, 113; female sexuality in, 102–9; heteronormative narratives in, 108–9; intersectional feminism in, 137; intersectionality in, 89, 96, 113; LGBTQ identities in, 108–9; music in, 109–10; neoliberal feminist narratives in, 105; promotion of, 112; racial assumptions by White people in, 92; racial inequality in, 110–11; racial privilege in, 97–98; reconfiguring of stereotypes of black women, 86, 88, 91–96; representational feminism in, 102; resistance of controlling images of black women in, 91–96; romantic relationships in, 102–9; structural racism in, 90; therapy in, 101–2; use of rap music, 92–94; white liberal feminism in, 96–97; white privilege themes in, 99; workplace setting, 96–102. *See also* black women
intersectional feminism: in advertising campaigns, 11; commodification of, 11; in *Insecure*, 137; scope of, 10–11; white feminism and, 76
intersectionality: for black women, 86; in conspicuous feminism, 87; feminism and, 10–11; in *Insecure*, 89, 96, 113; #MeToo Movement and, 86; streaming platforms and, 38–39; white feminism and, 76

James, Etta, 127
Jessica Jones, 39
Jewish comedy traditions, in *The Marvelous Mrs. Maisel*, 71
Jewish women, Jewish identity for: in comedy, 71; in *The Marvelous Mrs. Maisel*, 77–78; stereotypes of, 78. *See also The Marvelous Mrs. Maisel*
Johnson, Jo, 49
Johnstone, Joel, 64
Jones, January, 32–33
Jordan-Zachery, Julia, 88
Joyce, Lisa, 92, 98
Judd, Ashley, 4
Julia, 25

Kaling, Mindy, 19, 31, 86
Kappel, Aaron, 75–76
Kavanaugh, Brett, 117
Kavka, Misha, 40
Keller, Jessalyn, 5
Kelley, David E., 42, 55
Kelly, Liz, 47–48
Kelly, R., 86
Kerns, Joanna, 27
Kidman, Nicole, 41–42, 44–45, *46*, *50*, 133
Killing Eve, 3, 33
Kirby, Luke, 69
Kohan, Jenji, 19, 37–38
Kravitz, Zoe, 41
Krefting, Rebecca, 70

Lagerwey, Jorie, 20
LA Law, 26
Lamar, Kendrick, 109
Landay, Lori, 23
Landgraf, John, 20
Lauer, Matt, 17
Laverne and Shirley, 21
Lavin, Linda, 25
Law and Order: SVU, 31
Lawrence, Jennifer, 4, 7
Lean In (Sandberg), 101–2
Leave it to Beaver, 22
Lemonade (Beyoncé), 96
Lentz, Kristen, 34
Leung, Rebecca, 86
Levi, Zachary, 60, 67
Levy, Yael, 105
LGBTQ identities: in *Insecure*, 108–9; in *The Marvelous Mrs. Maisel*, 79; queer women, 137
Lindgren, Simon, 135
Little, Judy, 70
Little Fires Everywhere, 3
Lorde, Audre, 89
Lotz, Amanda, 19, 29
Louis-Dreyfus, Julia, 31
Lynch, Jane, 61
Lynn, Susan, 64

MacKinnon, Kate, 1
Mad Men, 32–33, 35
Manne, Kate, 49, 118–19
Mare of Eastown, 3
The Martha Stewart Show, 32
Martin, Trayvon, 109
The Marvelous Mrs. Maisel, 14, 34, *74*, *78*, 136; beauty ideals in, 66–67, 69–70; Bruce in, 69, 71, 73; comedy as gendered space, 60–61, 69–75; conspicuous feminism in, 61, 67, 75, 81–82, 102; critical acclaim for, 60; domestic identity in, 59; domesticity ideals in, 62–69; economic privilege in, 61–62, 76–77, 80–81; female empowerment in, 82; female Jewish identity in, 77–78; feminine appearance in, 66–67, 69–70, 76; femininity ideals in, 62–69, 72–74, 81–82; gender dynamics in, 60, 67; gendered spaces in, 59–83; homosexual themes in, 79; Jewish comedy traditions and, 71; Joan Rivers as model for, 64, 71, 73; misogyny themes in, 60; motherhood themes in, 64–65, 81; power dynamics in, 60; production design of, 63–64; racial dynamics in, 78–79; self-actualization themes in, 63; transgression of femininity in, 72; white feminism in, 75–83
The Mary Tyler Moore Show, 13, 24–26; career advancement as theme of, 21; quality television era influenced by, 34–35
masculinity. *See* black masculinity
maternal abuse, 54
matriarchy thesis, 95
Matte, Gerard, 71
Maude, 25
McCann, Hannah, 74–75
McClain, Leo, 60
McClain, Leroy, 69
McCulley, Mason, 96
McFayden, Ian, 71
McGowan, Rose, 9
#MeToo Movement: *Big Little Lies* (TV series), 44–45, 50, 57; conspicuous feminism and, 3–9, 39; expansion of, 87; on Facebook, 4; failures of, 134–35; female empowerment through, 83; feminist advertising campaigns influenced by, 8; against gender inequality, 2; *The Handmaid's Tale* influenced by, 39; as hashtag activism, 6, 135–36; incentives as element of, 2; *Insecure* and, 113; intensification of, 4–5; intersectionality and, 86; Milano role in, 3; in popular media, 10–12; in popular television narratives, 3,

133; primacy of whiteness in, 86; privilege and, 55; quality television era and, 33–40; against sexual abuse, 2; in social media, 135; stand-up comedy impacted by, 82; visibility narratives and, 55; Women's Marches influenced by, 4
Milano, Alyssa, 3–4
Miller, Bruce, 116, 119
Miller, Quinlan, 23
Minaj, Nicki, 94
The Mindy Project, 31, 86
Minghella, Max, 123–24
misogyny, 2; in *The Handmaid's Tale*, 118; in *The Marvelous Mrs. Maisel*, 60; race and, 55; of Trump, 4; on Twitter, shared experiences of, 4; towards women with power, 49. *See also Big Little Lies*; *specific topics*
Mizejewski, Linda, 61
Modleski, Tania, 108
Moeggenberg, Zarah, 39
Montgomery, Elizabeth, 24
Moore, Kenya, 89
Moore, Mary Tyler, 22–23
Moorti, Sujata, 54
Moran, Claire, 105
Moriarty, Liane, 41
The Morning Show, 17
Moss, Elisabeth, 115, 121, *122–23*
motherhood, traditional ideals of, 51; cult of motherhood, 32; "happy housewife" trope, 22–24, 42–43; in *The Marvelous Mrs. Maisel*, 64–65, 81
Moyer, Kate, 115
Moynihan, Daniel Patrick, 95
Mrs. America, 3, 134
multichannel transition period, for television industry, 21, 26–30; corporate takeover of networks, 26; expansion of cable television, 30
Munford, Rebecca, 30–31, 33
Murphy Brown, 26–27

Nash, Jennifer, 87
Nash, Meredith, 36
Nasser, Larry, 134
National Organisation of Women (NOW), 24
Negra, Diane, 29
neoliberal feminism, 101–2; in *Insecure*, 105
neoliberalism: conspicuous feminism and, 7–8; in *The Handmaid's Tale*, 129. *See also* white liberal feminism
Netflix, 3, 19–20, 37–38. *See also specific shows*
network era, of television industry, 21–22. *See also specific networks*
Newman, Omarosa Manigault, 89
Nicolson, Paula, 47
Noel, Y'lan, 103
"Nolite te bastardes carborundorum," 120, 129
NOW. *See* National Organisation of Women
Nygaard, Taylor, 20

One Day at a Time, 25
oppression, of women, 2–3
Orange is the New Black, 13, 37–38, 39
Orgad, Shani, 12, 137
Orji, Yvonne, 85

Paltrow, Gwyneth, 4
panopticon, Bentham and, 12
Parker, Mary Louise, 32–33
Parker, Sarah Jessica, 30
patriarchal structures: in *Big Little Lies* (TV series), 47–48, 55; in *The Handmaid's Tale*, 117–18, 130; race and, 55
peak TV era, 20, 39
Pompeo, Ellen, 31
popular feminism: Beyoncé as symbol of, 6; body positivity and, 19; commercial appeal of, 7; commodification of, 7; as concept, 6–7; cooptation of, 7; economic

appeal of, 7; female empowerment as foundation of, 6–7, 43; media visibility of, 6; Rivers, N., on, 18
postfeminism, 28–33; *Ally McBeal* and, 29–31; choice and, 28–29, 36–37; cult of motherhood and, 32; gender identity and, 11; individuality and, 28–29; institutionalization of, 28; postmodern feminism as distinct from, 29; primacy of whiteness in, 10; proper femininity and, 31; as rewriting of classic feminism, 29; scope of, 29; in *Sex and the City*, 29–31, 90, 108–9
postmodern feminism, postfeminism as distinct from, 29
post-network era, for television industry, 21; antihero narratives, 35
The Practice, 30
Press, Joy, 37
privilege, for White women: #MeToo Movement and, 55. *See also* economic privilege
"problem with no name," 23–24
Probyn, Elspeth, 33
Projansky, Sarah, 46

quality television era, 13; *Big Little Lies*, 56; conspicuous feminism and, 33–40; definition of, 34–35; HBO and, 34–37; *The Mary Tyler Moore Show* as forerunner of, 34–35; #MeToo Movement and, 33–40; Netflix and, 34. *See also specific shows*
The Queen's Gambit, 3
queer women, 137

Rabinovitz, Lauren, 18
race: in abuse narratives, 53–57; as commodity, 89; female solidarity and, 54–55; in *The Handmaid's Tale* (TV series), 129–30; in *The Marvelous Mrs. Maisel*, 78–79; maternal abuse and, 54; misogyny and, 55; patriarchy and, 55. *See also* black women
racial inequality: in *Insecure*, 110–11; #SayHerName movement, 86–87, 111
racial politics, of Beyoncé, 11
Radner, Gilda, 71
Rae, Issa, 19, 31, 85, *93*, 133. *See also Insecure*
Rape, Abuse, and Incest National Network (RAINN), 134
rape culture, in stand-up comedy and, 82
rape narratives, in *Big Little Lies* (TV series), 49
rap music: feminist reclaiming of, 93–94; in *Insecure*, 92–94
Rashad, Phylicia, 27
The Real Housewives of Atlanta, 89
Real Housewives franchise, 32
Reed, Donna, 22–23
representational feminism, 102
resilience: gendered qualities of, 122; in *The Handmaid's Tale* (TV series), 117–31
resistance. *See* female resistance
Rhimes, Shonda, 38, 104. *See also How to Get Away with Murder*; *Scandal*
Rivers, Joan, 64, 71, 73
Rivers, Nicola, 7, 90; on popular feminism, 18
Roar, 133
Robertson, Pamela, 73
Roe v. Wade: legalization of abortion under, 24; overturning of, 8–9, 133
Rose, Charlie, 17
Roseanne, 28
Ross, Marion, 24
Rothwell, Natasha, 87
Rottenberg, Catherine, 7–8, 102
Rowe, Kathleen, 28, 70
Ryan, Maureen E., 5

Saddiq, Raphael, 109
Sampson, Kendrick, 110
Sandberg, Cheryl, 101

Saturday Night Live, 1–3, 2, 8
#SayHerName movement, 86–87, 111
Scandal, 31, 94–95, 104
Schreiber, Michele, 68
Schumer, Amy, 1–3, 2, 82
Sciorra, Annabella, 10
Scott, Ellen C., 106
Seales, Amanda, 87
Second Industrial Revolution, 5
second wave feminism: backlash against, 26–28; challenges to domesticity as sole female identity, 24; doctrine of feminine domesticity and, 62; feminist tropes, 20; Friedan and, 23–24; gender equality as focus on, 17–18; "happy housewife" trope, 22–24; National Organisation of Women, 24; on television, 20–26; "unruly woman" type, 28; Women's Equity Action League, 24; women's rights movement and, 21
self-actualization, in *The Marvelous Mrs. Maisel*, 63
Sex and the City, 13; ambiguous feminism and, 18; *And Just Like That . . .* and, 38; construction of feminism in, 36–37; female sexuality in, 103, 106; parody of, 1–3; postfeminist narratives in, 29–31, 90, 108–9; quality television era and, 36; single women narrative in, 92; white feminism in, 90; whiteness as element of, 43, 90–91
sexism, dismantling of, 3
sexual abuse: allegations against Weinstein, 3, 9–10, 44; #MeToo Movement against, 2; in rape narratives, 49. *See also Big Little Lies*
sexual assault and harassment, conspicuous feminism and, 12
sexuality. *See* female sexuality
sexual violence: in *Big Little Lies* (TV series), 45–48, 53; in *The Handmaid's Tale* (TV series), 116; rape culture and, 82
Shalhoub, Tony, 60
Sharp Objects, 39
Sherman-Palladino, Amy, 19, 59–60, 75; production design style, 63–64. *See also The Marvelous Mrs. Maisel*
"Silence Breakers," 4
Silverman, Gillian, 91
Silverman, Sarah, 71
Simone, Nina, 124
single women narratives: in *Fleabag*, 3, 92; in *Sex and the City*, 92
Six Feet Under, 32
Skarsgård, Alexander, 41–42
Sobande, Francesca, 108
social media, #MeToo Movement in, 135
Solomon, Sarah, 39
The Sopranos, 32, 35, 39
Sorvino, Mira, 10
Spacey, Kevin, 4
Spangler, Lynn, 18, 22, 28
Springer, Kimberley, 88–90
stand-up comedy: #MeToo Movement impact on, 82; rape culture and, 82
Stapleton, Jean, 24
Stay Woke, 97
Steinem, Gloria, 18
Stelters, Brian, 17
Stewart, Martha, 32
streaming platforms, 19–20; branding for, 38–39; intersectionality and, 38–39. *See also specific platforms*
Streep, Meryl, 42, 47, 56
Strong, Brenda, 42
Strong, Cecily, 1
structural racism, in *Insecure*, 90
Sturtevant, Victoria, 61
Surviving R. Kelly, 86
Swift, Taylor, 7
Sykes, Wanda, 79

Tasker, Yvonne, 29

television: multichannel transition period, 21, 26–28; network era, 21–22; peak TV era, 20; post-network era, 21, 35; quality television era, 13; second wave feminism on, 21, 23–26; streaming platforms, 19–20. *See also* cable networks; female representation; *specific networks*; *specific shows*; *specific streaming platforms*
That Girl, 21, 24
The Theory of the Leisure Class (Veblen), 5–6
third wave feminism, 18
13 Reasons Why, 39
Thirtysomething, 26
Thomas, Clarence, 133
Thompson, Robert J., 35
Thorburn, David, 35
TIME magazine, 4; popular feminists as cover stories, 18
Time's Up initiative, 134
Tometti, Opal, 110
Tomlinson, Barbara, 11, 126
To Pimp a Butterfly (Lamar), 109
Top of the Morning (Stelters), 17
trans gender queer elements, in *I Love Lucy*, 23
trauma themes, in *Big Little Lies* (TV series), 44–53
Trump, Donald, 117; misogyny of, 4
Twitter, misogyny experiences shared on, 4

Ugly Betty, 89
Unbelievable, 39
"unruly woman," 28, 70

Valenti, Jessica, 129–30
Vallée, Jean-Marc, 42, 55
Vance, Vivian, 22–23
Veblen, Thorstein, 5–6
Veep, 31
victim blaming, in *Big Little Lies* (TV series), 53

violence: domestic, 51–53; in *The Handmaid's Tale*, 118–19. *See also* sexual violence
visibility, of feminist narratives, 9–15; Foucault on, 12; #MeToo Movement and, 55

Waller Bridge, Phoebe, 19
Wanzo, Rebecca, 91–92
Washington, Kerry, 31
Wasserstein, Wendy, 71
Waters, Melanie, 30–31, 33
Watson, Allan, 94
WEAL. *See* Women's Equity Action League
Weeds, 32–33
Weinstein, Harvey, 2; sexual abuse allegations against, 3, 9–10, 44. *See also* #MeToo Movement
Welang, Nahum, 93
West, Cornel, 95
Westworld, 39
white feminism: intersectionality and, 76; in *The Marvelous Mrs. Maisel*, 75–83; in *Sex and the City*, 90
white liberal feminism, in *Insecure*, 96–97
whiteness, primacy of: in *Big Little Lies* (TV series), 43; in *Girls*, 90–91; in #MeToo Movement, 86; in postfeminist culture, 10; in *Sex and the City*, 43, 90–91. *See also* privilege
white privilege: in *The Handmaid's Tale*, 129; in *Insecure*, 97–98. *See also* privilege
Wiley, Samira, 124
Williams, Janice, 95
Williams, Porsha, 89
Williams, Robert, 86
Williams, Vanessa, 89
Wisseh, Assatu N., 95, 100
Witherspoon, Reese, 41
women. *See* black women; women's rights movement

women creators, on television, 19. *See also specific people*
Women's Equity Action League (WEAL), 24
Women's Marches, #MeToo Movement as influence on, 4
women's rights movement, second wave feminism and, 21
Wong, Ali, 82
Woodley, Shailene, 41, *50*
Woods, Faye, 92
workplace settings: code switching in, 99–100; female ambition in, 101–2; gendered hierarchies in, 101; in *Insecure*, 96–102. *See also* gendered spaces; stand-up comedy
Wyatt, Jane, 22–23

The X-Files, 30

#YesAllWomen, 4
"You Don't Own Me" (Gore), 120

Zegan, Michael, 60
Zimmerman, George, 109

About the Author

Anna Marie Bautista is lecturer in American studies, gender studies, and comparative literature at the University of Hong Kong. Her teaching and research interests include various aspects of film, television, and popular culture studies, particularly representations of gender.

Lightning Source UK Ltd.
Milton Keynes UK
UKHW011420110123
415174UK00004B/48